T0244282

HOUSE OF
HUAWEI

HOUSE OF
HUAWEI

THE SECRET HISTORY
OF CHINA'S MOST
POWERFUL COMPANY

EVA DOU

PORTFOLIO · PENGUIN

Portfolio / Penguin
An imprint of Penguin Random House LLC
penguinrandomhouse.com

Most Portfolio books are available at a discount when purchased in quantity for sales
promotions or corporate use. Special editions, which include personalized covers, excerpts,
and corporate imprints, can be created when purchased in large quantities. For more
information, please call (212) 572-2232 or email specialmarkets@penguinrandomhouse.com.
Your local bookstore can also assist with discounted bulk purchases using the Penguin
Random House corporate Business-to-Business program. For assistance in locating a
participating retailer, email B2B@penguinrandomhouse.com.

Image credits may be found on pages 389–90.

BOOK DESIGN BY CHRIS WELCH
MAP BY DANIEL LAGIN

LIBRARY OF CONGRESS CATALOGING-IN-PUBLICATION DATA

Names: Dou, Eva, author.
Title: House of Huawei : the secret history of China's most powerful company / Eva Dou.
Description: [New York] : Portfolio / Penguin, [2025] |
Includes bibliographical references and index. |
Summary: "The epic story of Huawei, China's most powerful company, and
its reclusive founder, Ren Zhengfei" —Provided by publisher.
Identifiers: LCCN 2024028798 (print) | LCCN 2024028799 (ebook) |
ISBN 9780593544631 (hardcover) | ISBN 9780593544648 (ebook)
Subjects: LCSH: Hua wei ji shu you xian gong si—History. |
Telecommunication—Management—China. |
International business enterprises—China. | Ren, Zhengfei, 1944–
Classification: LCC HE8430.H83 D68 2025 (print) | LCC HE8430.H83 (ebook) |
DDC 338.8/872139167—dc23/eng/20240716
LC record available at https://lccn.loc.gov/2024028798
LC ebook record available at https://lccn.loc.gov/2024028799

ISBN 9780593852262 (international edition)

Printed in the United States of America
1st Printing

To Ma Ding

As a military man I have known many clever and truly outstanding strategists. I have rarely come across an individual more strategically oriented than Ren.[1]

—*Admiral William A. Owens,*
former vice-chairman of the Joint Chiefs of Staff

CONTENTS

PART II

PART III

THE PEOPLE'S REPUBLIC OF CHINA

A NOTE ON NAMES

The Chinese names in the text are transliterated in the pinyin system, which has been used in China since the 1950s. In pronunciation, a *zh* can be approximated by the English *j* (Ren Zhengfei = "Rin Jung-fay"), an *x* by the English *sh* (Ren Moxun = "Rin Moh-shyun"), and a *q* by the English *ch* (Zhou Daiqi = "Joe Dye-chi").

Surnames precede given names in Chinese, and this often remains the case in anglicized versions. Some Chinese individuals who move abroad choose to adopt the Westernized convention of putting surnames second.

Many Huawei executives have adopted English names for their

professional work, and this text frequently uses English names for broader accessibility.

The Cast of Characters lists executives by prominent titles they have held that figure into this story. Huawei's executives tend to rotate roles and responsibilities every few years, and some have since progressed to other titles.

CAST OF CHARACTERS

The Ren Family

Ren Zhengfei / 任正非: Founder of Huawei Technologies Co., the world's largest supplier of telecommunications equipment.

Meng Wanzhou / 孟晚舟 (a.k.a. Cathy Meng and Sabrina Meng): Daughter of Ren Zhengfei and Meng Jun; Huawei's chief financial officer.

Ren Moxun / 任摩逊: Ren Zhengfei's father; dean of Duyun Normal College for Nationalities and principal of Duyun No. 1 Middle School.

Cheng Yuanzhao / 程远昭: Ren Zhengfei's mother; math teacher at Duyun No. 1 Middle School.

Steven Ren (a.k.a. **Ren Shulu** / 任树录): Ren Zhengfei's younger brother; Huawei's chief logistics officer.

Zheng Li / 郑黎: Ren Zhengfei's younger sister; a finance executive at Huawei.

Meng Jun / 孟军: Ren Zhengfei's first wife.

Meng Dongbo / 孟东波: Meng Jun's father and Ren Zhengfei's first father-in-law; Sichuan Province's vice-governor.

Ren Ping / 任平 (a.k.a. Meng Ping / 孟平): Son of Ren Zhengfei and Meng Jun.

Yao Ling / 姚凌: Ren Zhengfei's second wife; mother of Annabel Yao.

Annabel Yao (a.k.a. **Yao Anna** / 姚安娜 and Yao Siwei / 姚思为): Daughter of Ren Zhengfei and Yao Ling.

Carlos Liu (a.k.a. **Liu Xiaozong** / 刘晓棕): Meng Wanzhou's husband.

Key Huawei Executives

Sun Yafang / 孙亚芳: Huawei's chairwoman from 1999 to 2018.

Guo Ping / 郭平: One of Huawei's three rotating chairpersons; member of the company's early engineering team; oversaw Huawei's international M&As and legal cases.

Ken Hu (a.k.a. **Hu Houkun** / 胡厚崑): One of Huawei's three rotating chairpersons; oversaw Huawei's international cybersecurity.

Eric Xu (a.k.a. **Xu Zhijun** / 徐直军): One of Huawei's three rotating chairpersons; led Huawei's wireless division during its early internationalization.

Zheng Baoyong / 郑宝用: Huawei's chief engineer in early years and later an executive vice president; also president of Huawei's US division in the late 1990s.

Li Yinan / 李一男: Huawei's "boy genius" engineer in the early years; founder of the rival router maker Harbour Networks.

William Xu (a.k.a. **Xu Wenwei** / 徐文伟): Senior Huawei executive and board member who did chip engineering for the company's early telephone switches.

Chen Zhufang / 陈珠芳: Huawei's party secretary from the late 1990s through around 2007.

Zhou Daiqi / 周代期: Huawei's party secretary starting around 2008.

Jiang Xisheng / 江西生: Early Huawei executive who negotiated the exit of the company's five original investors.

James Yan (a.k.a. **Yan Jingli** / 阎景立): Huawei's first US representative in the 1990s.

Matt Bross: British Telecom CTO who selected Huawei for its first major contract in the West in 2005; later joined Huawei as global CTO.

Teresa He (a.k.a. **He Tingbo** / 何庭波): Head of Huawei's chip unit, HiSilicon.

Wen Tong / 童文: Huawei's lead 5G scientist; former head of Nortel's Network Technology Labs.

Charles Ding (a.k.a. **Ding Shaohua** / 丁少华): Huawei's chief US representative during the House Permanent Select Committee on Intelligence's 2012 hearing on Huawei and ZTE.

Richard Yu (a.k.a. **Yu Chengdong** / 余承东): Huawei's smartphone head.

Catherine Chen (a.k.a. **Chen Lifang** / 陈黎芳): Head of Huawei's public affairs during the US-China trade war; her husband, Cao Yi'an, was one of Huawei's early engineers.

Domestic Rivals

Shen Dingxing / 沈定兴: Founder of Zhuhai Telecom; one of Huawei's original five investors.

Wan Runnan / 万润南: Founder of the Stone Group Corporation, China's most promising early private tech company, dubbed "China's IBM"; he went into exile in France after supporting pro-democracy student protesters in Tiananmen Square in 1989.

Wu Jiangxing / 邬江兴: Military engineer who developed the "04 switch," China's first homegrown advanced digital telephone switch, in 1991; founder of the switching company Great Dragon; he was a director of the Information Engineering Academy of the PLA's General Staff Department, a title that Ren Zhengfei has been mistakenly cited as holding.

Hou Weigui / 侯为贵: Founder of ZTE.

Liu Chuanzhi / 柳传志: Founder of Lenovo.

International Industry Executives

John Chambers: CEO of Cisco when the company filed an intellectual-property lawsuit against Huawei.

Bruce Claflin: 3Com CEO; set up a joint-venture company with Huawei to help it defend itself against the Cisco lawsuit.

Mike Zafirovski: Motorola COO who tried to negotiate a merger with Huawei in 2003.

William A. "Bill" Owens: Former vice-chairman of the Joint Chiefs of Staff; former Nortel CEO; represented Huawei in its 2010 bid for a place in a Sprint contract.

Daniel "Dan" Hesse: Sprint Nextel CEO.

Chinese Government Officials

Note: The title of China's top leader fluctuated before 1997. Mao Zedong led China under the title "chairman of the Communist Party of China" from 1949 until his death in 1976. After a brief interregnum, Deng Xiaoping took over the helm under a range of titles, including "paramount leader," then just "comrade" in the years before his death in 1997. Since then, starting with Jiang Zemin, the nation's top leader has ruled as "general secretary of the Chinese Communist Party" while also doubling as the nation's "president" on a staggered schedule. For instance, Xi Jinping became China's leader in November 2012, when he assumed the post of general secretary of the Chinese Communist Party, then gained the additional title "president of China" in March 2013. The premier is the nation's number-two official.

Mao Zedong / 毛泽东: Founder of the People's Republic of China, chairman of the Communist Party of China (CCP), and the nation's leader from 1949 until his death in 1976.

Deng Xiaoping / 邓小平: China's leader from 1978 to 1997. He retired his formal government titles in the late 1980s but continued to be regarded as the nation's de facto leader until his death. He is credited with engineering China's economic renaissance through market reforms following Mao's Cultural Revolution.

Zhao Ziyang / 赵紫阳: China's premier from 1980 to 1987 and general secretary of the CCP from 1987 to 1989. He was deposed after sympathizing with the pro-democracy student protesters of Tiananmen Square in 1989. Earlier in his career, he was the leader of Sichuan Province as it began its experimentation in market reforms.

Li Peng / 李鹏: China's premier from 1987 to 1998. A security hardliner who backed the use of force against the Tiananmen Square protesters in 1989.

Hu Yaobang / 胡耀邦: General secretary of the CCP from 1982 to 1987. His death in April 1989 sparked student protests in Beijing that escalated into the Tiananmen Square protests.

Jiang Zemin / 江泽民: General secretary of the CCP from 1989 to 2002. He oversaw China's freewheeling boom in private business, as well as the nation's 2001 entry into the World Trade Organization (WTO). Outranked by Deng Xiaoping during the first part of his tenure as general secretary, he became China's top leader following Deng's death in 1997. Ren's meeting with Jiang in 1994 is often cited as an early highlight for Huawei.

Zhu Rongji / 朱镕基: China's premier from 1998 to 2003. He was a leading proponent of China's economic liberalization and negotiated the country's entry into the WTO. Following Zhu's visit to Huawei in 1996, the company gained easier access to financing from the state-owned banking system.

Hu Jintao / 胡锦涛: China's leader from 2002 to 2012, he presided over a period of rapid globalization. Ren Zhengfei accompanied him on a state visit to Iran in 2001.

Wu Bangguo / 吴邦国: China's vice-premier from 1995 to 2003 and chairman of the Standing Committee of the National People's Congress from 2003 to 2013. He was one of Huawei's supporters in Beijing and the official whom the company sought out for help when it came under scrutiny from national auditors in the early 2000s.

Wen Jiabao / 温家宝: China's premier from 2003 to 2013.

Zhang Gaoli / 张高丽: China's vice-premier from 2013 to 2018. He visited Huawei in 1998 during his tenure as Shenzhen's party secretary.

Xi Jinping / 习近平: China's current leader and general secretary of the CCP since 2012.

SELECTED PHOTOS

A street in Shenzhen, China, on August 3, 1981, a year after the city was named the nation's first "special economic zone," giving it the green light to experiment with capitalism. Bicycles were still the most common mode of transportation.

Huawei's founder, Ren Zhengfei (right), speaks with China's premier, Wen Jiabao, at Huawei's software development center in Bangalore, India, on April 10, 2005.

Huawei's founder, Ren Zhengfei (front row, second left), speaks to former vice-premier Wu Bangguo (center) and the International Telecommunication Union's secretary-general, Yoshio Utsumi (front row, third right), at the Huawei booth of a trade show in Hong Kong on December 3, 2006. Eric Xu, who became one of Huawei's three rotating CEOs, stands (first row, left). Wu was one of Huawei's supporters in Beijing.

Guo Ping (front row, right), who started out as one of Huawei's earliest engineers and later became one of the company's three rotating CEOs, meets with Ewon Ebin (center), Malaysia's minister of science, technology, and innovation, in Kuala Lumpur, Malaysia, on June 18, 2013, as Huawei signs an agreement with the Malaysian government to promote digital education.

Huawei's longest-serving chairwoman, Sun Yafang, meets with Egyptian president Abdel Fattah el-Sisi in Cairo, Egypt, on April 13, 2017. Sun handled many of the company's high-level diplomatic meetings.

Ken Hu (left), one of Huawei's three rotating CEOs and head of the company's international cybersecurity policy work, meets with the Czech Republic's prime minister, Andrej Babiš, in Davos on January 25, 2019, as the Czech government announced it was studying potential cybersecurity risks in Huawei's equipment.

Meng Wanzhou, Huawei's CFO and eldest daughter of founder Ren Zhengfei, meets with former Italian prime minister Mario Monti (left), in Milan, Italy, on May 9, 2018.

An employee of Chinese mobile operator China Telecom shows a Huawei 5G base station on the roof of a high-rise in Shenzhen, China, on January 21, 2019.

Huawei's founder, Ren Zhengfei (second left), shows China's leader, Xi Jinping (second right), around the company's offices in London on October 20, 2015. Huawei has benefited from Xi's Belt and Road Initiative for global infrastructure construction.

A man inspects Huawei surveillance cameras displayed at the China Public Security Expo in Shenzhen, China, on October 29, 2019. Huawei is a major global vendor of video-surveillance systems.

Huawei displays its Safe City surveillance system at a trade show in Barcelona, Spain, on November 15, 2016. The system allows authorities to view footage from individual surveillance cameras, as well as traffic information and other analytics, on a big screen.

Annabel Yao (front row, second right), *the youngest daughter of Huawei's founder, Ren Zhengfei, attends Le Bal des Débutantes in Paris, France, on November 24, 2018. Yao studied computer science at Harvard University but decided to pursue a career as a pop singer and an actor.*

A building inspired by Germany's Heidelberg Castle sits on Huawei's sprawling Ox Horn Campus in Dongguan, China. The 1.2-square-kilometer grounds of the R&D center were designed to look like twelve European cities and regions in miniature.

A row of caryatids, Greek-style pillars sculpted to look like women, in a hall where Huawei receives guests at the company's headquarters in Shenzhen, China.

Huawei's CFO, Meng Wanzhou, leaves her house in Vancouver, British Columbia, on May 8, 2019. While under house arrest, she was allowed outside with a tracking anklet and a security escort.

Huawei's CFO, Meng Wanzhou, arrives in Shenzhen, China, by chartered flight on September 25, 2021, after spending nearly three years under house arrest in Canada. The following year, she was promoted to rotating CEO of Huawei, a title she shares with two others.

AUTHOR'S NOTE

This is a work of journalism, which means that nothing is invented or fictionalized. Much of the dialogue and many of the details are drawn from official meeting minutes, speech transcripts, video recordings, government reports, and other contemporaneous records. Some information is also derived from the recollections of firsthand participants. Details on sources can be found in the endnotes, which are accessible at www.houseofhuawei.com /endnotes.

The goal of this project was to chronicle the historic path of the most successful company in China's modern history, Huawei Technologies, in the belief that it could contribute to the conversation about how we arrived at this current moment in history—and what comes next.

This is an independent project, which means it does not have the endorsement of, and was not commissioned by, Huawei, any other tech company, or any government. Penguin's Portfolio imprint was the sole source of funding. *The Washington Post* supported the endeavor through a book leave. This book also draws on interviews and research I did as a reporter for *The Post* and *The Wall Street Journal*.

The reconstruction of this narrative was made possible through the generous time and insights of many industry executives, policymakers, and scholars of China. I have tried to faithfully reflect the diversity of their perspectives in these pages. Any errors, misunderstandings, or oversights are solely my own. I hope that readers will enjoy their foray into the astonishing world of telecommunications as much as I did mine.

HOUSE OF
HUAWEI

INTRODUCTION

The woman's flight from Hong Kong arrived in Vancouver on December 1, 2018, at 11:10 a.m., a few minutes ahead of schedule.[1] Dressed comfortably in a dark hooded tracksuit and sneakers,[2] her shiny black hair hanging loose around her shoulders, she was planning a quick stop at one of her family homes, then heading on to Buenos Aires. As it happened, the most powerful men and women in the world were gathering just then in the Argentine capital for the G20 summit. It was—by her account—a coincidence.

As she stepped off the Cathay Pacific flight at the Vancouver International Airport, something was not quite right. An officer was checking passports as the passengers emerged from the jetway at gate 65. When she reached him, she showed him her Hong Kong passport, a fairly new one, her seventh in eleven years. The officer called over a colleague, who asked her to hand over her mobile phones. Her lawyers would later say she could have resisted. But she was jet-lagged and caught off guard, so it didn't occur to her to resist. She handed over her iPhone and a red-cased smartphone made by her father's company. The officers put them into a thick bag designed to block cell-phone signals and make it difficult for anyone to wipe them remotely.

After following her to baggage claim, the two officers rifled through her luggage, pulling out more electronics: a pink MacBook, a rose-gold iPad, a 256-gigabyte USB drive. One of them asked her for the phones' passwords and scribbled the numbers on a loose sheet of paper. The questioning continued. One hour passed, then two. Finally, three hours after she'd gotten off the plane, a third man appeared and told her she was under arrest. She was facing charges of fraud in the United States.

"You're saying you're going to arrest me?"

"Right."

"And then send me to the United States?"

"Right."[3]

It was now undeniable that this was not a random airport check. This was a highly planned operation. As the officer explained that they were going to book her into jail and fingerprint her, he advised Huawei's CFO, Meng Wanzhou, also known as Cathy Meng, also known as Sabrina Meng, to get a lawyer.

Huawei had been on Washington's radar for some time. The company had emerged as China's leading high-tech firm, trouncing its Western rivals in bids for major contracts on the strength of its sales team's ferocious "wolf culture." Huawei was now number one in the lucrative trade of building the "pipes" that made up the world's phone and internet networks. Its pockets seemed endlessly deep, as it scooped up top engineers from across the globe.

Meng Wanzhou's father—Huawei's reclusive founder, Ren Zhengfei—was a corporate legend in China. He had a reputation as a long-term strategist, and his military-esque aphorisms were widely quoted. Starting from humble beginnings, Ren had worked his way up through the military before setting up a humble telephone switch venture that had shot straight to the top. It was either an astonishing feat of innovation or, as some people muttered, too good to be true. There were rumors about the company pursuing obscured projects in Iran and North Korea. There were fears that Huawei products might contain "back doors" that could let overseas spies burrow their way in. There were questions of whether the company was controlled by China's government, despite Huawei's protests that it was an independent, privately owned company. Some US officials, with a touch of melodrama, were calling Huawei no less than the greatest threat to American democracy.[4]

Ren protested that he couldn't possibly be involved in such things. He was, he said, only a maker of pipes—a humble vocation not unlike that of a plumber. Not everyone saw things this way. Sure, Huawei might make pipes of a sort, but it was not water flowing through them. What flowed through these pipes was telephone calls, emails, internet traffic, text messages, video calls, corporate accounting, medical records, wills and testaments, love letters, family photographs, police intelligence, government secrets. In a word: data. The most valuable commodity of the information age. And Huawei was the largest supplier of these pipes—by a long shot.

And there was something else here. The question of Huawei wasn't merely a question of business; it was also a question of belief. When the Soviets had sent Sputnik 1 into the skies in 1957, it had shaken

Americans to the core. There was nationwide soul-searching: How could Moscow have gained the technological edge with its stodgy Communist methods? The collapse of the Soviet Union seemed to put that debate to rest, affirming the brittleness of Communist rule and the superiority of Western liberal democracy. As for China, it had been a technological leader centuries ago, inventing the compass, gunpowder, and paper. But it had fallen behind in the fifteenth century, and the prospect that it would ever catch up again seemed unlikely. Until now. The world was having another Sputnik moment. And this time the Sputnik was Huawei.

Huawei was filing more patent applications than any other company on earth. Huawei was number one in 5G. Huawei was number one in smartphones. It was breaking ground in artificial intelligence. It pulled in more in annual sales than Disney and Nike combined, and it employed more people than Apple. The rise of such an absolute corporate juggernaut was not supposed to be possible through Communism. But it had happened. It was the kind of thing that made people reconsider what they knew to be true. They were reconsidering if free trade really made everyone wealthier. They were reconsidering if history did end with Western-style democracy. They were reconsidering if the source of innovation really was college dropouts' garages and not the state picking winners and losers. Because if so, then how did a company like Huawei exist?

D ays after Meng's detention, Beijing struck back. Two Canadians, both named Michael, were detained in China, thrown into solitary detention, and accused of espionage. The simmering

US-China trade war had exploded into full-fledged hostage diplomacy.

Amid the fear and uncertainty that followed, something strange happened. Invitations began trickling out to major news organizations: *The New York Times*, *The Washington Post*, CNN, BBC. They were all invited to come to China and meet Ren Zhengfei himself. It was the first time in his life that Huawei's secretive founder had thrown open his doors to the foreign press. So it was with a great deal of intrigue, and a little trepidation, that the journalists arrived, one after another, in the megacity of Shenzhen on China's southern coast.

As they drove through the smoggy outskirts of Shenzhen, the sea of factories must have seemed to go on forever. There was one assembly line after another, churning out yo-yos, ziplock bags, scuba wet suits, electric toothbrushes, ultrasonic plastic welders, arch-support insoles, and everything in between. This was the place called the world's factory floor. Finally, the foreign reporters emerged at a lakeside hill. This was where Ren had built his Garden of Eden. There was a life-size replica of Versailles, with statues of white horses galloping around a fountain at its entrance. Nearby, the red turrets of Heidelberg Castle soared. A little red train chugged cheerfully from castle to castle. One hundred and fifty Russian painters had been hired to paint the walls and ceilings of the massive halls with Renaissance-style murals. In one hall, there was a re-creation of the caryatids from Delphi, the mysterious female figures holding up the sky with their heads. Exquisitely dressed young women playing the lute. There was also a sprawling vista of the Battle of Waterloo. Outside, black swans glided on a lake—a reminder from Ren to his employees to always be on the lookout for a "black-swan event," a term for an extremely unlikely but disastrous occurrence.

"Welcome," the Huawei staffers said, "to Huawei's R&D campus."

Now out walked Ren himself. If you believed some folks in Washington, he was one of the most dangerous men in the world. He didn't look so standing before them: a wizened little old man in a blue leisure suit and pastel shirt, spouting aphorisms and jokes through a translator.

The visiting journalists were keen to ask Ren about his background, about Huawei's ownership, about the psychedelic vision of the European castles, about Huawei's business in Iran, about the detention of his daughter. But most of all, they wanted to ask him over and over, in every possible permutation, the unanswerable question: Did Huawei help the Chinese government spy?

"We are a company that sells water taps and pipes," Ren said. "How can anyone ask for water from a hardware store like us?"[5]

PART I

A country without its own program-controlled switches is like one without an army.[1]

—Ren Zhengfei, July 20, 1994

1

The Bookseller

Ren Moxun[1] sold "good books."[2] That was what he and his friends called patriotic literature. They were seeking to inspire their countrymen to heroism at a time when it was urgently needed. They'd considered names like Advancement Bookstore and Pioneering Bookstore before finally settling on July Seventh Bookstore. The reference was obvious: Earlier that year, on July 7, 1937, Japanese troops had crossed the Marco Polo Bridge, captured the capital, and continued their invasion of China. World War II would not come for Europe for another two years, when Adolf Hitler invaded Poland. But here in China, the war was already upon them. Ren Moxun opened up the bookstore in the small town of Rongxian,[3] in southern Guangxi Province, and threw himself into the war effort.

Ren Moxun was around twenty-seven at this time, and he had a high forehead, long cheeks, and bushy eyebrows.[4] The only one among his siblings to have attended university,[5] he cultivated a professorial air and wore horn-rimmed spectacles. He revered books, schooling, and the written word, a predisposition he would pass down to his seven children.[6] At the time he opened his bookstore, reading was still a hobby for the privileged elite. If you pulled five people off the street at random, you'd be lucky if one could read.[7] Chinese script was difficult to learn: it had no alphabet, and you had to memorize each word, one by one. Still, there was enough interest in Rongxian for a bookstore. Ren Moxun stocked revolutionary titles[8] from a supplier in Guilin: Karl Marx's *Das Kapital*, Vladimir Lenin's *The Proletarian Revolution and the Renegade Kautsky*, the complete works of the modern Chinese thinker Lu Xun. He and his colleagues placed a bench at the front so that frugal students could sit and read for free.[9] Outside the bookstore, they propped up a blackboard to scrawl news of the war, something of an unofficial village newspaper. They started a political reading club too, which gathered for spirited discussions.

In his day job, Ren Moxun served as an accountant for a Nationalist military factory supporting the fight against Japan. The Nationalists, China's rulers at the time, were also embroiled in a civil war against Mao Zedong's Communists, who were seeking to overthrow them with the help of the peasantry. As they fought Japan's invasion, the two sides had brokered a delicate truce, an agreement Ren Moxun strongly endorsed. When one faction of Communist revolutionaries in his town began advocating to end the détente with the Nationalists, he denounced them as traitors.[10] These were tense times. People disagreed on what was the right path for the nation, on who was friend or foe, on whether a book was a "good book" or not. One day in March 1938, some Nationalist officers searched the bookstore and pulled out a big pile of books that they demanded not be sold. Ren Moxun and his colleagues found a clever workaround.[11] They piled the banned books into a vitrine and scrawled a sign on it: INSIDE THIS CABINET ARE BANNED BOOKS. As it turned out, the books inside the cabinet sold briskly.

The July Seventh Bookstore was shut down by the Nationalists in the second half of 1939. Its owners held a fire sale to get a last batch of good books out to the people.[12] Ren Moxun considered traveling to Yan'an to join Mao's Communists but found the roads impassable. So he crossed to the rolling hills of the neighboring province, Guizhou, where he found work as a teacher.

Guizhou Province is a hilly region slightly smaller than Missouri, set inland from China's southwestern border with Vietnam. Monsoons sweep the subtropical region each summer, watering the terraced paddies of sticky rice. Cold drizzles continue through the winter. The area's indigenous people were the Bouyei, who spoke their own language and also inhabited northern Vietnam. For centuries, China's emperors considered the area an impoverished borderland[13] where even cooking salt was sometimes in short supply.[14] Even in the modern day, Guizhou retains the reputation of a hardship posting for officials.

In Guizhou, Ren Moxun met a seventeen-year-old named Cheng Yuanzhao. With big brown eyes,[15] round cheeks, and a broad smile, she was also bright and good with numbers.[16] They married, and Cheng Yuanzhao soon became pregnant.

Their son was born in October 1944,[17] and they named him Ren Zhengfei. It was an ambiguous name. *Zheng* meant "correct," and *fei* meant "not." "Right or wrong" would be a fair translation. It wasn't like the common, straightforward boys' names. *Jiabao* meant "family treasure." *Jianguo* meant "build the nation." But what did a name like his mean?

Japan's occupation of China ended abruptly the year after Ren Zhengfei's birth, when the Americans dropped atomic bombs on Hiroshima and Nagasaki. For all the efforts of Ren Moxun and his compatriots, it was America's superior bomb technology that ended the Japanese occupation. In China, there would not yet be peace. Civil war resumed between the Nationalists and Communists. Ren Moxun and Cheng Yuanzhao had six more children, all while both parents worked teaching local students in spare conditions, under the glow of kerosene lamps.[18] Cheng served for a period as an elementary school principal.[19]

In 1949, Mao Zedong emerged victorious. It was clear that Ren Moxun had picked the wrong side by working for the Nationalists during the war. It wasn't yet clear how dire the consequences would be for his family.

On a foggy morning in 1950, Ren Moxun rode a horse-drawn carriage into the town of Zhenning.[20] The name Zhenning meant "town of peace," but Ren Moxun, seated in the middle of the cart and surrounded by three armed men who kept their Mauser guns trained outward, arrived with some trepidation. The fog was so thick the men could see only a few meters ahead on the winding dirt road, and they feared that unfriendly locals might attack them. Officials had tasked Ren Moxun with launching a new middle school for Bouyei children in Zhenning, one that would teach them the Mandarin Chinese language and help integrate them into the nascent Communist republic. Mao's new government was seeking to solidify its control over a sprawling territory that, for most of its history, had been not a unified whole but self-governing fiefdoms speaking different tongues. A unifying language was not just a linguistic issue but a political one.

Ren Moxun and his colleagues began setting up a new boarding school, going door-to-door to recruit students across the countryside. Fewer than half of the students spoke fluent Mandarin.[21] Many of the older residents didn't speak Mandarin at all. Ren Moxun and his staff learned conversational Bouyei. Attendance was a challenge for students who had to travel a great distance.[22] Many families also couldn't afford the school fees. Ren Moxun and his staff came up with a solution: the students and faculty would make up the budget shortfall through part-time farming.[23] He got the government to give them an acre of land, where the students planted crops and raised pigs. The labor of the students and teachers enabled the school to cover its costs, including meals and a free blue uniform for each student.

Mao's officials believed they were extending a civilizing influence to the nation's frontiers—Guizhou in the south, Inner Mongolia in the north, Tibet and Xinjiang in the west. The residents didn't necessarily see it that way. They had lived for centuries with their own languages and customs, and they were now being compelled to assimilate. There were those who did not like Ren Moxun and his school either. After someone threatened to kill him with a hand grenade—the precise reasons are unclear—the school was issued four rifles to protect the staff and students.[24]

One of Ren Moxun's objectives was to inculcate his students with the right beliefs. "Principal Ren, your guiding ideology must be clear," a visiting official instructed him. "You must make clear who the enemies are, who we are, who are our friends." Ren Moxun organized rallies for the students to denounce their enemies.[25] The enemies at home were the oppressive landlords. The enemies abroad were the Americans, who were waging war against North Korea, one of China's allies. Ren Moxun reported that the "scoundrels" hidden among the teachers were successfully caught through these criticism sessions, which were often intense, with students bursting into tears. In the anti-America sessions, students offered up secondhand accounts of atrocities committed by US troops in the area, presumably when they had passed through during World War II. One student said a US soldier had shot a farmer for sport near the Yellow Fruit Waterfall. Another said a classmate's sister had been dragged into a jeep and raped. It was hard to say what, exactly, had happened years ago with US soldiers, but the resentment against America was certainly real.

Ren Moxun was a man of quiet ambition, and by age forty-five, he was beginning to gain national attention for his work. In 1955, a prominent linguistic journal published a paper of his on teaching Mandarin Chinese to Bouyei children.[26] He outlined their successes in connecting with their pupils by learning their tongue. He noted that the Bouyei language had been changing rapidly since Mao came to power, with new terms like *landlord* and *land reform* added. His paper impressed officials at the Ministry of Education enough that they dispatched officials to visit his school. In the autumn of 1955, he was also invited to attend the landmark linguistic conference in Beijing where officials made the controversial decision to simplify the Chinese written language to boost literacy. Arriving in the nation's capital, he posed proudly for a photo on a tree-lined walkway of Beihai Park.[27]

After returning home to Zhenning, Ren Moxun was promoted to dean of the new Duyun Normal College for Nationalities, a teachers' school for local ethnic minority students. His son Ren Zhengfei, then a middle schooler, was astonished when they moved to the county seat and saw the department store. It was his first time seeing a two-story building.[28]

When Ren Moxun took up management of Duyun Normal College for Nationalities in 1958, Mao had just launched an ambitious national campaign dubbed the Great Leap Forward. The previous autumn, the Soviet Union had launched the world's first artificial satellite, Sputnik 1, a technological feat that stunned the world. The Soviet Union's leader, Nikita Khrushchev, set a goal of surpassing the US in industrial output in fifteen years. Mao was inspired to follow suit, declaring that China would catch up with the United Kingdom in fifteen years.

To meet such an astronomical goal, all of China would have to suspend business as usual for an emergency industrialization push. Duyun Normal College for Nationalities was no exception. Ren Moxun was ordered to halve the four-year curriculum to make time for steelmaking. His staff and students would work nights making steel while continuing their daytime classes, a grueling schedule.[29] The exhausted students could only catch up on sleep during the day, and their coursework suffered.

Some steel was produced in the nationwide drive, but a lot of the amateur efforts came to naught. As farmers neglected the fields and melted farming tools to try to meet steel quotas, the crops failed. By

1959, starvation was widespread across Guizhou Province and the nation. In some Guizhou towns, grain rations were reduced to several tablespoons per person per day.[30] Ren Moxun pleaded with local authorities to increase the students' rations, arguing that they needed more food to complete their workloads. They stretched their rations by growing radishes in the schoolyard and gathering acorns to grind into meal. The dean had Communist Party members among the staff—seen as the most morally upstanding employees—take turns guarding the pantry from theft.[31]

Outside the schoolyard, the situation was even more dire. Local authorities across Guizhou were receiving reports of a swelling sickness.[32] Farmers' abdomens were ballooning with fluid until it killed them. Investigations determined that the cause was starvation. By one historian's estimate, 10 percent of Guizhou's population died from the famine, one of the highest death rates in the country.[33] The famine coincided with local unrest: At one point, officials instructed Ren Moxun and his students to disperse a crowd of angry ethnic minority villagers, which they did with reluctance. It is not clear what the villagers were protesting.[34]

Ren Moxun's own family was struggling to put enough food on the table for their seven children. The family foraged wild roots, tasting them gingerly, unsure if they were edible.[35] They ate wild castor beans, which gave them diarrhea. Ren Zhengfei had been an excellent student in middle school, but now he found it hard to concentrate. In his sophomore year of high school, he had to retake the final exams.

As Ren prepared for the grueling college entrance exam, the gaokao, his mother encouraged him by slipping him an extra corn cake now and then to ease his hunger pangs.

Excerpted from a 1959 booklet about the Chongqing Institute of Architecture and Engineering, this photo shows a campus building designed and constructed by students.

In 1963, Ren Zhengfei was accepted to the Chongqing Institute of Architecture and Engineering (later merged into Chongqing University).[36] This was not an elite school like Tsinghua or Peking University in the capital. But for a small-town student who had just survived a famine, it was good enough indeed. Chongqing was a major inland city in Sichuan Province, which was known for its mouth-numbingly spicy cuisine and its surrounding bamboo forests, where giant pandas roamed. As a temporary wartime capital for the Nationalists in the early 1940s, it had munitions factories, heavy industry, and engineering schools.

The Great Leap Forward and the famine had ended, but Ren's college experience was still not a normal one. Mao thought young people were spending too much time with their noses in books. They should be learning by building things with their hands, with the peasantry as their tutors. In early 1964, Mao ordered universities to thin out curriculums, making room for students to learn through practical work.[37] The professors at the Chongqing Institute of Architecture and Engineering were obliged to turn lectures into reading handouts and allow students to take open-book tests. Teams of students were sent out for stints on construction sites.[38] Mao also ordered universities to participate in nationwide defense preparations, with students run through militia drills.[39]

On the morning of May 14, 1966, students awoke to find all classes suspended for three days.[40] Mao announced that class enemies had infiltrated the Communist Party and had to be rooted out. The Cultural Revolution had begun. At Ren's university, students and teachers were told to write "big-character posters," handwritten signs denouncing individuals as counterrevolutionaries. Before long, some four thousand posters papered the campus.[41] By the summer, the professors were in terror as growing numbers of them were denounced. More and more of Ren's classmates wore the red armbands of the Red Guards, Mao's youth paramilitary organization, which was spearheading the hunt for counterrevolutionaries.

As was happening elsewhere across the nation, Red Guards at Ren's university overthrew the administration, forcing the professors to turn over the keys and official seal. They overthrew the Chongqing government as well. Teachers and students fled. Management of the college remained in chaos for the next two years. In February 1967, some fellow students at Ren's university kidnapped

Luo Guangbin, a local writer.[42] The Red Guards locked Luo up inside a room in the physics building on campus, denouncing him as a traitor who wrote reactionary novels, until he leaped from a window to his death.

Beyond the campus walls, Red Guards were staging deadly battles[43] in the streets of Chongqing as rival factions fought for dominance. The students had broken into the city's military factories, seizing rifles, heavy artillery, and even tanks. Six middle schoolers and a college student were killed in a shootout on August 4, 1967.[44] Four days later, a Red Guard clash along a riverbank left 24 dead, 129 wounded. Chongqing was becoming one of the bloodiest sites of the Cultural Revolution. Some 1,700 Red Guards and civilians had been killed in the city by the time the violence receded in 1968, according to an independent historian's estimate.[45]

Ren Zhengfei watched from the sidelines with fear and a little envy.[46] His father's bad political background meant that he could not join the Red Guards even if he wanted to. Instead, he buried himself in books, reading deeply on math and philosophy, as well as self-studying three foreign languages. Ren received letters from his mother periodically; they were largely banal, repeating party slogans. Mail was not private, and people were careful about what they put to paper. It was only through a friend who had met a student from his father's school that he heard his father, too, was enduring brutal persecution.

Principal Ren Moxun's background was all wrong. He'd grown up in material comfort, his father a successful ham maker in coastal Zhejiang Province.[47] The family had lived in a sprawling 1820s estate that was sometimes called the "Thirteen Rooms of the Ren Family."[48] On the outside, the two-story home looked simple, with whitewashed walls and a gray-tiled roof in the common style. But the interior betrayed the family's wealth and status: there were intricately carved wooden beams and balconies that surrounded a central courtyard, or siheyuan.[49] This bourgeois background was now a problem for Ren Moxun, along with his work at a Nationalist factory during the war. He had joined the Communist Party in 1958, but that was far too late to expiate these other sins.[50]

Ren Moxun was hauled onto a platform in the school cafeteria, his hands tied, his face smeared with black ink, the tall hat of shame denoting a counterrevolutionary placed on his head.[51] "Studying is useless!" people shouted. "The more knowledge you possess, the more reactionary you are!"[52]

One of Ren Moxun's students demanded the principal admit that he'd instilled feudalist thinking in the students, such as by quoting Confucius. According to a recollective essay by Feng Jugao, a different student, when Ren Moxun tried to deny the accusation, the accuser rushed forward with a wooden stick and beat him until the stick broke.[53] "I can't say if the wooden stick was weak, or if Principal Ren's backbone was strong," Feng wrote. "But the wooden stick broke in two across Principal Ren's back." Feng recalled his mother being aghast, saying that the students who beat the principal would get their karmic punishment.

Ren Moxun was put on a truck with other "rightists" and driven around town with a sign looped around his neck as a warning.[54] One of his colleagues—the school's party secretary, Huang Xuanqian—couldn't endure the torments and committed suicide.[55] Ren Moxun also considered ending his life, but he didn't want to die before his name was cleared, as it would leave his wife and children with a cloud over them. "If he died," Ren Zhengfei explained, "his children would have to carry this political burden. . . . He endured a hundred tortures, but he would not kill himself."[56] Ren Moxun was sent to a labor camp.[57]

"The Cultural Revolution was a disaster for the nation," Ren Zhengfei later wrote. "But for us it was a baptism. It made me politically mature, so that I wasn't just a simple bookworm."[58]

Universities nationwide were banned from matriculating any new students between 1966 and 1976. Ren Zhengfei's younger siblings were shut out, but through the random luck of his birth year, he'd been able to eke out a college education. In 1968, Ren graduated with a major in heating, gas supply, and ventilation engineering.[59]

The year of Ren's graduation, Mao began his "rusticated youth" campaign, sending millions of urban youths to the countryside to be reeducated by laboring alongside the peasantry. Some of the young people were obliged to farm for years—planting corn, hoeing potatoes— before they were allowed to resume their lives back home. Many others never made it back, having put down roots in the countryside by the time they were allowed to return to the cities.

Ren was also assigned to rural labor, but he was luckier than many. Guizhou Province was a stone's throw from the border with Vietnam, and for several years already, Mao had been funneling artillery, shells, tanks, radio transmitters, and telephones to Hanoi to aid Vietnam's fight against the Americans. The hills of Guizhou provided good air cover, so the Chinese military had burrowed in there, building secret air bases and camouflaged factories. Whatever the political rhetoric against science, Mao needed an enormous number of trained engineers to keep the gears turning in the proxy war. And so as Ren left university, he found himself assigned to the familiar hills of Guizhou, not to hoe potatoes or to make steel but to help build a secret military production site code-named 011.[60]

2

The Factory in the Cave

REN'S MILITARY YEARS:
1968-1982

Guizhou Province is a land of hills and caves. The thin top-soil sits on pale limestone, eroded over the eons by rain.[1] As underground sinkholes collapsed, they formed an ethereal terrain of caverns, hills, and valleys. Guizhou's city builders flattened some of the hills and filled in some of the valleys, but there were too many, so they had to build around them. Persistent fog shrouds the region. In ancient times, superstitious travelers from the north believed it to be noxious vapors that caused disease. But now Mao's troops saw the land from a new perspective: it was the perfect spot to hide a fighter jet factory.

The project was dubbed 011, and long after it had ceased operation, people still found it mysterious. "'It was a secret unit of China's in Guizhou,'" the local state-run newspaper, *Anshun Daily*, reported residents saying decades later.[2] "'People say it was a military factory that manufactured aircraft.'" According to one former employee, it didn't have a regular address for receiving mail.[3]

Ren Zhengfei arrived at Base 011 following his 1968 college graduation. After spending his teenage years in deprivation and turmoil, he had emerged a compact young man, with the same tall forehead, triangular eyes, and bookish bent as his father. He tended toward melancholy, and he would have a lifelong habit of fearing worst-case scenarios. The worst was happening to many people in the Cultural Revolution, but Ren had been lucky. He'd arrived in one of the few places in the nation where he could continue scientific studies without fear of political peril: the military.

Beijing had ordered Base 011's construction[4] in 1964, as the Vietnam War raged to the south. China's leaders were anxious to avoid open war with the US, but there was a real risk that the war would spill over the border. So they ordered the construction of Base 011 and other installations as part of a sweeping military-industrial production campaign. Guizhou was not directly on the border but not far removed either. US intelligence observed three new Chinese air bases being constructed.[5] Across the province, residents were ordered to dig bomb shelters. Deng Xiaoping, a senior official who would become one of the nation's longest-ruling leaders, visited the area himself to survey the preparations.[6]

Base 011 wasn't a single manufacturing site; it was a network of dozens of factories scattered across caverns outside the town of Anshun in central Guizhou. The dispersed setup made it harder to see from the air—harder, too, to sabotage. The project covered more than half a square kilometer and cost a staggering 1.1 billion yuan ($160 million in US dollars based on current exchange rates).[7] More than 2,000 employees of the Shenyang Aircraft Corporation were transplanted from the far northeast to set it up, and there were plans for 35,500 people to work there at full capacity.[8] Officials had originally hoped that planes could start rolling out of Base 011 in 1968, the year of Ren's university graduation. But the schedule was delayed, as rebels seized control of the facility during the Cultural Revolution.[9] Beijing officials were impatient about the delays, ordering Base 011 to produce fighter jets by 1970.[10]

According to Ren, he had to work two years as a cook first, since he was an "intellectual" who required reeducation. From there, he progressed to plumber, then to technician. In his spare time, he said, he self-studied electronics. Asked if his work there was related to communications technology, he replied, "What I did back then had nothing to do with communications. I was just an ordinary construction worker, just like today's migrant workers in cities."[11]

At first, living conditions were primitive. The dorms had been hastily erected by piling stones into walls without mortar, so the wind and wet whistled straight through. With no plumbing, workers drew their drinking water straight out of rice paddies.[12] "You cannot imagine how tough it was back then," one worker recalled to a local magazine. "We all bunked together in the shabby stone houses, and we were hungry."

To Huawei's detractors, Ren's military past would be viewed as his original sin. It led to all the other questions about how closely the company was linked to the Chinese government and the party. It was a reason why officials in Washington began taking an interest in Huawei in the late 1990s, recalled James Lewis, who was working at the US Commerce Department on international technology issues.[13] "That was one of the questions," Lewis said. "How strong is his connection back to his former employers?"

Huawei would downplay Ren's military tenure over the years. "Mr. Ren's military service did not involve Chinese signal intelligence in any way," a Huawei executive told the US Federal Communications Commission (FCC) in a sworn declaration.[14] Huawei said that Ren's work at Base 011 took place through the Second Company of the State Construction Commission's Third Bureau.[15] "This company constructed buildings for the 011 factory, but was not actually part of the military. With this company, Mr. Ren was not a soldier," Huawei's statement said.

Huawei was probably right in that Ren's military background was not the key factor in understanding the company's later connections with China's government. Over the years, Huawei's business interests would become intertwined with those of Beijing in numerous ways that did not have any apparent connection to Ren's early days as an army engineer. But there is no doubt that Ren's experience in the military helped shape his worldview. He would inculcate Huawei with a military-esque culture, running new hires through army-inspired boot camps and emphasizing discipline and personal sacrifice. He peppered his speeches with military analogies and references to famous battles. Years later, he still carried himself with a soldier's bearing.

At some point after his university graduation, Ren was introduced to a young woman named Meng Jun, who was the daughter of Sichuan Province's vice-governor, Meng Dongbo.[16] According to a history of the Red Guards in Chongqing by the Chinese historian He Shu, Meng Jun had been a student at the Chongqing

Medical College.[17] A fellow student recalled her as tall, bespectacled, and not a great beauty, but carrying herself with a noble bearing.[18] "I don't know what she saw in me," Ren said, "because she was already somebody and I was nobody."[19]

Jun meant "military," and it was an odd name for a young woman. But in Mao's China, it had become trendy for young women to take on militant names and tomboy styles. Mao had outlawed the crippling practice of foot-binding for girls and encouraged women to take their places on the battlefield and on the assembly line. Mao's wife, Jiang Qing, a former movie star, eschewed makeup and jewelry and wore loose, androgynous clothes. Young women across the nation imitated her. Ren described Meng Jun as "very tough."[20]

While Ren's bad political background had ruled him out of membership in Mao's youth paramilitary group, the Red Guards, Meng Jun was exactly the kind of upstanding youngster whom officials wanted to recruit into the organization. She was appointed deputy political commissar for the Mao Zedong Thought Red Guards, or Thought Guards, a Chongqing-based branch of Red Guards backed by the local government.[21] Ren has said that Meng Jun led some three hundred thousand Red Guards.[22]

Meng Jun's father, Meng Dongbo, was a large-framed man with a toothy smile[23] and the proletarian background that higher-ups found trustworthy.[24] He'd been raised by his impoverished grandfather in Wuxi, as his widowed mother worked in Shanghai to try to pay off the family's debts. As a schoolboy in the days of Nationalist rule, Meng Dongbo had begun working for an underground Communist cell, taking on the dangerous task of delivering secret notes sewn into the lining of his jacket. Meng Dongbo was a quick study, and he even picked up some English during a stint working at British American

Tobacco in Shanghai as a teenager. After joining Mao's troops in Yan'an in 1938 at the age of nineteen, he swiftly rose through the ranks.[25] By the time Mao launched his Great Leap Forward steel-making drive in 1958, Meng Dongbo was head of metallurgy for Sichuan,[26] China's most populous province. Under orders from his bosses, he oversaw Sichuan's construction of thousands of primitive kilns to smelt iron across the countryside, a disruption of farming that contributed to the deadly famine that followed.[27]

By the time the Cultural Revolution was beginning in 1966, Meng Dongbo was Sichuan's vice-governor.[28] As Mao became paranoid of enemies hidden within the party's ranks, he ordered a purge of senior officials. Meng Dongbo's boss, Li Jingquan, the tan, gap-toothed Sichuan chief, was now public enemy number one, with massive public rallies held to criticize him.[29] Li was thrown in prison[30] after being accused of ideological crimes ranging from opposing the construction of a factory that would print Mao Zedong's writings[31] to reading salacious novels from the library.[32] His deputies were also implicated. One poster that hung in the street accused Meng Dongbo of scheming to help Li organize pro-government worker groups.[33]

Meng Dongbo was "brutally persecuted and criticized," according to the *Sichuan Daily*, the state-run provincial newspaper.[34] He was sent to a labor camp[35] along with thousands of other officials, where they were stripped of their titles and called "cadets." The cadets planted crops, fed pigs, built houses, and dug wells.[36]

His daughter Meng Jun also suffered. She and the others in the government-backed Thought Guards had quickly come under attack from more radical student groups that accused them of being puppeteered by corrupt officials. Meng Jun was pressured into denouncing the local government and the Thought Guards, according to several

A 1967 public rally in Chengdu to denounce Sichuan's then party secretary, Li Jingquan.

accounts.[37] The Chongqing Red Guard factions soon deteriorated into deadly firefights in the streets.

The upheaval of the Cultural Revolution had been a great equalizer. In another time, it might have been unlikely for a small-town school principal's son to find himself in the orbit of a vice-governor's daughter. But with both their fathers in labor camps, Ren Zhengfei and Meng Jun began courting. At their wedding, Ren's siblings, who had been assigned to manual labor like digging sand and building railroads, scraped together a modest sum of cash for a gift.[38]

On September 18, 1970, Base 011 delivered on Beijing officials' demands. Its first fighter jet, a Shenyang J-6 III, based on a Soviet design, made a successful test flight.[39] It was a small plane, cigar-shaped, with an engine under each wing and a clear bubble around the cockpit. That first flight must have been a magical moment for everyone there. From caves in the backcountry, they had produced a hulking piece of metal that could float through the air.

Base 011 became more sophisticated over the years. One former employee recalled a unit of technological intelligence officers conversant in foreign languages working there on research projects ranging from jet engine construction to mining explosives.[40]

In 1972, Ren and Meng Jun welcomed their first child, Meng Wanzhou. *Wanzhou* meant "evening boat," and the name was part of a Chinese idiom describing a beautiful scene at sunset. Days later, Richard Nixon set foot in Beijing, a historic first visit to Communist China by a US president. The United Nations had also recognized Mao's People's Republic of China after years of clinging to recognition of the defeated Nationalists, who had fled to the island of Taiwan at the end of the civil war. After decades of being international pariahs, China's Communists were finding acceptance into the world.

By 1974, Ren had been transferred to Xi'an, the ancient gate of the Silk Road and the capital of Shaanxi Province, to train at the Xi'an Instruments Factory,[41] which made thermometers, pressure gauges, and other specialized gadgets used in scientific labs and industry. It was there, through a university lecture by the Chinese computing pioneer Wu Jikang, that he learned about computers for the first time.[42] Ren didn't understand much of the lecture, but he felt inspired.

That same year, Ren was dispatched to Liaoyang in the frigid northeast, a remote site about one hundred miles from China's border with North Korea, as part of a construction arm of the People's Liberation Army called the Engineering Corps.[43] His wife stayed behind in Chengdu with their two-year-old daughter, Meng Wanzhou, whom Ren affectionately nicknamed Piggy.[44] Their son, Ren Ping, was born about a year into Ren's Liaoyang posting. He had only a month's home leave each year, preventing him from forming a closer bond with his children.

Ren's troops had been tasked with helping China manufacture nylon and polyester, which had been invented in the United States in the 1930s[45] and which were still mysterious foreign textiles that no Chinese company could produce. This was a top-level project ordered by Mao himself.[46] If China could weave textiles out of petrochemicals, it could alleviate the dire shortage of cotton cloth, which was still rationed. Ren himself had grown up without enough shirts: as a high schooler, he had to wear the same thick shirts year-round.[47] Nylon was also useful for the military, with US troops using it for everything from parachutes to aircraft fuel tanks to flak jackets.

A number of foreign companies had lobbied for the lucrative factory project. In a nod to diplomatic considerations, Mao's government awarded the contract to France's Technip and Speichim: France had been the first Western power to recognize Mao as China's leader.[48] The project was hailed as the largest ever between France and Mao's China.[49]

There were ambitious plans to build a factory town with capacity for hundreds of French engineers and some seventy thousand Chinese workers. But when Ren and his colleagues arrived, there was still no housing, and they had to camp in the grass.[50] Ren later said he ended up in Liaoyang because the government was having trouble staffing the project. "No team answered the call," he said. "Therefore, the government had to mobilize military teams to build the factory."[51] Some of the workers were also drawn from reeducation camps for local officials, who were promised a second chance if they worked hard.[52]

The project was woefully behind schedule. The construction teams had neglected to first lay down the pipes for carrying corrosive chemicals, which had to run underneath everything else. When they realized their mistake, they had to tear everything up and start again. "It was a mess," the factory's party secretary, Qi Yushun, recalled.[53] The delays were so severe that the project was publicly criticized in the *People's Daily*, the party's mouthpiece paper in Beijing, as an example of the failures that resulted from the "reactionary nature" and "wolfish ambition to restore capitalism" of Deng Xiaoping—then a senior Beijing official who was in the process of being purged from Mao's inner circle.[54]

The staff dorms had been constructed hastily, and the walls soon cracked, letting the chill wind through. They shivered in the cold in their dark-green cotton uniforms. The hot water supply was spotty in the dorms. It was hard to even get vegetables beyond pickled cabbage and radish in the cold months,[55] let alone grape wine, a privation felt deeply by the French engineers stationed in Liaoyang for the project.[56] Still, Ren was appreciative of his time there. "The factory was like an oasis in the desert," Ren later said. "It was really difficult to find a place in China at the time where reading technical books wouldn't be treated as a political mistake."[57]

Ren's unit was assigned to test and calibrate the imported French factory equipment. These devices were things like differential pressure transmitters, gauges that measured the rate of flow through a pipe.[58] To test them, Ren needed a machine that could produce a precise amount of air pressure, with any variations smaller than a twentieth of a percentage point. Ren's team had only crude Soviet-made mercury gauges from the 1950s. After learning about a precision version made by the US company Ametek with a floating ball over a nozzle, Ren determined that he would make his own, becoming obsessed with the research project.[59]

"He was so devoted to his research that he worked night and day, and lost all track of time," read a profile of him in the PLA Engineering Corps' internal newspaper. "As a result, he was suffering from hair loss, insomnia, and bad appetite. Wrinkles were deeply etched on his forehead already, though he was only at the age of 33."[60]

3

A New Start

CHINA'S ECONOMIC REFORMS
BEGIN: 1976-1984

The fortunes of the Ren and Meng families changed abruptly on September 9, 1976. At 4:00 p.m., radios across the country carried the solemn announcement that Mao Zedong had died. Within weeks, Mao's wife and her allies had been arrested. The Cultural Revolution was over.

It was a new lease on life for Ren Zhengfei's father, Ren Moxun, and his father-in-law, Meng Dongbo. Both had suffered in labor camps and were now allowed to resume their work and lives. Ren Moxun was sixty-six. It was bitter for him to accept that some of the prime years of his career had been lost so senselessly. "Like Don Quixote, they set up all sorts of imaginary enemies," he wrote about the campaign. "They endlessly pursued a 'class struggle' that distorted facts."[1] His wife, Cheng Yuanzhao, had also survived, but she had severe hearing loss after a bout of untreated tuberculosis.[2]

Ren Moxun emerged from the Cultural Revolution with a demotion. Freed from the labor camp, the former university dean was named principal of Duyun No. 1 Middle School in 1979.[3] The school was in a sad state. Red Guards had trashed much of its equipment, which symbolized old ideas and old customs. Most of the desks and chairs had gone missing. Teachers had tried to hide cartloads of the school's books, but these had been found and burned. Around half the teachers, some thirty instructors, had been denounced and persecuted. Two math teachers had been killed, and a history teacher had died of illness during forced labor.[4] Well into his sixties, Ren Moxun was past retirement age in China, but he did not want to retire. He could finally work again. "I am proud of the political caliber of the older generation," he later wrote. "As soon as they were let out of the labor camps, as soon as they'd recovered organizational life, they worked as hard as they could."[5]

In Duyun, first the farmers were allowed to keep extra crops after paying state quotas,[6] and then others could start small businesses.[7] At the local department store, sales of plastic slippers, hot water thermoses, wristwatches, and sewing machines surged.[8] It was a sudden change for everyone, adults and children alike. Ren Moxun followed the official line, teaching his students that their system in China was fundamentally different from exploitative capitalist systems overseas. "Capitalists provide workers with electric refrigerators and cars on credit, putting 8% to 12% interest on the bill, and tell you to pay in installments," Ren Moxun taught the students. "After paying for several months, if you can't pay anymore, they'll take the stuff back. They won't return your money."[9] His pupils studied an essay by a Chinese woman living in Japan who described the heavy burdens of life in a capitalist system. She wrote that she had to change outfits several times a day to avoid being ridiculed or losing her job. One student remarked that they now understood why people changed outfits so often in foreign movies. "In the past we thought it was a luxury, but now we understand it's nothing to envy."[10]

In around 1977, when Meng Wanzhou was about five, she was told that she was being sent to live with her father's parents in Guizhou.[11] It was a common arrangement for elderly grandparents to take on the child-rearing in Communist China, with both women and men working outside the home. It is unclear why the decision was made for Meng to go to her paternal grandparents instead of staying with her mother's politically connected parents in Chengdu.

Meng struggled to adjust in Guizhou, far from her parents. Her grandparents lived more simply. Candy was a rare treat, and there often wasn't meat for dinner. Her grandparents enrolled her two years early in Duyun No. 3 Elementary School, where she struggled to keep up with the older students. Math homework was especially painful. Her grandmother would help her with her sums but would occasionally remark, "How does Feifei have such a dumb daughter!"[12]

Meng's view of herself as a bad student lingered into adulthood. "When I was in grade school, I was very, very dumb. I couldn't sing and I couldn't draw, and I was the kind of student that teachers didn't like," she wrote in an essay published internally at Huawei.[13] Recalling her mother's patience with her, she quoted an idiom: "Mothers don't mind if their children are ugly."

After his release from the labor camp, Ren's father-in-law, Meng Dongbo, was reinstated as Sichuan's vice-governor. Sichuan was now the focus of the nation's reforms. Deng Xiaoping—the diminutive Sichuanese official whom Mao had purged and whose "wolf-ish ambition to restore capitalism" was used as a scapegoat for the delays at Ren's nylon factory—had now emerged as the nation's new leader. Deng indeed believed that Mao's communes and political witch hunts were wrongheaded, and that Western-style capitalism would save the nation. Deng encouraged his home province, Sichuan, to start experimenting under the new party secretary Zhao Ziyang, a long-faced man with a widow's peak.

As one of Zhao's deputies, Meng helped dismantle the communes and restore private farming across Sichuan. In 1980, they launched the radical experiment of letting several Sichuan factories operate privately, managing their own accounts and keeping their profits after paying a state profit tax.[14] A cotton mill, a clockmaker, and a print shop were among the first. When the editor of the *People's Daily*, the party's press organ, visited from Beijing, Meng discussed with him how far they could push the reforms, and the two even floated the idea of the government charging the businesses rent.[15]

As China opened up to the world, they were hosting a growing stream of foreign visitors. Officials from Switzerland, Yugoslavia, Zaire, and North Korea arrived in Chengdu in quick succession, with Zhao, Meng, and their colleagues preparing banquets in the guests' honor.[16] There was even an American visitor, Helen Milliken, Michigan's first lady, who arrived in 1982 to sign a friendship pact between Michigan and Sichuan Province.[17]

In 1979, Meng got a rare chance to see the world through a three-week tour of Britain, Switzerland, and France along with Zhao and nine other Sichuan officials.[18] After years of wearing plain clothing in line with the Communist ethos, Meng donned a sky-blue Western-style three-piece suit for the trip.[19] It was an eye-opening excursion.

They saw up close how market economies operated, meeting with senior officials like British Foreign and Commonwealth Affairs Minister Peter Blaker.[20] They found it remarkable how different countries specialized in different crops based on their climates, trading for greater wealth: grapes in arid parts of France, wheat on England's sunny east coast. Upon their return, Zhao advocated for China's provinces to adopt a similar system of trade. These international encounters must have fired up the imaginations of Meng Dongbo's family members at a time when overseas travel was strictly controlled.

Later on, Ren would rarely mention his first wife and first father-in-law. Perhaps it was awkward to acknowledge a high-level political connection when Huawei had cultivated the myth of being a scrappy little company that had always pulled itself up by its own bootstraps. In truth, having a certain amount of political patronage was probably a requirement for survival in China's chaotic early market economy. And a vice-governor was not that high up the ladder, comparatively speaking: Wan Runnan, the founder of Stone Group, China's leading high-tech company of the 1980s, had married the daughter of Liu Shaoqi, the nation's head of state himself.[21]

There was never any proof that the Meng family's political connections helped Ren get Huawei off the ground—and indeed Ren and Meng Jun divorced around the time that he was starting the company. But the Meng family's standing must have opened political doors to a young Ren that otherwise would have remained closed, and helped open the mind of a schoolteacher's son to audacious dreams.

A Floating-Ball Precision Pressure
Generator, *Ren Zhengfei's 1979 book about
his pressure generator invention.*

After much effort, Ren succeeded at building a precision air-pressure generator in 1977. His breakthrough was well timed. With Deng Xiaoping as the nation's leader, scientific research was suddenly encouraged. News of Ren's invention was splashed across state media. "Only a few countries in the world with advanced industry are able to manufacture it," the official Xinhua newswire boasted.[22] Ren published a slim paperback book of equations and diagrams to explain how the pressure generator worked.[23] "Compared to the American company Ametek's products, it's at an advanced level," he wrote. "It fills a blank space in our nation's technology."[24]

Ren had previously found himself passed over for promotions and awards due to his family's suspect political background. Membership in the Chinese Communist Party would have helped with career advancement, but he had not been able to join. In Deng's China, Ren now found himself getting a second chance. When Deng held the nation's first National Science Conference in March 1978, a thirty-three-year-old Ren was invited, making him one of the youngest among the six thousand scientists and engineers in attendance.[25] In a rousing speech, Deng told the scientists that they were not part of the bourgeoisie, as they had been previously labeled, but part of the working class. "Everyone who works, whether with his hands or with his brain, is part of the working people in a socialist society," Deng declared.[26] The scientists' applause was thunderous. Some pumped their fists in the air. Many eyes were wet.[27] "We were moved to tears because we were finally recognized as the 'sons' of this country," Ren later recalled. "We were overjoyed to be part of the working class rather than the capitalist or intellectual class."[28]

The National Science Conference of 1978 proved pivotal to Ren's career: it allowed him to join the Chinese Communist Party.[29] During the conference, an official impressed by Ren's potential took it upon himself to make a phone call to push for him to be allowed into the club. In response, the PLA Engineering Corps assigned Xu Guotai, a journalist for the corps' internal newspaper, to probe Ren and his family background. Xu was impressed and charmed by Ren's dedication to his research and ended up serving as a reference for Ren's membership application.[30] Xu also penned a favorable profile of Ren for the corps' newspaper that praised him for persevering with his research during the Cultural Revolution, despite the political risks of being seen as an intellectual.[31] "Neither the pressure from the Gang of Four nor the well-intentioned persuasion of his relatives, friends and colleagues stopped him from study and research," the profile said. "He loves his country, its people and science more than his family and himself."

In February 1979, the Engineering Corps' newspaper carried an article by Xu on the front page: INVENTOR OF THE PRECISION PRESSURE GENERATOR REN ZHENGFEI JOINS THE PARTY. The article said that Ren Zhengfei of Troop 00229 had honorably joined the party after multiple failed applications, and after his family members had suffered false accusations due to the interference of the "Gang of Four." It noted that Ren had been promoted to the role of "Engineer."[32]

Ren would later tell colleagues at Huawei that he had wasted time in those years when he was outside the establishment. "As a soldier for all those years, I didn't join the party. My life was full of adversity," he told his staff. "When I think of all that wasted time, I wonder, *How could I have been so naive and ridiculous that I didn't understand at all being open, compromise, and shades of gray?*"[33]

With the bulk of the construction of the Liaoyang factory complete, Ren's unit began moving south in November 1978.[34] The destination was Jinan, the capital of Shandong Province, a cultural hub famed for its bubbling natural springs. Troop 00229 set up a research institute in Jinan,[35] and Ren was appointed deputy director, with a staff of about twenty.[36] This move had the benefit of uniting Ren's family. His wife received preferential approval to join the military in Jinan,[37] and the couple were rejoined with their children. Meng Wanzhou, who was around seven years old, was enrolled in an elementary school on the city's rural outskirts.[38] She considered it a happy period, a time when she was under little pressure to study and often played in the fields, catching grasshoppers.[39]

Ren worked to commercialize his pressure generator, coordinating with factories in Taiyuan, Dalian, Shenyang, and the Jiangsu Province county of Yangzhong.[40] One local official in Yangzhong recalled him speaking excitedly about competing in the nascent market economy, saying that a sales team should be like a pack of wolves: "The wolves must be hungry if they are to voluntarily hunt for food and compete for food," he remembered Ren saying. "We must encourage salespeople to proactively go on the offensive, to go on more work trips and visit customers, to fight for more sales, to win more bonuses."[41]

In September 1982, a thirty-seven-year-old Ren attended the Twelfth National Congress of the Chinese Communist Party, a twice-a-decade meeting where the nation's top leaders made governance plans for the next five years.[42] At the time, it was an enormous honor to be invited. It would later become a liability for Ren, with foreign officials questioning how close Huawei's ties were to the party. Later on, Ren would avoid appearances at high-level government meetings.

The congress also marked the abrupt end of Ren's military career. Deng was making a tectonic shift toward private enterprise, and this included the decommissioning of the PLA Engineering Corps.[43] For Ren, there was excitement about the nation's progress but also reluctance to give up the only career he had ever known.

With the end of the army's Engineering Corps, Ren and Meng Jun were assigned to work on the southern coast in a place called Shenzhen, where an experimental "special economic zone" was being built from the ground up. The children, Meng Wanzhou and Ren Ping, were sent for a second time to live with Ren's parents in Guizhou.[44]

Eleven-year-old Meng Wanzhou had fallen behind in schoolwork while living in Jinan, and back under her grandparents' watch, she struggled at first. She was enrolled at Duyun No. 1 Middle School, where her grandfather was the principal and her grandmother taught math. On her first test, she scored the lowest grade in the class, an embarrassment to her and her grandparents.[45] Her grades improved over time. She once even got a perfect score on a geometry test. When she was selected as the head of a city youth committee, her mother mailed her a sky-blue outfit, writing that she would look like a little white dove flying free.

Ren Moxun retired from Duyun No. 1 Middle School in the summer of 1984 at age seventy-five.[46] By then, he was often in ill health,[47] but he refused to stop working. Appointed head of the Cultural and Historical Materials Committee of the Duyun City People's Consultative Conference, Ren Moxun set about compiling a history of the local schools. One day, one of his old students visited him and recalled the struggle session where a classmate had beaten Ren Moxun with a wooden stick until it broke. Ren Moxun smiled grimly. "I have to thank that piece of wood," he said. "Had it been sturdier, I surely would have been beaten until there was something wrong with me."[48]

4

The Special Economic Zone

In the early 1980s, a vast construction zone was materializing on the southern coast of China. This new city being built from scratch, the Shenzhen Special Economic Zone (SEZ), would cover 126 square miles, nearly the size of Philadelphia. Not long ago, it had been mostly just grassland here, surrounding a sleepy town that stank from garbage-filled ditches.[1] Now the city's first skyscraper, the Guomao Building, was materializing at the astonishing pace of one floor every three days. Local officials proudly declared that this was *"The Shenzhen speed!"*[2] China was embarking on its grand experiment in capitalism, and Shenzhen was ground zero.

The Shenzhen SEZ was not designed like a traditional Chinese city, a circle surrounded by a circular wall, ideal for defense against invaders. It was a long, thin strip,[3] extending west to east along mainland China's border with the British colony of Hong Kong. On a map, it looked like a snake, its long belly lying across the border, its tail curling to the east around Mirs Bay, its head jutting westward into a promontory aptly called Shekou, or Snake's Mouth. Such a city was not built for the convenience of its inhabitants. Denizens had to jostle around on a bus for hours to get from one side to the other. The SEZ's form followed its function: it was to be a buffer zone between China and the rest of the world, one that would absorb capital and technology from Hong Kong and let it percolate into a safe zone while minimizing the spread of capitalism's "moral corruption" to the rest of the nation. If the experiment proved unsatisfactory, it could be shut down; the SEZ was walled off from the rest of China by barbed-wire fences,[4] the entrances patrolled by paramilitary guards.

Ren has alternately recalled arriving in Shenzhen in 1982 and in 1984,[5] and either way, he would have been approaching forty. It was exhilarating and disorienting. Ren was astonished to discover that average laborers in the city made some five hundred yuan a month, more than double what he had been making as a mid-career military engineer.[6] He learned about a foreign style of shop called a "supermarket" and strolled the gleaming aisles of one for the first time.[7] A sweet, fizzy drink called Pepsi was rolling off the assembly line at the city's first joint-venture factory with an American company.[8] Yet amid the wonders, Ren was also nervous. A new world was opening up, but it was unclear if he could keep up. "People of my age group were the most worthless," he reflected. "We didn't understand computers, and our English was not good."[9]

Shenzhen was a city for young people. There were fortunes to be made if you could remake yourself fast enough, and if you were willing to take the risk. The young people in Shenzhen took their fashion cues from the British colony of Hong Kong, just across the border, switching out their plain blue Mao suits for dandy black Western-style suits and scandalously short skirts with stockings. At night, they snuck fishbone antennae up onto their roofs to watch uncensored Hong Kong TV shows, then retracted the antennae in the morning to circumvent crackdowns.[10] They took pride in their worldliness, calling the rest of China "the inland." A growing number of them were getting the opportunity to study abroad, and they came back fluent in foreign languages and with the latest in technical training.

Ren was assigned a job at a company called South Sea Oil Shenzhen Development Service Co.[11] This was a subsidiary of the state-owned enterprise South Sea Oil Corporation, which was building a modern harbor in Shenzhen's Shekou district to support offshore oil-drilling projects in the South China Sea. Ren's subsidiary was tasked with the construction of peripheral facilities, including manufacturing zones, shopping centers, and modern apartment complexes.[12] Housing was badly lacking. Meng Wanzhou later recalled her parents living in a "thatched hut" during this time: "When it was raining heavily outside, it would be raining lightly inside; when the neighbors spoke, you could hear everything clearly."[13]

Ren's tenure at the company was short and undistinguished—little is known about what exactly his role was there, and there are no apparent local press records of his work, in contrast to the laudatory clippings from his time as a military engineer. One rare report of his work there came from Chen Zhufang, an administrator at what was then called the Huazhong Institute of Technology in the inland city of Wuhan. After she discussed with Ren the possibility of setting up a technological joint venture between Huazhong and South Sea Oil, she came away with a favorable impression. He was a handsome guy, she thought, with a pronounced military bearing, and it was clear that he had high ambitions.[14] Ren would later persuade her to join Huawei. She worked for years as the secretary of its internal Communist Party committee, an important role serving as a liaison between the company and the government.

Ren would later acknowledge he had made mistakes as a deputy manager at South Sea Oil.[15] Indeed, he maintains he was fired after getting tricked in a business deal and losing money for his employer.[16] "Some people offered to sell us TVs, so we gave them money but didn't receive TVs in return," Ren later said.[17] He said he spent a lot of time reading legal books and trying to claw back the funds. No corroborating or alternate account of the incident has emerged from his former colleagues.

Ren was facing personal challenges during this time as well. His relationship with his wife, Meng Jun, was unraveling, and the two decided to divorce.[18] It is unclear what prompted it, though Ren's years away in the military could not have helped. It was still rare to divorce in China, with much of society considering it shameful. But divorce rates were rising nationwide, as some progressive Chinese no longer felt required to remain in unhappy unions.[19]

As Ren floundered, someone at Shenzhen's Science and Technology Bureau suggested he try starting a company.[20] Ren was forty-two when he founded Huawei Technologies Co. His first career as a military engineer had ended, and not by choice. His brief second career in the state sector was also at a close. Now Ren decided to make the jump and become that intriguing, scandalous, and dangerous thing: a *capitalist*.

Shenzhen legalized the establishment of "minjian" (unofficial or, more literally, "among the people") private technology companies in February 1987 under a pilot program. Applicants poured in from across the country—professors and engineers from Beijing to Kunming.[21] The idea of running your own company in the SEZ was exciting—and risky. Seventy-five percent of the first batch of entrepreneurs asked their state employers for temporary unpaid leave, with the option of reprising their old jobs if their startups didn't work out.[22]

Ren founded Huawei as a minjian company on September 15, 1987, with twenty-one thousand yuan pooled between himself and five investors. At first, Huawei did not have its own products. It assembled and sold simple telephone switches, fire alarms, and other products on contract for others. Huawei printed out pamphlets touting telephones as the economic engine of the new age, akin to railroads and canals in the eighteenth century: *Wishing you an early start on the road to success. Electronic communications are the catalyst for your career.*

Huawei's first office was in a residential building built by South Sea Oil in the standard style, with eight floors and a balcony on each unit for drying clothes.[23] An early employee recalled finding his way there in 1989 based on Ren's business card, which said that Huawei occupied the eighth and ninth floors of the South Sea Oil complex, building 16, District A. "When I got to the ground floor of that building, I realized the building didn't have nine floors," he said. "It was only an eight-story building. I thought for sure it was a shell company, scammers."[24] He later discovered a shabby greenhouse-like structure on the roof. Another early employee who arrived for a job interview recalled Ren telling him to wait while he took a quick shower to cool down.[25]

One long-standing curiosity about Huawei's origins is the silence surrounding its original five investors. None of the five has publicly recounted their version of events. For decades, even the names of these investors would be a mystery to the outside world.

In 2019, Huawei finally disclosed them to the *Los Angeles Times*: Zhang Xiangyang, a member of the Shenzhen Bureau of Development Planning; Wu Huiqing, an accountant at a Shenzhen petrochemical company; Chen Jinyang, a manager in the trade department of Shenzhen's state-run China Travel Service; Shen Dingxing, founder of Zhuhai Telecom; and Mei Zhongxing, founder of Shenzhen Sanjiang Electronics Co.[26] Little is known about the first three. Shen and Mei appear here and there in archival records.

Born in Shanghai and eight years older than Ren, Shen had worked at the telecom bureau in Yining, in China's far-west Xinjiang region, then at a military telecommunications factory in southern Guilin before moving to the southern coast and wading into entrepreneurship.[27] Shen had launched his own startup, Zhuhai Telecom, just across the bay from Shenzhen after developing a telephone switch called the BH-01. The BH-01 was something called a private branch exchange, or PBX, a microwave-sized box that could hook up twenty-four to eighty telephones. In those days of scarce telephone lines, a small business or hotel would use a PBX to hook multiple telephones up to a single line.

Shen quickly became a minor business celebrity, with his BH-01 lauded as a highlight in local innovation. The city of Zhuhai showered him with $40,000 in cash, a new apartment, and an Audi luxury sedan as a prize for his invention. Some were scandalized that a supposedly Communist government would throw money around so vulgarly. Local officials defended it as being in line with Deng's mandate for bold economic experimentation. Huawei struck a deal to manufacture and sell the BH-01 on Zhuhai Telecom's behalf, along with the switches of Hung Nien, a Hong Kong company.[28] Shen's company was a key early source of technological know-how for a fledgling Huawei.

Mei came to Shenzhen after spending years in the cold far-northeastern province of Liaoning working for Liaoning Radio Factory No. 3, a state-owned fire-alarm manufacturer, according to a profile in *China Entrepreneur* magazine.[29] In 1985, Mei and six colleagues moved south to Shenzhen to set up a joint venture for Liaoning Radio Factory No. 3. "After the first month, the seven of them didn't even have any salary," the profile said. "But they still worked during the day, at night, and also on holidays. . . . Three months later, they finally developed their first ionization smoke detector."

According to local records in Shenzhen, Mei's joint-venture company, Shenzhen Sanjiang Electronics Co., soon branched out from fire alarms into chips for audio recorders and video-surveillance systems,[30] fields that Huawei later also ventured into. Shenzhen Sanjiang Electronics was half-owned by the state-run factory in Liaoning that had dispatched Mei, with the other half owned by a subsidiary of South Sea Oil, the South Sea Oil Shenzhen Development Service Co.[31] This was Ren's employer before he founded Huawei. It meant that Mei and Ren had been colleagues at South Sea Oil, though it isn't clear whether or not they knew each other or worked together there.

One more detail about Mei—a key one—would not emerge until 2021. The Chinese scholar Tian Tao, who had studied Huawei in great detail for years, published a volume of his transcribed interviews with Huawei executives, writing that recent health troubles had sparked his wish to share his research with others.[32] Tian's interviews offered many fresh insights into the company's early history, including this remark from the early Huawei executive Jiang Xisheng: "When the company was first founded, Mr. Ren wasn't even the chairman. Mei Zhongxing was the chairman."[33] In all these years of Huawei telling its story to the world, this looked to be the first mention that Mei was Huawei's first chairman. It was a notable omission from Huawei's story of itself.

In local government yearbooks, Mei continued to be named as the legal representative of Shenzhen Sanjiang Electronics, the South Sea Oil subsidiary, at least through 1989, a couple of years after Huawei was founded.[34] This suggested, perhaps, that Ren's break with his former state-run employer may not have been as clean and simple as often told.

In retrospect, one might guess that the invisibility of Huawei's original investors in later years might have something to do with this messiness. Huawei was founded at a time when the rules of China's new market economy were still emerging, and business ties were often a convoluted web. Later on, as Huawei sought to introduce itself to the world as a clear-and-simple private company, this early history became inconvenient. Huawei's executives stopped talking about it.

T here was something that Ren had not told his original investors up front: He had no intention of remaining a contract manufacturer. He wanted to build his own telephone switch.

Ren arrived in the inland city of Wuhan in the spring of 1988 in search of engineers.[35] Dubbed "the Chicago of China,"[36] Wuhan was a bustling industrial city on the Yangtze River. The Huazhong Institute of Technology had been founded here in the 1950s,[37] and three decades later, conditions at the university were still spare: Students bunked six to a room in the dorms and took cold-water showers.[38] There was no air-conditioning or heat. But there was a professor who was knowledgeable about telephone switching, and Ren hoped he could help Huawei build a switch.

At Huazhong's main entrance stood a sixteen-meter-tall white concrete sculpture of Mao Zedong, one arm raised.[39] During the Cultural Revolution, the institute's president and his wife had been accused of showing insufficient reverence to images of Mao. He was sent to a labor camp; she was locked in the university cafeteria for two months.[40] The hulking Mao statue was erected around that time, and there it stayed. After the Cultural Revolution, the institute had experienced a renaissance. The university president, Zhu Jiusi, had declared ambitions to build a Chinese MIT.[41] He'd sent his professors around the world to study the latest technologies.[42]

Ren had crossed paths with the institute in the early 1980s, when its administrators had sought out a partnership with Ren's employer, South Sea Oil.[43] Now Ren had come to see a professor named Zhou Xi, who had recently developed software for tabulating users' telephone fees.[44] In Professor Zhou's lab, Ren met a twenty-two-year-old graduate student with large eyes, a tan complexion, and a dense thicket of hair. His name was Guo Ping.[45] A native of Ganzhou in Jiangxi Province,[46] the nation's capital for navel oranges, Guo was curious about the Shenzhen Special Economic Zone on the southern coast. So was his girlfriend, which helped seal the deal.[47] Guo agreed to go to Huawei for an internship.

Guo found himself invigorated by the work. He was thrown straight into the deep end of switch engineering, and he crammed to try to catch up. "At the time I hadn't even used a telephone to make calls that many times, and somehow I was responsible for switches," he said.[48] After his internship, Guo worked at the electric power bureau in Wuhan, but he found it uninspiring.[49] He was soon back at Huawei.

When word got out that Ren was building his own switch, there was disagreement among Huawei's investors, some of whom preferred the company to remain a contractor. The precise sequence of events is fuzzy, but around this time, Shen, one of Ren's five original investors, abruptly cut Huawei off from further supply of the BH-01 switch, which Huawei had been selling on contract.[50] The Huawei executive Jiang Xisheng recounted to scholar Tian Tao that there was intense conflict at a 1990 Huawei shareholder meeting, after which little trust remained between Ren and his investors.[51]

Huawei's first switch was called the BH-03, and Ren has admitted that there were more than a few similarities to Shen's BH-01, a copycat phenomenon not uncommon during that Wild West era of lax to nonexistent intellectual-property protections in China. Once, in an internal speech, Ren recalled that his engineers used a copier to make "exact one-to-one printed copies" of circuit boards to make the BH-03, explaining that they were struggling to find a way to fulfill customers' orders after their supply was cut off.[52] He also remembered an official at the Petroleum Ministry urging him to first stake his claim in the market, then sort out the rest later. "What you need to control is the market," the official told Ren. "No one can keep hold of the technology in the long run. It will be opened up, don't worry."[53] The Ministry of Posts and Telecommunications later ordered Zhuhai Telecom to license its switch technology to other companies. "Our imitation was also legalized," Ren said.[54]

M eng Wanzhou had rejoined her parents in Shenzhen by the late 1980s, enrolling in a new high school run by South Sea Oil.[55] She was a familiar presence at Huawei, using the printer in her father's office for her homework and chatting with the engineers, whom she called, respectfully, "uncle."[56] At age sixteen, she decided to adopt her mother's surname, which was not uncommon in the new Communist China, with its emphasis on gender parity.[57] It's unclear why she made the change.

Youth unrest was stirring in Shenzhen and across the nation. "Everyone's thinking was really lively," Jiang told Tian, remarking on Shenzhen in that era.[58] At least some of the young workers in Shenzhen—and even some local officials—saw their experiments in economic reforms as being linked to political change, including Western ideals like free speech and democracy. In 1988, Shenzhen made national headlines when local workers clashed with Beijing scholars over their motivation, with the young people declaring that they worked only for profit, not patriotism. Shenzhen officials defended the young people's right to free speech, with one saying they "could not allow speech to become a crime."[59] In an even more startling act of disobedience, the *Shenzhen Youth News*, a local state-run paper, ran a front-page editorial that called on the nation's leader, Deng Xiaoping, to retire.[60]

Then came the turmoil of 1989. The protests began in April in Beijing, with gatherings to mourn the death of General Secretary Hu Yaobang, seen as a reformer and a symbol of anti-corruption. They quickly snowballed into calls for democratic elections and for eighty-four-year-old Deng to step down. Protests broke out nationwide, from Shanghai to Gansu, with students staging a hunger strike in Beijing's Tiananmen Square. As Reuters reported, some one hundred thousand factory workers, engineers, students, and other residents marched through the streets of Shenzhen on May 22 in support of the Beijing students.[61] Shenzhen University's students gathered more than twenty thousand signatures in a petition calling for Deng's resignation.[62]

The Stone Group's founder, Wan Runnan (right), and his wife, Li Yu.

The student protesters had influential supporters. Among them was Shenzhen University's founder and president, Luo Zhengqi, who joined in the calls for Deng's resignation.[63] In Beijing, the nation's preeminent tech entrepreneur, Wan Runnan, also threw his support behind the students. Wan's company, the Stone Group, was China's breakout success story in the nascent private sector, with the press nicknaming it "China's IBM." Wan believed that private enterprise could help push the government toward political change. He sent the protesters food and drink and even helped them broker meetings with the government. Zhao Ziyang, who had spearheaded economic reforms in Sichuan Province in the late 1970s and been the boss of Meng's grandfather, was also sympathetic to the students. As general secretary of the Chinese Communist Party, Zhao was now China's top leader on paper, and he favored a nonviolent resolution. But Deng Xiaoping, still in control behind the curtain, overruled the pacifists.

Shenzhen residents woke up on the morning of June 5, 1989, to shocking news across the front of the *Shenzhen Special Zone Daily*: MARTIAL LAW TROOPS QUELL COUNTERREVOLUTIONARY RIOT. The article cast the pro-democracy protesters as the instigators, saying they had kidnapped and beat soldiers to death. But even this sanitized version acknowledged that students had been killed.

Zhao was deposed and put under house arrest. Police began a nationwide crackdown. Political dissidents from across the country flooded into Shenzhen to make a dash for the safety of Hong Kong. Wan, the Stone Group's founder, snuck into Shenzhen under a friend's ID a few days after the crackdown. Luo, the Shenzhen University president who had supported the protesters, came to see Wan at his hotel, with the two bewailing the calamity.[64] Wan made it safely into

Hong Kong a day before Beijing put out a warrant for his arrest, accusing him of a criminal attempt to overthrow the government. In Beijing, military troops took up residence in the Stone Group's offices and shut down the company's think tank, which had advocated for democratic reforms.[65] Wan would never be able to return to China.

Meng graduated from high school in 1990 and enrolled as an accounting major at Shenzhen University. The school had a reputation for radical open-mindedness: Luo had allowed his students to run their own "court" to determine punishments for peers' infractions, and even to launch their own bank.[66] Now it was under tense control. Luo was fired and cast out of the party for supporting the calls for Deng's resignation.[67] Amid rumors that Luo was being held in isolation to prevent him from fleeing, Luo's successor confirmed that he was "studying" at his home on campus due to his political misunderstandings.[68] Police questioned students involved in the protests.[69]

For Meng—and her cohort at Huawei—the events at Tiananmen must have been a formative experience. Many in her generation would grow up to retreat reflexively from political expression. Former Huawei spokesman William Plummer, who worked with Meng on preparations for some finance conferences, called her "very conservative." "I think she has sort of an old-school 'I don't want to do something wrong, I might be punished' attitude," he said. "In certain environments, like China, being punished can be bad. She's a smart woman, but she had this guardedness. She's her father's daughter."[70]

As for Ren, he was practical. He told his staff that patriotism was a fundamental requirement for working at Huawei. "The company requires every employee to love their motherland, to love this nation of ours that is just starting to rejuvenate," he wrote in a letter to new employees in 1998. "In no time or place may you do anything that disappoints the motherland or disappoints the nation."[71] He counseled younger workers that they could not be too idealistic. "True, absolute fairness does not exist. Your hopes cannot be too high in this regard."[72]

Ren would later describe freedom as the understanding of objectivity. Freedom, Ren said, was a train running back and forth on a track without overturning.[73]

5

A Homegrown Switch

Ren Zhengfei looked out the window of the conference room and threatened to jump.[1] If this project failed, he told the scrawny young engineers gathered around him, he'd fling himself out. He and his team were trying to build their first advanced telephone switch, and they weren't sure if they could succeed. He had arranged financing for the project at usurious rates. They would either succeed or go bankrupt trying.

Ren's team had been making simple analog switches that could handle forty, eighty, or, at most, a couple hundred phone calls at once.[2] Their early attempt at a more complex one-thousand-line switch was a failure, suffering from serious cross talk, dropped calls, and a tendency to catch fire from lightning strikes.

Now, in 1993, they were trying to build a digital switch that could handle *ten thousand* telephone calls at once. This would catapult them into the big leagues. They would no longer be selling to hotels and small offices; they would be selling directly to the telephone switching centers for entire cities. And instead of the traditional analog switching technology, they were attempting to make the jump to digital switching, which converted the sound of people's voices into zeros and ones, allowing the data to be transmitted more efficiently.

Ren had built a promising engineering team by this point, even if many of his engineers were very young. Two engineers in particular were becoming indispensable to Huawei's early R&D efforts, both of them graduates of the Huazhong Institute. The first was Zheng Baoyong, a sturdily built twenty-nine-year-old with a round face and a booming voice.[3] Ever since Guo Ping had recruited him from the Huazhong Institute,[4] Ren had taken to him like a brother, nicknaming him A-Bao, teasing him gently for his illegible handwriting,[5] and declaring him the equal of ten thousand others in engineering ability.[6] In Huawei's employee numbering system, which accorded roughly with seniority, Ren was Employee No. 0001, and Zheng was Employee No. 0002. The other engineer was Li Yinan, a pale, spindly "young prodigy" who had joined Huawei in the summer of 1993. Li had been part of an early enrollment program for gifted youngsters at the Huazhong Institute and had graduated early. Li was so frail-looking that a visiting senior government official commented that he should eat more.[7] But he quickly made a name for himself as a brilliant engineer. Li would win a string of government prizes, including "Outstanding Technology Worker" from Shenzhen's Science and Technology Bureau, and number two in a national contest. Ren promoted him rapidly and took him under his wing, almost like a godson.

Ren had rented the third floor of an industrial building on Shenzhen's outskirts for his fledgling R&D team.[8] There was no air-conditioning, only electric fans, and they took cold showers to try to keep cool. They rigged up nets to try to escape the ferocious mosquitoes. A dozen cots lined the wall. The engineers worked day and night, flopping down on mattresses to sleep for a few hours when they reached exhaustion, which led to the saying that Huawei had a "mattress culture."[9] One engineer worked so hard that his cornea detached, requiring emergency surgery.[10]

After dinner, the engineers would pull up their stools and Ren would sit there telling war stories. He hadn't fought in the famous battles himself, but he recounted them vividly. He told them about the Battle of Triangle Hill during the Korean War, in which Chinese soldiers won a costly victory over US and UN troops. "He told it with great passion and enthusiasm, and we listened with such excitement our blood was practically boiling," a Huawei executive recalled in an essay.[11]

Starting in Huawei's early days, Ren asked employees to purchase shares in the company. He badly needed the cash to fund Huawei's budding R&D projects, and he believed that the shares would make employees feel invested in the company's success, encouraging them to work harder—similar to the reasoning behind the stock options offered by Silicon Valley startups to founding executives. Accounts of Huawei employees buying shares date back to at least 1989. According to early finance manager Zheng Aizhu, she and her husband gave Ren their life savings—eight thousand yuan—when they joined Huawei in February 1989. Ren gifted them seven thousand yuan worth of shares on top of that. "We had tied our entire family's fate to the company," she said.[12]

These were not ownership shares in the modern sense. Employees couldn't use their shares to vote out management, nor could they sell their shares to others. If they left the company, they could only sell them back to the company at a low price. This stock was simply a way to share the wealth with employees in the form of dividends. There wasn't exactly a legal basis for Ren to be issuing these shares, with Chinese corporate law still nascent. But no one was stopping him.

By 1991, Huawei had ten million yuan in fixed assets and was churning out eighty million yuan worth of switches a year.[13] It had 105 employees, the majority of whom were shareholders. That year, Huawei's shareholders did something curious: after proudly launching themselves in 1987 as one of Shenzhen's first wave of "minjian" private tech companies, they voted unanimously to stop being one.

From 1992 to 1997, Huawei would be a jitisuoyouzhi, or a "collectively owned enterprise," something that was neither "private" nor "state-owned" in the modern senses of the words. Indeed, such companies were most similar in spirit to the Mao-era communes: Beijing defined them as "socialist economic organizations whose property is collectively owned by the working people, who practice joint labor, and whose distribution method is based on distribution according to labor."[14] While collectively owned businesses had been used in the countryside to mixed success, China's national government had, in 1991, just formalized guidelines for urban collective companies.

Putting on the "red hat" of a collective was popular among startups then as a way to obtain political protection.[15] The Stone Group— hailed as "China's IBM" in the 1980s—had been a trailblazer in this regard, successfully switching to a "collectively owned enterprise" in 1986.[16] The 1991 national guidelines stipulated that collectively owned enterprises could enjoy preferential treatment in national policies and apply for loans from specialized banks.[17] The guidelines also ordered government authorities nationwide to incorporate the companies into their economic plans in order to ensure the success of the urban collective economy. It remains unclear why Ren and his team decided to switch to a jitisuoyouzhi, though it's likely that the broader financing opportunities were attractive. Ren would later recall the business environment being challenging in the wake of the 1989 Tiananmen crackdown, with Western nations putting financial sanctions on China. "The Chinese economy was in a downward slide for three years," Ren said in an internal speech. "The economy was really bad then, almost on the verge of collapse."

Such a system was implemented at Huawei, and local officials pointed to the company as a success story. After Huawei made the switch to collective ownership, its corporate charter stipulated that 40 percent of after-tax profits would be divvied up as dividends among the shareholders (who were also the employees), local officials reported. Another 30 percent would go into the company's "common reserve fund," which was set aside for the company's expansion and could not be touched for dividends or employee bonuses. The other 30 percent would go into a "welfare fund." Huawei's new charter also spelled out how assets would be distributed among the employee shareholders if the company went under.

Many of the quirks of jitisuoyouzhi lingered on as part of Huawei's management style, even after the company became a limited liability one in 1997. The national guidelines for collectively owned companies called for "democratic management," with workers involved in supervising their elected factory manager through a workers' committee. They also required remuneration of employees according to the principle of distribution according to work, and dividends to shareholders in years where there were profits. A trade union had to be set up to represent the workers' interests.

What "democratic management" meant in a company was that the CEO—or "factory manager"—did not have complete control. Under the guidelines, the factory manager was required to "love the collective" and "connect with the masses," and if they did not, the workers' committee could vote them out. The guidelines specified that the workers' committee was the authority within the company. For major management decisions, the factory manager had to submit a proposal for the approval of the workers' committee. It's unclear exactly how the power was divided in Huawei's case, though the local Shenzhen officials wrote that Huawei was complying with democratic management by instituting a shareholder committee, a board of directors, and a CEO.

China's leaders had distrusted foreign telecommunications gear from the start, suspicious that it was a tool of colonialism and surveillance. In 1865, Prince Gong, the ruling regent of the Qing dynasty, said as much in a letter to the Russian minister in Beijing, turning down his request to put up telegraph lines: "They are extremely inconvenient," Prince Gong wrote. "Therefore, they can never be introduced."[18]

Telegraphs would indeed be introduced, then telephones, but the rollout was slow. By the time Deng Xiaoping was beginning to open up the economy in the late 1970s, many people were still relying on telegraphs and paper mail. High-level government officials each had their own secure red desktop telephone, which only connected to the others and worked much better than those among the public.[19] For everyone else, it was still common for an entire neighborhood to share a single phone, with no expectation of privacy.[20] In 1979, all of Shenzhen had only two public telephones.[21]

The 1980s saw a telephone boom. Shenzhen jumped from 1,500 registered telephones in 1982 to 43,876 in 1988, with telephone numbers upgraded from four to six digits.[22] Demand was still far outpacing supply: the city's wait list for telephones ran 37,500 units long. With no domestic company able to make the switches, Chinese telecom bureaus could only buy foreign. "The People's Republic is described as 'a gold mine,'" an executive at Northern Telecom, the Canadian switchmaker later renamed Nortel, declared to a Canadian newspaper in 1985. Sweden's Ericsson and Japan's Fujitsu were leading the sales, aided by their home governments offering huge sums in financing.[23] "In the early days, there was very little money. It was very much a diplomatic game. It was governments and their national champions going to China, doing this complicated dance, and looking to find some advantage," recalled Ken Zita, who was a China-based telecom analyst in the 1980s.

Beijing wasn't letting the foreign switchmakers in for free: it was demanding that the companies share some technology with a Chinese partner through a joint-venture partnership. It was hardly a secret that Beijing officials hoped they could learn what they needed to become self-sufficient. The first company to get in line was Bell Telephone Manufacturing Company, a Belgium-based arm of the Bell Telephone Company, which agreed to share technology through a joint venture, Shanghai Bell.[24] Shanghai Bell enjoyed massive sales, leaving everyone else scrambling to follow suit. In the industry, people debated whether China would succeed in learning how to make these advanced technologies. Former Canadian ambassador Guy Saint-Jacques recalled Canadian companies being confident that they could stay a step ahead by transferring only older generations of technology to China while enjoying the sales bonanza. "I always compare this to running toward a cliff. At some point, you will fall down," Saint-Jacques said.[25] But Ren felt that the foreigners weren't so simplistic. "Their trick for transferring technology is they expect that after a few years, you will need to import it again, and then import, import, and, again, import," he once remarked. "In the end, you are not self-sufficient."[26]

Then, in 1991, China made its first breakthrough in ending its dependence on foreign telephone switches. This achievement was not made by Huawei. It was made by a round-faced Chinese military engineer named Wu Jiangxing. Wu's "04 switch" was the first in China that could handle thousands of phone calls at once, the kind of large-scale switch needed to run the central telephone exchanges for cities. The breakthrough was perhaps not solely due to domestic innovation. One Chinese tech official later recalled in his memoir visiting a military research institute in 1988 and being told that the military engineers were busy studying the source code of a foreign switch they had acquired "by a chance occurrence"; they were working on a project that he said led to the 04 switch.[27] But however it had happened, China could now build a telephone network without being at the mercy of foreigners.

The breakthrough galvanized Ren's engineers at Huawei. They decided that they would also try to build an advanced switch akin to the 04, even though the prospects of success were uncertain. One of

Ren's engineers managed to visit the 04 switch factory in Zheng-zhou, where the staffers let him take a close look at the device, per-haps arrogantly assuming he could never build such a thing himself.[28] Through an industry contact, Ren also managed to arrange a tour for some of his engineers to see AT&T's new ten-thousand-line switch in the northern Chinese city of Changchun.[29]

But they needed financing for such an ambitious R&D project, and it was hard to convince the banks, which were state-owned and risk-averse.[30] Ren's solution was to launch a joint-venture company called Mobeco Telecom Co. Ltd. in April 1993.[31] *Mobeco* was a portmanteau of the names of the three forefathers of telecommunications: Samuel Morse, Alexander Graham Bell, and Guglielmo Marconi.[32] The sev-enteen founding investors in Mobeco were provincial and municipal telecom bureaus, which had put a combined thirty-nine million yuan into the venture, and Huawei promised them 30 percent annual re-turns, issued in the form of "dividends" on the shares.

Internally, Ren and his team dubbed their new advanced digital switch the "06"[33] to one-up AT&T's flagship No. 5 switch. But this was bravado. It was unclear if they could even make a functioning digital switch, let alone one that could one-up anyone else's.[34]

Huawei's presence in the United States began during this pe-riod, as Ren and his team struggled to build their switch. A switch had thousands of pieces that needed to be sourced from doz-ens of specialized companies.[35] And many of the best component suppliers were in the United States.

Huawei set up a subsidiary in Santa Clara, California, called Ran

Boss Technologies on March 4, 1993.[36] The origins of the subsidiary's name are unclear, though Ren once said *Ran Boss* meant "the head of the goddess of the sea," a possible reference to the Norse sea goddess Rán.[37] One account by a former Huawei manager claims the unit was named in tribute to "Boss Ren," which infuriated Ren when he discovered it.[38] In any case, they hoped that Ran Boss could help them keep abreast of the latest technologies. "This marks the real beginning of Huawei's international expansion," Huawei's main internal newspaper reported.[39] "Ran Boss will mainly serve as an R&D base in the United States, so that we can improve our technical level faster, and guarantee the development of products at an internationally advanced level." Ren flew over to launch the unit and to visit potential suppliers. His delight in traveling the United States on these early trips would become an indelible part of Huawei's story. Talking to journalists, Ren recalled flying to the States with $10,000 in cash sewn into his coat, as he didn't know how much things cost.[40] He was astonished at the vastness of Central Park in New York, the quiet of the Boston suburbs, and the opulence of Las Vegas. Ren marveled at how IBM's four-hundred-square-mile campus went on and on.[41]

A Huawei engineer named Yan Jingli, or James Yan, was appointed as the company's first US representative. He toured trade shows, met with component suppliers, and sent dispatches about the latest trends. "The CD-ROM has become a new type of gift for people when celebrating Christmas, New Year's and birthdays," Yan reported back after one convention.[42]

One key supplier that Huawei landed was Motorola. The US high-tech company was keen on expanding its China business. Tony Kwong, a former sales executive for Motorola's Hong Kong–based chips business, recalled meeting Huawei's chief engineer at the time,

Zheng Baoyong, in 1993.[43] Zheng told him Huawei was working on a rival to the 04 switch and wanted Motorola's help, Kwong said. Kwong was impressed by Zheng's vision and ambition. *This is a bunch of guys I would personally like to work together with*, he thought.

Kwong persuaded his superiors at Motorola's headquarters to take Huawei seriously and put it on their priority customer list. That meant Huawei could get free component samples for development and early access to new products, putting it on a level playing field with international brands. Huawei ended up using Motorola chips almost exclusively in its "line cards," the circuitry that connected to each telephone line in the switch. It was a win for Huawei and a win for Motorola.

During his US travels, Ren was particularly struck by Las Vegas. When he arrived in the city to attend the Consumer Electronics Show, he was dazzled by Caesars Palace, a vision of ancient Rome with its Corinthian columns, gladiators, and winged horses. It was "so beautiful and luxurious," he thought. Taking in the glow of the neon lights at night, Ren believed that Las Vegas might be the most beautiful city in the United States.[44]

By May 1994, Huawei had a prototype of its advanced digital switch, which looked like an enormous row of filing cabinets filled with wires. The company had settled on naming it the "C&C08," with eight being a lucky number in China. The ampersand-linked Cs, Huawei executives would explain to visitors, stood for both "City & Countryside" and "Computer & Communication."[45]

They set up their first test unit in Yiwu,[46] a short drive from the

Ren family's ancestral village in Zhejiang Province, where they had managed to wheedle the local telecom officials into giving them a chance. At first, the switch didn't work. The engineers brought the quilts from their hotel to the switchroom, camping out there night after night to try to fix it. Li Yinan described it as being as finicky as "a coquettish little woman."[47]

But Huawei had supporters rooting for it to succeed. Officials from the Ministry of Posts and Telecommunications took time from their weekends to help the engineers troubleshoot. Wu Jichuan, the telecommunications minister himself, had visited Huawei in December 1993 and encouraged Ren's team. Wu told them that even though the nation was purchasing technology from abroad, the ultimate goal was to build Chinese brands. "For some critical technologies, after we introduce, digest, and absorb them, we must Sinicize them with Chinese characteristics."[48]

At an industry convention in Beijing in October 1994, Huawei's team was bursting with pride that Huawei was the only Chinese company whose booth stood in the hall for international companies, alongside Siemens and Nortel. The Huawei booth featured the lyrics of "L'Internationale," the international socialist anthem, which called on workers to stand up and throw off their shackles:

There are no supreme saviors
We want neither gods nor emperors
To build a new life
We must only rely on ourselves.[49]

6

A Shared Interest

On a Sunday afternoon in June 1994, Ren Zhengfei made his way to the Shenzhen Guesthouse[1] to rendezvous with Jiang Zemin, general secretary of the Chinese Communist Party, who was on a brief stopover in the Special Economic Zone. Huawei's C&C08 switch still had glitches, and it had yet to pass government certification for mass production. But local officials had placed their trust in Ren, selecting him as one of only eight Shenzhen entrepreneurs to meet the nation's leader.

Ren was already proving to be politically adept, able to gauge how the political winds would blow and position Huawei accordingly. His father's persecution during the Cultural Revolution would have made him more sensitive to the potentially dire consequences of misreading the political direction. His meeting with Jiang would reflect his attunement to the needs of Beijing—and to the business opportunities that they presented.

Sixty-seven-year-old Jiang wore oversize rectangular glasses and combed his hair into a stiff, similarly boxy shape. As an engineer by training who had done an exchange stint at a Soviet auto factory early in his career, he was interested in technology. Jiang had been one of the Beijing officials in charge of the launch of the Shenzhen Special Economic Zone in 1980, and he had served as electronics minister. With his technical background, Jiang hadn't originally been destined for the top, but he'd made an unexpected ascent after Zhao Ziyang was sidelined following the Tiananmen crackdown of 1989.

In the summer of 1994, Jiang was preoccupied with China's efforts to become a founding member of the World Trade Organization, which was set to launch on January 1, 1995. Washington was obstructing Jiang's WTO bid.[2] The Clinton administration had declared that there was nothing to be discussed until China cleaned up its rampant piracy of Western movies, music, and other intellectual property. It was true that China's 1990s economic boom had been freewheeling, allowing many people to bootstrap their way into small fortunes overnight, but it had not been without legal and safety problems. Just that morning, Jiang had visited hospitals across the bay in Zhuhai to meet with survivors of a collapsed textile factory, the second such deadly accident in the area in two weeks.[3] China's leaders had acknowledged that the nation needed to clean things up in order to gain acceptance on the world stage, and part of that meant evolving its own R&D.

So as Ren described Huawei's R&D advances, Jiang listened with keen interest, calling him "Old Ren" in a show of fondness and even taking notes when Ren spoke about the company's chips research.

Ren waxed eloquent about the importance of the nation developing its own telephone switching technology. "A country without its own program-controlled switches is like one without an army," Ren declared, delivering what would become one of his most famous sayings.[4] Jiang thought it well said and replied approvingly.[5] Ren added that because of the national security imperative, the software of such systems should be government-controlled: "Program-controlled switches are related to national security," he said. "Its software must be held in the hands of the Chinese government."[6]

A local magazine reported that Jiang was also presented with Huawei's company oath, which read:

> Our feet stand on our forefathers' dream of prosperity
> Bearing the hope of national rejuvenation
> We are an honest and progressing force
> Aiming toward the advanced technology of the United States
> Following Japan's great management
> According to the glorious tradition of the Chinese nation
> Building our team at a high level with high quality
> To better serve the motherland and the people.

According to the magazine, Jiang quipped that they should add a line to the oath: *We must learn the meticulous hard-working spirit of the German people.*[7]

Two days after the meeting, Ren penned an optimistic report to his staff.[8] General Secretary Jiang had talked "many times" about telecommunications policy during their meeting, he wrote. Top leaders understood their complaints: that it was an unfair playing field because foreign switchmakers were getting tax exemptions domestic vendors could not access, and that foreign switchmakers had enormous financing support from their own governments in ways Chinese startups did not. "The country will soon be canceling the practice of foreign switchmakers using commercial loans to get exemptions from customs duties and value-added tax," Ren wrote. "The domestic industry will be protected, so that domestic and foreign industry are on a level playing field."[9]

Following Jiang's visit, their obstacles began to melt away. In November 1994, the Shenzhen-headquartered China Merchants Bank announced a new financial product: "domestic buyer's credit," an equivalent to the kind of loan that foreign switchmakers were touting to Chinese telecom operators to get them to buy overseas wares. The first company in the nation able to offer domestic buyer's credit to its customers was Huawei.[10]

O n April 3, 1995, the Ministry of Posts and Telecommunications approved Huawei's C&C08 switch for mass production.[11] Telecom specialists from across China had participated in the review, along with officials from the electric power ministry, the Guangzhou military staff, and the Ministry of Public Security's cybersecurity bureau. The experts had pointed out problems, like the colors of components being inconsistent, the design inelegant, and some of the labels incorrect. Still, Huawei's C&C08 passed the review. The company could commence selling it to telecom bureaus across the nation. Some of Huawei's overseas rivals weren't impressed either. One Western executive who peeked under the hood of a C&C08 thought it looked suspiciously like AT&T's No. 5 switch.[12]

Now it turned out there was a new use for Mobeco, the joint venture Huawei had set up to finance its development of the C&C08. Mobeco's investors—the municipal telecom bureaus—were also in charge of picking the switches for their cities' central telephone exchanges. Huawei said they would achieve "common prosperity" through the venture and touted the prospect of an IPO. Huawei's then vice-chairwoman, Sun Yafang, described it like this: "We created a community of shared interests with the telecom operators and the government departments overseeing them."[13] In the modern day, such an arrangement might be considered a conflict of interest. But in China's early capitalist era, few rules existed around things of this sort, and even fewer were being enforced. By the end of 1994, Huawei was Guangdong Province's top-selling private tech company.[14]

Mobeco had started out with seventeen provincial and municipal telecom bureaus whose employees were shareholders, including in the capital, Beijing, and in cities across the country, among them Chengdu, Nanning, and Taiyuan. This list would grow quickly, with other municipalities keen to join the profit-sharing deal. Huawei talked up Mobeco as having the support of senior officials, including Guangdong Province's boss, Xie Fei, who hoped it could quickly become competitive against foreign companies.[15]

Mobeco was tasked with manufacturing Huawei switches, including the C&C08. Its articles of association set the initial production target at 740,000 lines, with an aim to expand capacity to three million annually. In the articles, Huawei also pledged a technology transfer to its state-owned partners: it said that after three years, it would exclusively transfer its program-controlled switching technology to Mobeco, with an option to transfer other technology as well.[16]

In a December 1994 meeting with Zhang Jinqiang, vice-minister of the Ministry of Electronics Industry, Ren also offered to share technology with the national government and give it an ownership stake in a project.[17] He gave Zhang a written proposal outlining a collaboration between Huawei and the government. While Huawei has not explained what, exactly, this proposed collaboration meant, the way Ren described it made it sound a lot like the one with Mobeco. "Our stance is very simple," Ren said. "One, we are willing to share everything for joint production. Two, in thinking from the perspective of the national interest, Huawei can give up its controlling interest. If Huawei's switches are used, Huawei can hold the controlling share and manage it in the short-term, and after setting up the system, gradually open it up." Ren also said Huawei was willing to "open up" its software to the nation. Zhang said he would bring the proposal back to Beijing for discussion. It's unclear if the proposition ever went forward.

In any case, the success of Mobeco prompted Huawei to expand the model, and it set up a network of joint ventures with local governments across the country. Forty-nine-year-old Li Yuzhuo, who had been Mobeco's chairman, was put in charge of this effort, reporting to Sun. Li understood the importance of government relations: he'd previously worked at the Stone Group, and his boss there had had to flee the country for sympathizing with the student protesters at Tiananmen. Li described the joint ventures as a way to acquire "blood relations" with the telecom authorities so that Huawei would be on a more even footing with state-owned rivals like Great Dragon and Datang.[18] "After setting up the JVs, it all became easy," Li wrote in a memoir. He recalled an official at their joint venture with Sichuan Province's government saying, "Now that we are partners, we're all one family," then pledging to rip out forty thousand lines of foreign switches and replace them with Huawei ones. "Without needing to open my mouth, twenty-seven million yuan was sent to our account."[19]

The local officials were pleased with the culture of efficiency that Huawei brought to the joint ventures, whipping their slowpoke factory workers into shape. They were also happy with the profit sharing, as Huawei's sales skyrocketed. In 1992, Huawei's sales were at 100 million yuan. This jumped to 410 million in 1993 (after Mobeco was founded), 800 million in 1994, and 1.5 billion in 1995.[20] And it kept on going up.

After retiring from Duyun No. 1 Middle School, Ren Moxun and his wife, Cheng Yuanzhao, lived for a while with their son Ren Zhengfei in Shenzhen. The elderly couple were frugal. They scoured the markets late in the day for discounted produce.[21] They filled up water bottles when going out to avoid having to purchase overpriced drinks. They were reluctant to turn on the air conditioner, even on sweltering days.[22]

After a period, they moved to the subtropical city of Kunming, where one of their daughters lived.[23] While the precise timeline is unclear, Ren Zhengfei had remarried at some point and was building a new family in Shenzhen. This second marriage may have taken place around 1994, according to a speech Ren gave in January 2009, in which he praised his second wife, Yao Ling, for "fifteen years of silent devotion to the family."[24] Yao Ling was a petite and graceful young woman, much younger than Ren, with almond-shaped eyes and a winsome smile. Some news reports referred to her as Ren's former secretary,[25] though this has not been confirmed by the company. Ren had called Meng Jun "very tough"; he called Yao Ling "gentle and capable."[26] Ren claimed that the two got along, mentioning once that his first wife had arranged the marriage certificate for his second marriage.[27]

In Kunming, Ren Moxun busied himself with penning a book on how to teach Mandarin to ethnic minority students who didn't grow up speaking the language.[28] The rules of Chinese grammar were instinctive to anyone born into them, but they were complicated to explain. Ren Moxun counted up sixteen rules for how to use the particle *de* (的), which connects an adjective or descriptive phrase to a noun in some situations but not others. You didn't need *de* to connect the noun to the adjective in *duli yundong* (independence movement) or in *hutu sixiang* (muddled ideology), Ren Moxun observed, but in other cases, it was necessary. For instance—and here Ren Moxun rattled off a few phrases that came to mind:

"Nengchi de shanlihong" (the hawthorns that are edible).
"Da riben guizi de gushi" (a story of battling the Japanese devils).
"Guoqu de rizi" (the days of the past).
"Zhengzhi guashi de ren" (a person who puts political considerations first).

Ren Moxun passed away in June 1995, at age eighty-five, in Kunming.[29] He had fallen ill after consuming a drink from a street vendor.[30]

Years later, Ren Zhengfei would ask someone to help him procure a copy of his parents' dang'an, their official dossiers.[31] The party kept one for each person, tracking their employment, political history, social activities, appraisals by colleagues, and other information. He said his friend was moved to tears after reading his parents' confessions to the party. "All their lives, they followed the revolution," Ren wrote.

H uawei was playing host to a growing stream of visitors out of Beijing. Officials were keen to support a rising star in the tech realm.

When Vice-Premier Zhu Rongji, the famed economic reformer, came to visit in 1996, he gave Huawei's staff a thumbs-up[32] and encouraged them to go abroad. "You young people are great!" he said. "As long as China's program-controlled switches make it overseas, there will definitely be buyer's credit provided." He told them that domestic switchmakers would also continue to enjoy support in the home market against foreign rivals. Shenzhen's party secretary, Li Youwei, was thrilled when he heard that Zhu was continuing to praise Huawei after returning to Beijing. "As far as we know, he has not expressed such an opinion about any other company," he exclaimed.[33]

The visitors also included Wang Qishan,[34] chairman of the China Construction Bank, and a local official named Zhang Gaoli,[35] both of whom would one day enter the government's top ranks under Xi Jinping. Zhang encouraged Huawei's engineers to set their sights higher. "You must not be satisfied with the status quo," he told them.

Many of the officials were particularly interested in Huawei's chip design center, founded in 1991. Chips were the brains inside all computing devices—from consumer gadgets to military systems to telephone switches—and the industry was dominated by US companies. Chips R&D was particularly expensive due to the microscopic precision required for circuits. In 1996, Huawei was one of eight companies selected by Beijing for a $1 billion national semiconductor development program.[36] Speaking with Premier Li Peng that year, Ren had said Huawei was interested in setting up a "state-owned, privately operated" chipmaking venture.[37] He called chipmaking a "national activity." "Developed nations use some silicon wafers and exchange them for a large amount of our peanuts," Ren once remarked. "We have long felt this is an unequal exchange."[38]

Since Ren's meeting with Jiang in 1994, much more government support had been pledged. At the end of 1994, Zhang told Ren that in the next five-year economic plan, half of telecom operators' switch purchases would be reserved for purely domestic companies like Huawei.[39] "The way I look at it," Zhang said, "it's not that important what type of ownership structure a company has. The important thing is if it's Chinese. So we at the Electronics Ministry want to support a business like yours." China would have 84 million telephone lines' worth of switches in operation by 1995, and officials planned to more than double that to 174 million lines' worth by 2000.

Beijing came through with sales for Huawei and its crosstown rival, ZTE. In June 1996, China's official Xinhua News Agency reported that the Ministry of Posts and Telecommunications had held a nationwide switch-ordering fair in which Huawei and ZTE emerged with 3.14 million lines' worth of switch orders, 62 percent of the total. "The transactions represented the country's total demand for the first half of the year," Xinhua said. The Xinhua report also noted that Huawei and ZTE were set to receive state aid in a program sponsored by the State Economic and Trade Commission.

Financing was also coming through. The People's Bank of China offered Huawei loans, with the bank's president, Dai Xianglong, declaring that it was forming an "unbreakable bond" with Huawei.[40] He said the bank would encourage its customers to use Huawei products.

In 1995, Shenzhen, inspired by Silicon Valley, launched its first venture-capital firm to invest in startups. Ren was invited to speak at the launch. "Without the government's attention and support, it's impossible to achieve rapid high-tech development," Ren told the crowd. "And the more intense the competition, the more state intervention is required. This is what is required by the high-tech industry, and what is required for national security."[41]

Chinese officials had also begun promoting Huawei's switches abroad. Vice-Premier Li Lanqing was extolling Huawei's switches to foreign governments and inviting Huawei executives to accompany him on diplomatic trips. On a 1995 trip to eastern Europe, Vice-Premier Li brought along Huawei C&C08 switches as diplomatic gifts.

The growing interest from Beijing raised the specter that Huawei could be nationalized. Becoming a sluggish state-owned enterprise was something Ren was anxious to avoid. Others also warned him against it. "You must never become state-owned," one official told him. "If that happens, you guys will die."[42] After Vice-Premier Zhu's visit, when his aides followed up to offer more loans, Ren politely declined.[43]

As government officials came to visit Huawei, they were also interested in how the technology could be used for surveillance. Visiting in March 1996, Premier Li Peng—a hard-liner nicknamed "the Butcher of Beijing" overseas for his role in the brutal Tiananmen

Square suppression of 1989—asked Ren about a technology he'd seen in movies where investigators could log the phone numbers of criminals making phone calls.[44] He said that the Ministry of Public Security wanted this capability.

"Do you have this technology?" the premier asked.

"As soon as it rings, we know," Ren said. "In less than a second."

Li asked if Huawei was selling the technology yet, and Ren said that the company had the capability but hadn't rolled it out.

"I'm especially interested in the issue of call tracing," the premier said, "because national security is very important."

It's unclear what, if anything, came of Premier Li's inquiries into call tracing at Huawei. But the incident reflected that Huawei had been subject to security demands from Chinese authorities at the highest levels as early as the 1990s. This would be unsurprising, given the governmental utility of monitoring telephone calls. Wiretapping is something that every nation's government does to a greater or lesser extent. And in a few years' time, as phones became hooked up to the internet, Huawei's networks would become even more valuable. A lot more than phone calls would be flowing through.

7

Pack of Wolves

On January 28, 1996, Ren Zhengfei held Huawei's first "mass-resignation ceremony." Each head of a regional sales office was told to prepare two reports: a work summary and a written resignation. "I will only sign one of the reports," Ren said.[1]

"Dear Chairman," the resignation letter said,[2] "I have fought for the company's sales development and sacrificed my youth. But in the few years that I've worked on the sales front lines, my technical and business ability may not have kept up. . . . If through the process of examination and selection, the company identifies a more suitable person for sales work, I will sincerely resign from my current position."

Huawei had started out in rural markets, and many of its early sales managers were provincial in their experience and network of contacts. As Ren sought to go national and international, he decided to make the entire sales staff resign and reapply for their jobs. "The mountain goat must outrun the lion to not be eaten," he had told them ahead of the event. "All departments and sections must optimize and eat the lazy goats, the goats that do not learn or progress, and the goats with no sense of responsibility."[3]

Now Ren took the podium. "Being an executive at Huawei should be understood as a responsibility, a choice to sacrifice personal happiness," he said.[4]

The resigning sales managers were allowed to speak in turn, some choking back tears.

"As a Huawei person, I'm willing to be a paving stone," one said.[5]

"If I can't keep up with the pace of the company's development, I'm willing to let new people, and higher-level people, take over my job," another offered.

"My youth and ability are limited, and Huawei's future is long," a third said. "I can't hold back the company because of me."

In the end, Ren accepted the resignation of six of the twenty-six sales branch chiefs and turned over some 30 percent of the sales staff. Huawei executives would often cite the mass resignation as an example of who they were as "Huawei people."[6] They could go up or down according to the needs of the company. In whatever position they were assigned, they would humbly strive to improve themselves. They believed in the company's mission. They were willing to sacrifice.

Purges were a fixture in the Chinese Communist Party, seen as a way to test the mettle of cadres. At Huawei, too, Ren told his followers that demotions built character and that the demoted would only be stronger when they worked their way up again. "The bird that isn't burned to death in the fire is a phoenix," he often told them. Ren reminded them that paramount leader Deng Xiaoping himself had been purged thrice in his career, springing back each time. "Even Deng Xiaoping could go down and up three times. Why can't you go down and up three times?"[7]

R en had grown up in the Mao years, when there was no such thing as private-sector sales. Now he presented sales to his young followers in rousing terms, almost as a mystical vocation. "Sales work is special, complex, and noble," he told them. "You need the intelligence of a scientist, the insight of a philosopher, the eloquence of an orator, the ambition of a social reformer, and the optimism and persistent spirit of a religious man."[8] He said that the sales profession was a battlefield, even if there wasn't gunpowder or smoke. It was winner takes all, no mercy for losers. "Haven't you been dying to have a go?" he asked. "Haven't you been seeking all along your self-fulfillment? Then stand up bravely. This great era calls for unique heroes."

Many of them were eager for this opportunity to travel, find adventure, look smart in a suit. The reality wasn't quite as glamorous. Nearly all their sales were in rural areas and small towns at first. They were following the strategy that Mao had used to win the Chinese Civil War of "encircling the cities with the countryside."[9] They'd won over villages and towns in the beginning, building their strength to take on the big cities. "There was no secretary, no cell phone, no driver or private car," one of Huawei's early salespeople wrote in an essay.[10] They traveled alone by bus or train, hauling product information, contracts, some basic maintenance tools, and changes of clothes. Another sales rep recalled that they were required to stay in the field for a year before they could take a trip home to Shenzhen: "You could only return to headquarters if you were accompanying a very important customer."[11]

Ren now exhorted his sales team to develop a "wolf culture." "Wolves are really powerful," Ren told his staff. "They have a keen sense of smell, they are very aggressive, and they don't attack alone but in packs. As soon as one falls, another steps into the breach. They don't fear sacrifice."[12]

To win orders, they made bold promises. In a memoir, one former Huawei salesman wrote that his manager had instructed him to tell customers a switch would be ready soon when they both knew it would be months. "Do you think it's better for the customer to doubt the company or to doubt the ability of a single engineer?" his boss had reasoned.[13] Huawei would build a reputation for courting its customers relentlessly, loitering at hotels or airports to catch traveling officials, even waiting outside their homes. In 1995, China officially switched from a six-day workweek to a five-day one,[14] but Huawei's staff continued to work around the clock.

Despite the interest that Huawei had received from government officials, it was only one among many contenders, and not even the most favored one. In 1995, officials had set up a state-owned switch-making champion called China Great Dragon Telecommunication in an effort to combat the foreign switchmakers. Great Dragon was built around the military engineer Wu Jiangxing's breakthrough 04 switch and had been formed by merging eight smaller telecom companies. The government was pouring some $2.2 billion a year into the venture.[15] Also in 1995, the Xi'an Datang Telephone Co.—a venture set up by a state-run research institute and several Chinese graduates from US universities[16]—began mass production of its new switch, the SP30. And across town in Shenzhen, the Zhongxing Telecommunications Equipment Company—which would later be known as ZTE—had developed its ZXJ10 switch.[17] People called them the Big Four of China's domestic switchmaking, and they made quick work of eating into the foreign vendors' market share. Within a few years, the price of telephone switches in China had dropped from $300 per line to $70 per line. With so many contenders, and such thin margins, companies were always flaming out. In early 1996, a dozen of Great Dragon's 04 switches abruptly failed due to a software problem.[18] The company never recovered.

At the start of 1997, Huawei cracked into the Beijing market.[19] The nation's capital purchased twenty-four thousand lines' worth of Huawei's C&C08 switches, following other big cities like Tianjin and Guangzhou. "It is time to equip China's telecom trunks with domestic products," a Beijing official affirmed. Huawei's annual sales were now approaching half a billion dollars.[20] Huawei had started out as an underdog compared with its state-owned rivals. Now it was emerging as the frontrunner, so much so that the state-owned companies were crying foul. "They sell cheaply to get market share," an executive at Datang complained.[21] Great Dragon's Wu Jiangxing griped to Shenzhen's Science and Technology Bureau that the local government shouldn't just support privately owned companies.[22]

Huawei's growing success was attracting broader public attention, but the company remained something of a cipher. Beginning in 1993, it had begun sending an in-house newspaper, *Huawei People*, to telecom officials and other stakeholders, but it remained press-shy to the general public. Huawei executives accepted interviews rarely; Ren, never. When he was selected to be one of eight entrepreneurs featured in a local magazine spread, the other seven had professional portraits, with soft lighting and heroic poses. For Ren, the magazine's editors only managed to scrounge up some awkward snapshots. In one, he stands at the back of a meeting room with a mottled tie and a five-o'clock shadow, peeking out from behind the shoulder of the Shenzhen mayor, Li Zibin. "It seems," the editors wrote, "that Ren Zhengfei is never in the center of a photograph."[23]

Sales during China's unbridled 1990s capitalist boom involved all sorts of risks. Business was heavily based on guanxi, or personal connections. And building guanxi with prospective clients involved heavy rounds of drinking and lavish gifts. "At the beginning of opening up, there weren't strong regulations. Corruption was all over the place," Ren once said. "It was so difficult for Huawei to build its own clean team in this environment."[24]

Polite protocol for a business dinner involved breaking out the baijiu, a clear sorghum spirit that has an eye-watering 120-proof kick, and pouring out round after round of shots over a rotating parade of exquisite dishes. The protocol also involved getting drunker than your clients to show your respect for them. One early Huawei executive wrote about having to excuse himself for a vomit break while entertaining customers—not an uncommon occurrence. Others developed stomach or liver ailments. This seemed to happen particularly often in the far northeast, which had a reputation for heavy drinking. "The key staffer for this account is currently suffering hepatitis but refuses to come back to Shenzhen for medical treatment and insists on fighting on the front line through the ice and snow," Ren said in 1995 about a Huawei salesperson based in Yichun, close to the northeastern border with Russia.[25] At one point, Huawei's headquarters sent a shipment of propolis, a bee-made resin known for its healing properties, to northeast staffers whose stomachs were ruined by drink.[26]

Then there was the problem of bribery. Officials in China expected it, whether it was cash stuffed in red envelopes or other gifts. Over the years, a number of Huawei sales managers would be named in domestic bribery cases where telecom officials were found guilty of accepting cash, gift cards, or other enticements. Huawei described these as isolated incidents of employees disregarding the company's ethics guidelines. But luxurious gifts to officials were par for the course. An executive of the Canadian vendor Nortel recollected how his boss tasked him with delivering fifty bottles of Johnnie Walker Scotch whisky to Chinese government officials. "Ericsson had a (golf) coach they would offer up to their customers. He would fly in from Australia," an industry consultant recalled of the Swedish vendor.[27] Ericsson would later admit to the US Justice Department that it had splashed out tens of millions of dollars to cover gifts and perks, including Caribbean cruises, for Chinese customers.[28]

There was one curious report that emerged years later: In 2017, Li Jingxian, a former Chinese ambassador to Uzbekistan, published an essay in a local magazine. He wrote that on September 1, 1998, he'd met Ren for tea at Beijing's Jinglun Hotel, and Ren had asked him for advice about breaking into the Russian market. At the end of the meeting, according to Li, Ren's assistant handed him some pamphlets, and when he returned home and flipped through the pages, an envelope fell out. Inside, he said, were twenty US $100 bills. "I was so scared," he wrote. "I hardly slept all night." The next day, by his account, he turned the cash over to the Ministry of Foreign

Affairs along with a written note explaining the situation. A few days later, Huawei's chief representative in Beijing, Catherine Chen, telephoned to say that the cash had been returned. Ren himself called too, apologizing profusely for the confusion and claiming that the money was a personal gift to the ambassador to help him furnish his new apartment. "This bit of money has been earned through my own labor, and is very much clean," Li recalled Ren telling him. "It's absolutely not from the company's accounts."[29]

In any case, Huawei had a reputation for generosity and hospitality within the industry. It paid for government officials and telecom executives to travel the world for conferences and training sessions. When they visited Huawei's headquarters, they were greeted with lavish feasts. Ren told his sales managers to continue sending birthday cakes to retired telecom experts who had helped Huawei.

After he left government office, Li Zibin, former mayor of Shenzhen, was visiting the US in 2007 when there was a knock on his hotel door. He opened it to find Ren standing there, inviting him to dinner. Li was stunned. He wrote in his memoir that Ren told him, "That's just me, Ren Zhengfei. When you were in office for eleven years, our company didn't invite you to dinner once. But Huawei's people know to be grateful. You are our benefactor, and now that you are retired, I'm inviting you to dinner."[30]

The company's sales initiative had created a new crop of internal rising-star executives, whom Ren called Huawei's "heroes" for enduring long hours and harsh conditions in the field. Two of the most outstanding salesmen were Ken Hu and Eric Xu. Hu had come out of the Huazhong Institute, like so many of Huawei's other engineers, and joined the company in 1990. Early in his Huawei career, he was dispatched to the inland city of Changsha.[31] One of his customer's switches was mysteriously malfunctioning each night. After camping in the switchroom overnight, Hu discovered it was because rats were gnawing on the cables.[32] Xu had gotten a doctorate in Nanjing before coming on board at Huawei in 1993. "I didn't have any concept of sales or strategy," he said. "The representative office would get a phone call or a fax, and I'd rush out with my materials and slide projector. I went to virtually all the provincial capitals."[33]

Ren's younger brother, Ren Shulu, or Steven Ren, had spent some time working in TV and film production and joined the company in 1992.[34] Twelve years younger, Steven Ren was assigned to run Huawei's sales office in Lanzhou, a bustling city in the nation's far west, before returning to headquarters. Ren's sister Zheng Li would reportedly become a manager in Huawei's finance department.[35] Ren's other four siblings have remained out of the public eye; he has not mentioned what they went on to do professionally, and domestic press reports and biographies have omitted this particular as well.

The executive who rose the highest was Sun Yafang, who was elevated from marketing and sales president to Huawei's vice-chairwoman in 1994. She was an intense woman of around forty, with a hawkish nose and a stately bearing. She had overseen Huawei's "marriage" to the state through the joint ventures with provincial telecom bureaus and had led the mass resignation of the sales managers. People whispered that Madam Sun had worked for the Ministry of State Security, or the MSS, China's powerful civilian intelligence agency, before joining the company. Perhaps that had something to do with her rapid rise through Huawei's ranks, or perhaps not.

Sun's parentage and childhood circumstances are unclear. Some Chinese media reports say Sun grew up in Guizhou Province, where Ren was born, but Huawei hasn't confirmed this. What is known is that Sun went to university in Chengdu, the city where Ren's first wife, Meng Jun, grew up and where their daughter Meng Wanzhou was born. In March 1978, when Sun matriculated at the Chengdu Radio Engineering Institute (which, like many technical schools at the time, was run by the military), she became one of the 760 students in the first freshman class in more than a decade.[36] During the Cultural Revolution, the college entrance exam had been suspended nationwide for twelve years. Competition was fierce that year, with a decade's worth of students all competing for a spot. "She was very popular with her classmates," Mao Yuming, a fellow student, recalled to a local newspaper. "She often organized class group activities. She was one of the leaders."[37] In Sun's freshman year, the school hosted its first American visitor since before the Cultural Revolution: the Georgia Institute of Technology's president, J. M. Pettit.[38]

After university, Sun got a job in 1982 as a technician at the Xinxiang Liaoyuan Radio Factory,[39] also called Factory 760, in central Henan Province.[40] Set up by the military in the 1950s, the factory made radio tuners, tape recorders, and other equipment. It had also just begun an exciting pivot: making black-and-white TVs under the Melody brand amid a broad push for military suppliers to shift to consumer products.[41] Sun stayed at Factory 760 for only a year before becoming a teacher at the China Research Institute of Radio Wave Propagation in 1983 and then an engineer at the Beijing Research Institute of Information Technology in 1985.[42] Both of these are state-run institutes with low public profiles, and it's unclear what she did there. Unclear, too, is whether her work at the MSS came after her stints at these institutes or took place concurrently.

Sun's rise at Huawei was swift. A September 1993 issue of Huawei's internal magazine, *Huawei People*, mentions her being a sales manager who gave product demonstrations to visitors from around the country. "Our lightning-resistant chips are developed by our company and sent to the US for processing," she told them.[43] By March 1994, Sun had been promoted to president of the marketing and sales department, where she ran training boot camps for new sales staff in which they each got eight minutes to pitch Huawei products.[44] At the end of 1994, she was listed as vice-chairwoman of the company.[45]

Sun ran a tight ship, cracking down on excessive golfing among the managers.[46] "Huawei's sales staffers all know that if Madam Sun sees you without a tie on a convention floor, your fate will be a miserable one," a member of her team wrote about her. "Not to mention her fiery temper. The hurricane of her criticism will leave you with no possible hope to find an escape."[47]

Ren had proved willing to promote capable female executives, even as he sometimes expressed old-fashioned views on women in the workplace. "Many companies don't like hiring female employees, because female employees are inefficient and can't achieve the goals when they do things," Ren said in a speech to Huawei's secretaries around this time. "Female employees have a big shortcoming, which is they like to gossip and nag, which undermines unity. Originally, the purpose of hiring female employees was to add a lubricant to the management team. The main characteristic of male employees is their rigidity, and they are prone to producing sparks when they collide. With a layer of elastic sponge in between, there won't be sparks."[48]

Sun described Huawei as a "male society" where the most talented male engineers garnered the most respect. "I'm no hero," she once wrote. "But I'm a loyal inheritor of Ren Zhengfei's management philosophy. . . . Some people would say I'm the most similar person spiritually to Ren Zhengfei."[49]

8

Farewell to the
Paramount Leader

DENG XIAOPING'S DEATH AND THE
HONG KONG HANDOVER: 1997

A round 3:00 a.m. on the morning of February 20, 1997, Ren
Zhengfei learned that ninety-two-year-old paramount
leader Deng Xiaoping had died of pulmonary disease.[1] Deng
had been the leader who revived scientific research, who brought back
capitalism, who made it possible for a company like Huawei to exist.
It was the middle of the night, but there was not a minute to spare.
The death of a national leader was a moment of political peril: in the
spring of 1989, the gathering of mourners after the death of General
Secretary Hu Yaobang had turned into the Tiananmen democracy
protests. With Deng gone, it was also unclear if his successors would
maintain his path of economic reform. Huawei was a company that
rose to the political moment. Ren picked up the phone.

By 8:15 a.m., Huawei's fax machines were sending the emergency
notice to all corners of the company, including thirty-some domestic

branches; the US R&D subsidiary, Ran Boss; and the Hong Kong office.[2] Flowers were brought into the main office, fragrant boughs of pine and cypress. The finance department ordered black veils and white gauze to make crepe flowers. Mourning halls were set up in each of Huawei's three offices in Shenzhen. Some Huawei staffers rushed out to a print shop to make large color posters bearing Deng's image. Others arranged for more than a dozen TVs to be set up so that everyone could watch the memorial ceremony. The national flag was lowered to half-mast and would remain there for a week. Huawei's vice-chairwoman, Sun Yafang, was traveling in Israel with China's premier, Li Lanqing, and she rushed to the Chinese embassy to express her condolences.[3] At Ran Boss in the US, employees sent flower wreaths to the Chinese consulate in San Francisco.

Ren's daughter Meng Wanzhou, now twenty-five, had been a secretary in Huawei's marketing department for two years. As she got onto the shuttle that morning, it was misty with a chill wind.[4] Her solemn colleagues on the bus remained quiet. Perhaps if no one broached the matter, it wouldn't be true.

Deng had requested a shockingly understated postmortem arrangement: for his corneas to be donated to an eye bank, for his body to be dissected for medical research, and for his ashes to be scattered into the sea.[5] It was a pointed divergence from Mao Zedong, whose embalmed body remained on permanent display in Tiananmen Square. Deng's body would disappear, leaving no tombstone or memorial.

Despite official orders for low-key mourning, residents were gathering in the streets of Shenzhen, as they did across the nation. Beneath a large image of Deng near city hall, people piled wreaths and yellow chrysanthemums.[6] They hung strings of paper cranes from a railing.

Deng had ordered the bloody crackdown on the student protesters in Tiananmen Square. There had been calls for him to step down near the end. But looking back, people felt that, on balance, Deng had been a great leader: he had ended the Mao-era witch hunts, reopened universities, legalized private enterprise, and given a generation a new lease on life. At Huawei, executives devoted the entire forty-fifth issue of *Huawei People*, the company's main internal newspaper, to tributes to Deng. It was the only time ever that the newspaper was entirely dedicated to a single topic—and one with no direct relation to Huawei business, for that matter. "The four seas weep, the mountains and rivers have grown pale," James Yan, Huawei's US representative, wrote.[7] "His death is a great loss for all mankind," Ren's younger brother, Steven Ren, was quoted as saying.[8]

Meng Wanzhou also penned a memorial essay.[9] She wrote that two months earlier, her father had instructed her to carefully watch the documentary about Deng Xiaoping running on state TV, reminding her that politics was the highest form of economic management. "In the past, Deng Xiaoping was so far away from me," she wrote. "I'm just a twenty-five-year-old girl who has been living a peaceful life." She called for Huawei's employees to redouble their work efforts amid their grief. "Let us use tomorrow's success to comfort our beloved Comrade Xiaoping."

Five days after Deng's death, Huawei's three thousand employees stood in silence for three minutes along with people across the country as Deng's memorial service began in Beijing.[10] For many of them, Meng included, it felt tragic that Deng would be missing the return of Hong Kong, which he had worked so hard to achieve for years. By the joint declaration signed in 1984, the British would hand over control of Hong Kong to the People's Republic of China on July 1, 1997.

"With only a bit more than a hundred days remaining before Hong Kong's return, he has left us," Meng wrote. "This is not only a pity for him, but a pity for all the nation's people."[11]

Shenzhen was separated from Hong Kong by only the narrow river. Its wealthier sister city was never far from Shenzheners' minds. Ren told his early engineers that the day would come when their salaries were higher than those of Hong Kongers, a giddy prospect that they only half believed.[12] If Shenzhen was China's door to the world, then Hong Kong was the beginning of the rest of the world.

Huawei had done business with Hong Kong since its earliest days. It had been a contractor for the Hong Kong switchmaker Hung Nien, for which it assembled switches that were sold into the mainland market.[13] When it started designing its own switches, it relied on international suppliers through its Hong Kong offices. Huawei opened its Hong Kong branch office in September 1995, throwing a party at the Regent Hong Kong with more than 120 guests, including representatives from Texas Instruments, Siemens, and Panasonic.[14]

Hong Kong's telephone operators had generally purchased foreign switches up until this point, viewing mainland switchmakers with suspicion. "I felt a sense of shabbiness," one Huawei manager reported after a trip to the British colony.[15] He urged his colleagues to improve their attention to detail and dress sharper to match their Hong Kong peers. But as the handover approached, Beijing was pushing for closer ties with Hong Kong. Shenzhen officials were tasked with trying to find technological points of cooperation.

It was amid this current of political warming that Huawei made its breakthrough with Hutchison Telecom, Hong Kong's second-largest telephone operator, owned by the city's richest man, Li Ka-shing. Li had been born in the mainland, but he had moved to Hong Kong as a child, building a real-estate empire after getting his start making plastic flowers.[16] Li had been wary of doing business with the mainland, according to Simon Murray, Li's right-hand man from 1984 to 1993.[17] "What he said to me was, 'Simon, if we have a partner in China and we have a row, it will be us against the Chinese, and it will be very bad for us.'" But as the handover drew closer, Li was convinced that forging some mainland business ties would be favorable. When the Hutchison team visited Huawei's headquarters in Shenzhen,[18] Ren's team convinced them that Huawei could supply a network expansion much faster than rivals, and at only half the cost.[19] In June 1996, Huawei sealed a deal with Hutchison Telecom to supply twenty-five thousand lines' worth of C&C08 switches.[20] Huawei scrambled to deliver, shipping the switches just four months later in October and completing installation in December. Asked why Hutchison picked Huawei as a vendor, Murray said: "Why not? We had a very nice relationship with China. When I was there, we bought a port in Shanghai. Everybody in Hong Kong was doing business with China."

It was an important deal for Huawei: their first sales foothold outside the mainland. "This is an important event in Huawei's history," a Huawei manager wrote about the Hutchison project. "It symbolizes that we have taken our first solid step into overseas markets! With tears in our eyes, and dripping sweat, we almost broke our wineglasses from toasting!"[21]

Huawei was also expanding its horizons beyond switches. As the handover neared, Huawei launched a new product: a video-camera system that could be used for both conference calls and closed-circuit surveillance. China's government had begun adopting these systems in 1992 for virtual meetings, but only foreign companies made them. Officials were keen to find domestic alternatives. "Video conferencing is very suitable for China's centralized management system," said Qiu Zhenbang, director of the emergency communications department of the Ministry of Posts and Telecommunications, in a 1997 speech. "It is particularly convenient for party and government leaders."[22] In 1996, Huawei engineer Chen Qing had gone to San Jose to visit the industry leader in videoconferencing, Compression Labs, and scope out the situation. "Since they knew Huawei was also making a videoconferencing system, the entire meeting was spent in a hostile and unfriendly atmosphere," Chen reported back.[23]

Huawei's ViewPoint videoconferencing system, which began development in 1994, was deployed in Sichuan Province in early 1997, with the city of Nanchong adopting eight interconnecting sets for communication between its offices.[24] Other provinces followed. Huawei lauded it as the first time that a domestically developed videoconferencing system had been put to use in China and said it was interoperable with the American Compression Labs systems that the Sichuan government was already using. Huawei was also marketing the ViewPoint system for surveillance. It could be hooked up to as many as 960 video cameras at once, with the video feeds rotating in color on a big screen.[25] When an alarm was triggered by a feed, the big screen would switch to that display. The device was being manufactured by Mobeco, Huawei's joint venture with the municipal telecom bureaus, which had branched out from switches to power supplies and other gadgets.

This video system piqued the interest of China's military. There were obvious security advantages over foreign-made gear. In November 1996, Liu Huaqing, vice-chairman of China's Central Military Commission, stopped in at Huawei during a visit to People's Liberation Army troops stationed in Shenzhen to prepare for the Hong Kong handover.[26] Ren showed Liu and other military officials some of Huawei's products and answered their questions. Liu encouraged Huawei to "continue prioritizing national interests" as it built its company, according to an account in *Huawei People*. Huawei's ViewPoint video system was installed near the Guangzhou Military Region, a couple hours' drive northwest of Shenzhen, and also to the south at the Hong Kong Garrison.[27]

Ren had claimed consistently to his staff that their humble work in switches was tied to larger purposes, even to national reunification. "To resolve Hong Kong's return, and Taiwan's unification, a large amount of foreign exchange is necessary," Ren said in an internal speech in 1995. "China is a poor country. What can it use to attract people? . . . There's only the market. And they don't want the potato or onion market, only the high-tech market, especially the telecom market."[28]

With the big day approaching, Ren gave a speech to Huawei employees. "In a few days, Hong Kong will return to the motherland," he said. "The smoke of the Opium War has dissipated, but the ghosts of the Opium War still linger. The century of humiliation has taught us a truth, which is that weak countries will never be in 'the right.' When wolves want to eat sheep, they will always find a way to be in the right."[29]

A few minutes before midnight on June 30, 1997, three British military guards of honor marched stiffly up to a flagpole under the bright lights in Hong Kong's new convention center.[30] They drew down the Union Jack for the last time. At the stroke of midnight, three Chinese military guards replaced it with a crimson flag emblazoned with five yellow stars. China's leader, Jiang Zemin, stood watch, as did Prince Charles, British prime minister Tony Blair, and former British prime minister Margaret Thatcher, who had negotiated the handover with Deng over many years.

Hong Kong was the last major colony of the British Empire, which, at its peak, covered a quarter of the land on earth. India had won its independence in 1947, Sudan in 1956, and most other British colonies in quick succession thereafter. "It wasn't just the end, as it were, of the British Empire," Hong Kong's last British governor, Chris Patten, would later say of the handover. "It was the end of empire."[31] Among the departing British, there was trepidation that Beijing would not keep its promise to allow Hong Kong freedom of speech and other rights not allowed in the mainland. Across China, there was jubilation that the era of colonial rule was finally over.

Some eight thousand journalists had descended on Hong Kong.[32] China's state-run broadcaster, CCTV, had forty cameras rolling and two helicopters shooting aerial footage. Among the sea of cameras were some of Huawei's.

"During the Hong Kong handover, it played a key role," *Huawei People* reported of the company's ViewPoint system. "It transmitted a large amount of command information, and at the first instance sent through precious images like the handover from the British troops to the Hong Kong Garrison, and the Hong Kong Garrison raising the national flag."[33]

Ahead of the handover, Meng had given birth to her first child, a boy.[34] Little is known about her first husband, whom she appears to have avoided discussing publicly. But her mother, Meng Jun, had been on hand, feeding her soup and changing the boy's diapers. Many years before, Meng Jun had sent her children Meng Wanzhou and Ren Ping to be reared by their grandparents while she pursued a career. Now she took on the role of doting grandmother to the small boy, freeing up Meng Wanzhou to focus on her career.

Meng Wanzhou had begun her journey at Huawei as a secretary, handling tasks like printing documents and answering phones.[35] She was flustered by all the buttons on the phone switchboard. Her family aspired for her to climb the ranks, and following her post-childbirth recovery, she spent six months working at Huawei's Hong Kong office before returning to school.[36]

Meng Wanzhou's college history remains hazy. Some domestic news reports called her a high school dropout. Years later, at her first press appearance, Meng would say that the reports were wrong,[37] that she had indeed attended university and graduated in 1992, a curious account given that Shenzhen University would list her as matriculating in 1990, putting her time at the university at only two years. Meng's official bios at Huawei have never given specific details about her undergraduate studies or even noted if she obtained a bachelor's degree.

What is known for certain, however, is that in 1997, Meng went back to school to get a master's degree in accounting while her mother looked after her son. She did her degree at the Huazhong Institute in Wuhan, the alma mater of Guo Ping and many of Ren's other early engineers. "To let me better study and work, she silently took up all the responsibility of caring for the child," Meng Wanzhou wrote of her mother. She may have pursued the degree under her father's surname: In late 1997, two papers on financial management penned by a Ren Wanzhou were published in Chinese academic journals. One paper, about novel fundraising methods for state-owned enterprises, gave Ren Wanzhou's affiliation as the Huazhong Institute, while the other paper, on the MRP II and ISO 9000 business-management systems, gave her affiliation as Shenzhen Huawei Company. With the accounting degree in hand, she would be able to rise through the ranks at Huawei. She was soon busy juggling work and motherhood. "Each day when I return from work, my precious boy is standing in the doorway, and when he sweetly says, 'Mama,' my heart is about to shatter," she wrote. "The day's weariness evaporates."[38]

Huawei had survived its first decade. Ren's team had built one of China's first advanced digital telephone switches, relieving the nation from its dependence on foreign technology. He'd built a deep team of talent, with Sun Yafang, the female sales chief with an intelligence background; Li Yinan, the "young prodigy"; Zheng Baoyong, or "A-Bao," whom he viewed with brotherly affection; and Guo Ping, one of his earliest engineers, all helping him steer the ship as Huawei vice presidents. Several of his family members were now at Huawei as well, including his younger brother, Steven Ren, who was in sales, and his daughter Meng Wanzhou, in the finance department.

Ren was setting his sights higher. He wanted Huawei to become not just a Chinese business but an international business and a leader in its field. He also wanted to take back control: he had asked a deputy to start negotiating to buy out Huawei's five original investors.[39] To govern this growing corporate empire, Ren had recruited scholars to draft his own constitution, taking inspiration from the British constitutional monarchy. The age of kings and queens had waned. Now Huawei was fast becoming a dominion upon which the sun never set.

When Meng was young, her father would tell her stories about the old war heroes from Mao's army: Dong Cunrui, who went on a suicide bombing mission to destroy a Nationalist bunker; Liu Hulan, a fourteen-year-old female spy beheaded by the Nationalists after they failed to get her to betray her allies; Wang Erxiao, a thirteen-year-old cowherd killed by Japanese troops' bayonets after he was found to have helped Red troops escape; and Yang Jingyu, who alone held off Japanese soldiers for five days, despite having nothing to eat but tree bark and cotton.[40] Meng listened in thrall, half wishing that she, too, could become a war hero. "How could I understand at such a young age," she wrote, "what exactly is a hero?"

PART II

As we are a large, globalized company, major events
happening in any corner of the world may have
something to do with us.[1]

—*Huawei's* Management Optimization
newspaper, March 31, 2011

9

Iron Army

HUAWEI ABROAD: 1996-1999

On December 17, 1998, at twenty minutes after midnight, the eerie wail of air-raid sirens pierced the dark sky over Baghdad.[1] The horizon exploded with bursts of light as Iraqi antiaircraft guns sprayed fire. American B-52H planes were bombing the Iraqi capital.

At the Chinese embassy earlier in the evening, the mood was light.[2] No one seriously expected the Americans to attack. Still, just in case, embassy staff had distributed bulletproof vests and helmets. Now, with air-raid sirens screaming, everyone rushed to the basement. According to a Huawei staffer's account, the embassy turned off the lights to avoid drawing fire. Some wondered if it would be safer to declare themselves friendly bystanders by blazing the lights and flying China's red-and-yellow flag.

In the morning, the embassy's staff surveyed the damage. Some two hundred US Navy Tomahawk cruise missiles had been fired into what the Americans called "sensitive targets," sites suspected of being associated with the development of weapons of mass destruction.[3] The Chinese embassy was unscathed. A stray shell had exploded beyond its perimeter, and a piece of Iraqi shrapnel had landed on the empty garage. As they evacuated from the city by car, a Huawei employee saw a group of Iraqi residents standing in the street, looking up at the sky. "I suddenly thought of the scenes from China during the Opium War, when foreigners used their foreign guns and cannons to confront Chinese people armed with traditional weapons like knives," he later wrote. "How terrifying it is to be a weak and small country. And as a citizen of such a weak nation, what kind of humiliation will they endure?"[4]

Iraq was tricky territory for a company like Huawei. The country had been under United Nations sanctions since the 1990 Iraqi invasion of Kuwait, which meant that sales of telecommunications equipment into the country were largely blocked, with any exceptions under the humanitarian Oil-for-Food Programme requiring a UN waiver. Huawei was operating there but trying to keep a low-profile presence. A few years later, when asked by a Western journalist about the company's Iraq office, a Huawei executive said he was uncertain if it existed.[5] When Huawei had brought a prospective Iraqi customer to visit its headquarters in Shenzhen, it had taken pains to go under the radar. "At that time, it was difficult to send formal invitation letters to them through normal channels," one Huawei employee working in Iraq recalled, saying that a colleague had used their connections to help them secure a visa to China.[6]

It was easy to see why many of Huawei's engineers would feel sympathy for the sanctioned and downtrodden nations of the world.

The parallels to China's own recent past were only too clear. Because the Beijing government had turned its guns and tanks on students at Tiananmen Square in 1989, all of China's people had been punished for years with economic sanctions, including those who had supported the student protesters. Now, in Iraq, Saddam Hussein's reign meant that under UN dictum, no Iraqi resident could use a cell phone.

As Ren Zhengfei and his team looked out at the global telecommunications landscape, they saw a market dominated by the West.[7] America's Lucent Technologies—a direct descendant of Alexander Graham Bell's Bell Telephone Company—was number one in the world, with Sweden's Ericsson, France's Alcatel, and Canada's Nortel rounding out the heavyweights. There were plenty of smaller contenders too, all jostling for space: Britain's Marconi, Germany's Siemens, Japan's Fujitsu, Finland's Nokia, and Motorola and Cisco in the US.

To thread its way into this competitive market, Huawei began working for "rogue regimes." These controversial contracts would serve as the engine for the company's early global rise. But they would also put Huawei in Washington's crosshairs. For one thing, the National Security Agency, the signals-intelligence agency of the US, had relied on interception of radio communications to monitor countries like Iraq. As Huawei laid down fiber-optic cables to modernize the phone networks, the National Security Agency (NSA) found itself shut out from conversations it would have liked to hear.[8]

H uawei's journey into the international market began with the Third Taiwan Strait Crisis of 1995–1996. As tensions between the US and China ramped up, Beijing sought out closer ties with

Russia, leading to Boris Yeltsin and Jiang Zemin announcing a strategic partnership in April 1996.[9] Timed to the historic pact, China's National Science and Technology Commission arranged for Ren to go to Moscow to attend an international convention.[10] It would be Huawei's first major international event.

Ren understood that political winds had blown the door open for Huawei. "I believe it's not solely because our technical products are so exceptional, to the extent that the Russian government values us so much," Ren wrote. "It's more likely that we are benefiting from the influence of both General Secretary Jiang and President Yeltsin, as well as from the mutual desire of China and Russia to improve relations."[11] A Chinese diplomat who helped organize the trip wrote that Ren had "grasped the business opportunity hidden in this change in international relations."[12] Russia's state-owned TASS news agency reported that China's government had made a "special disbursement" to Huawei to open an office in Moscow, and that the office would also cover former Soviet countries like Ukraine and Belarus.[13]

Ren had grown up in the 1950s, when Soviet Russia was held up as a role model for China. Mao's industrial projects had relied heavily on Soviet expertise.[14] Ren had studied the Russian language in school,[15] and he'd read Soviet novels like *How the Steel Was Tempered*, Nikolai Ostrovsky's classic about a Bolshevik soldier.[16] "The Soviet Union's today is our tomorrow," the slogan went. He was now curious to see the heroic nation he'd heard so much about.

But by the time Ren arrived at the Moscow airport, the Soviet Union was no more, having lost the Cold War and collapsed in 1991. Ren saw a Russia devastated by hyperinflation. It cost twenty thousand rubles just for Ren to rent a couple of carts to wheel his luggage out of the airport.[17] Ren felt that the United States was partly to blame: Washington had coaxed the leader of the new Russia, Boris Yeltsin, to apply "shock therapy" to the economy with a rapid shift to capitalism, he wrote, but Washington did not follow through with the financial aid it had dangled. "They always give you some bait to get you to change some policies, but when you've made changes according to their demands, they raise further demands," Ren wrote. "You still cannot get 'sincere' help from the United States."[18]

For Huawei's coming-out-to-the-world moment at the Moscow convention, Ren and his team had prepared stacks of marketing materials and hired Russian water ballet dancers to staff the company's convention booth, which had China's flag displayed proudly at the front, along with the words CHINA HUAWEI.[19] The Chinese embassy had helped them with everything they needed, setting up meetings with Russian officials and organizing a reception and press conference at the luxurious Hotel Ukraina.[20] Ren had brought along his daughter Meng Wanzhou, who had joined Huawei a few years earlier and who tried to make herself useful on tasks like exchanging dollars for rubles.[21]

That visit resulted in Huawei's first international company, a joint venture with Russia's Ufa-based Beto company to produce Huawei's C&C08 switch. The factory would be tied up for years by regulatory red tape, as Russian officials found one reason after another for delays.[22] At the end of the day, the Russians remained wary about installing Chinese switches in their networks. "We are still unsure how much we know about Russia and if we can really open up the market," Ren wrote to staff.[23]

Huawei would continue to court Russia, China's neighbor to the north. Neither side really trusted the other, but Beijing and Moscow understood their fates to be intertwined. "The people of China and Russia will become wealthy," Ren wrote. "To be wealthy is not the birthright of the West alone."[24] Later, when a man named Vladimir Putin was elected president, Ren sent him a congratulatory message through a friend.[25]

I n January 1998, Ren's second wife, Yao Ling, gave birth to their daughter, Yao Siwei, or Annabel Yao, in the subtropical city of Kunming.[26] The city had become a new family hub for the Ren family: one of Ren's sisters lived there, and his parents had moved there after retirement. In the year of Annabel Yao's birth, Ren was fifty-three. His elder children, Meng Wanzhou and Ren Ping, were twenty-six and twenty-three. Ren had no intention of retiring anytime soon, but speculation already swirled over the prospect of a family succession. Former Chinese ambassador to Uzbekistan Li Jingxian reported asking Ren that summer, when they were on a flight to Beijing, if Meng Wanzhou might succeed him at Huawei.[27] He wrote that Ren brushed off the idea, citing his daughter's young age and remarking that she wasn't made of the right material for the job. As for Ren Ping, his father made him an intern at Huawei at a young age, but he appears to have had little interest in telephone switches. According to an account by a former Huawei executive, Ren Ping studied at China's University of Science and Technology in Hefei, then went to the UK for an MBA.[28]

Yao Ling moved to the UK with Annabel Yao and enrolled her in school there.[29] Annabel Yao described herself as a shy girl. "Each morning outside the nursery school, I would cry," she recalled in a documentary. "I would say, 'I don't want to go to school, I want to go home, I want to stay with Mama.'"[30] To build the shy girl's confidence, her mother enrolled her in a ballet class. Annabel Yao loved it. Soon she was being cast in starring roles.

While Annabel Yao would speak English fluently, having been exposed to it at a young age, the foreign language was a struggle for the rest of the family. Colleagues reported seeing Ren reciting English to himself at the office,[31] and they spotted Meng Wanzhou reviewing English vocabulary during breaks in meetings.[32] Across Huawei, contests and other activities were launched to try to accelerate English learning among employees. At the India office, executives instituted a small fine of a few cents for any engineers caught speaking Chinese during work hours.[33]

Ren was spending much of his time overseas wooing prospective clients. The veteran industry consultant Duncan Clark recalled an unassuming-looking Ren wearing a name tag and manning the Huawei booth personally at the GSM World Congress in the French city of Cannes in around 1996. "The big boys like Alcatel and Motorola—some of them even had huge yachts off of the Croisette," Clark recalled, referring to a scenic coastal strip of Cannes. "Siemens had a boat they would use to ferry their customers back and forth. And then there was little Huawei." Clark said he introduced Ren to executives from Vodafone, the major European mobile operator, at the convention.[34]

Ren often scheduled overseas work trips for Chinese holidays, considering it a way to squeeze out some extra time to work.[35] He felt apologetic for not spending more time with Annabel Yao, who had developed a fondness for stuffed pigs. The girl nicknamed Ren "Daddy Pig" and her mother "Mommy Pig."[36] As Ren recalled, "She wanted me to play games and spend more time with her, but I didn't. When I came back home from overseas, I was so tired that I would just lie on the bed."[37] Ren's constant travel took a toll on the marriage. His wife accused him of only caring about his company, not the family.[38]

C hinese officials were urging companies like Huawei to go abroad in preparation for China's entry into the World Trade Organization and providing preferential policies to support them. WTO membership would open the floodgates for foreign companies coming into China—and Chinese officials also wanted their own companies to have a running start overseas. "As China gets closer to entering the World Trade Organization, it is of great significance for the country to engage in investment and to actively participate in global market competition," one official said.[39]

In most countries, Huawei's executives encountered more than a little skepticism. Government officials all understood the importance of their telephone networks when it came to their economies and their national security. They weren't going to lightly hand them over to an unknown and untested switchmaker from China. As Ren and his team gradually began to land orders, they would chalk it up to sheer persistence. One of Huawei's internal newspapers recounted the company's manager in Saudi Arabia landing a contract because he continued to seek meetings with the Saudi Telecommunication Company (STC) for two years, earning the respect of Saudi executives.[40] Like many of Huawei's projects, the STC one was rocky at first, with Saudi officials phoning up Huawei to complain about network outages. Huawei stuck with it, and its services gradually improved.

After Huawei made an overseas stint a requirement for promotion in 1998,[41] it became a rite of passage for Huawei executives to do hardship postings in distant corners of the earth. When they returned to headquarters, they would swap stories from the trenches. Some had dodged bullets in war zones. Others had caught malaria or typhoid fever in swamps and hills. Or they had hobbled on frostbitten feet over desolate tundras. Some projects in sanctioned nations were cloaked in secrecy and code names.

One staffer posted to Burundi reported frequent power cuts, a T-shirt shortage due to the lack of a nearby market, and a close call with a hippopotamus.[42] Another recalled sticking it out through an Ebola outbreak in Sierra Leone, including offering to take a customer's sick employee to the hospital.[43] When civil war broke out in Libya, Huawei's staffers divided themselves into two teams so that they could keep the phones running on both sides.[44] "We must always remember," Ren told his staff following a deadly earthquake, "when phone service is down, we must run toward the switchrooms as fast as we can."[45]

Ren called his workers his "iron army."[46] He called his managers "generals," his engineers "soldiers," his sales teams "guerillas," and their salaries "rations." He sent new employees through military-esque boot camps to build discipline and camaraderie. He said Huawei's executives took their inspiration from the US military in choosing which staffers to promote: "Has this person been in combat? Has this person been in a live firefight? Has this person been wounded?"[47]

He rallied them with lines from a poem about soldiers' bodies returned from the battlefield: "Bury the bones at the green mountain / The bodies return wrapped in horse-skin shrouds."[48]

Eric Xu, the bespectacled PhD from Nanjing who had spent his early years at Huawei running from province to province with a slide projector, was now head of Huawei's international marketing department.[49] Some of his fellow executives called him "Little Xu" to differentiate him from another teammate, the larger-framed William Xu, or "Big Xu," who had been their early chips specialist. In 1999, Little Xu told the state-run *China Daily* that Huawei had representative offices in Moscow, Ukraine, Brazil, Columbia, Saudi Arabia, South Africa, and Nigeria, as well as an R&D foothold in Silicon Valley. He said they had also landed sales in Bulgaria, Uzbekistan, and Kenya. Huawei's Silicon Valley outpost—which was set up in 1993 under the cryptic name Ran Boss—had recently come out of stealth mode. In 1998, the unit reregistered as Huawei America Inc., with Huawei's executive vice president, Zheng Baoyong, listed as the subsidiary's president.

Huawei's fiercest rival in China was now ZTE, also based in Shenzhen. Outsiders were often surprised by the intensity of the vitriol between the two. One executive who had worked for both would describe Huawei and ZTE as being "at virtual war with one another," adding that "they love to sue each other and steal each other's customers."[50] Duncan Clark recalled that Huawei executives hated being associated with ZTE so much that "they would never even refer to them by name." The two companies' salespeople went to extreme lengths to outbid each other for contracts. One Western executive recalled ZTE staffers turning up on his doorstep when he was on the verge of signing a deal with Huawei. "You can't do this—we'll lose our jobs," one of them said. For years, Huawei and ZTE would be locked in bitter court battles around the world, with each accusing the other of intellectual-property infringement.

ZTE's founder, Hou Weigui, was born in 1941, three years before Ren. He had started his career at a state-run aerospace factory before being sent to Shenzhen to set up a chipmaking joint venture in the new Shenzhen Special Economic Zone. Like Ren at Huawei, Hou also had an early falling out with his original investors. He and much of his staff quit and started their own company, with China's Ministry of Aerospace Industry trying for a while to shut down the runaway company.[51] But Hou's ZTE prevailed. It was soon making a name for itself in telephone switches.

The two men were very different. While Ren was short and compact, with a fiery temper, Hou was tall, gangly, and mild-mannered. "Always smiling, he appears at ease. Most ZTE employees talk of his amiability," one state-media profile said about Hou.[52] Ren, on the other hand, was famous for his irascibility, with former colleagues recalling him angrily throwing reports on the ground in meetings, berating staffers until they cried, and once even chucking a binder at a subordinate's head.[53] Unlike Huawei, ZTE was majority state-owned, and its company culture was more bureaucratic and risk-averse. The local media likened ZTE's executives to oxen, Huawei's to wolves. This was sometimes an advantage domestically: when retired party historian Li Rui visited both companies in May 1998, he noted in his diary that Huawei had twenty-two hundred engineers—twice ZTE's head count—but that ZTE had less debt, making it a less risky enterprise.[54] But overseas, ZTE's state ownership was a major impediment to gaining trust from foreign telecom operators, who felt that Huawei might be more independent as an employee-owned company. One potential customer recalled a ZTE sales executive, confronted yet again with distrust over ZTE's state ownership, exclaiming in frustration that Huawei's employee shareholder system was a "facade."

Former Huawei executive Liu Ping claimed that ZTE and Huawei kept a very close eye on each other's operations.[55] "As soon as a high-level Huawei meeting was over," Liu wrote, "ZTE's leadership would have the meeting notes. Of course, Huawei would also know immediately that ZTE had gotten Huawei's meeting notes." To try to stem the leaks, according to Liu, they went so far as to draw up a list of everyone at Huawei whose spouse worked at ZTE.

As midnight approached on May 7, 1999, a US B-2 bomber flew over Belgrade. People nearby heard a whoosh as five guided missiles smashed into the Chinese embassy, reducing it to a flaming shell.[56] The blasts shattered windows a block away, sending glass shards flying. From the embassy ruins, bloodied staffers stumbled out in shock. Three journalists for Chinese state-run media lay dead. Washington called it an accident, claiming that the CIA had identified the wrong coordinates for a military target as part of the NATO bombing of Yugoslavia in the Kosovo War. But many in China did not believe it was an accident.

After the bombing of the Chinese embassy in Belgrade, Huawei's staff joined people across the nation in an outpouring of anger. "I hope the powers of global justice can defeat the crazy US and NATO," one Huawei employee wrote. "Every Chinese person should remember this day when the US and NATO incurred this new blood debt."[57] Huawei sent a message to the Chinese embassy in Yugoslavia, condemning the attack and offering two hundred thousand yuan to the relatives of those killed. The company offered to help orphaned children.[58] "Since 1949, the Chinese people have never lowered their heads," Huawei declared.[59] The scene in Shenzhen was subdued compared with that in Beijing, where thousands of protesters filled the streets outside the US embassy, hurling rocks, flaming US flags, and even Molotov cocktails. But Shenzhen still made a strong showing, hosting a political protest concert for ten thousand people under the slogan "Today the Chinese People Say No." Huawei employees joined a chorus of two thousand who sang patriotic songs at the event.[60] Such a large political gathering was a rarity in China, with authorities wary of allowing large protests since the 1989 tragedy in Tiananmen Square. This was an exception.

China's vice president, Hu Jintao, came on television to denounce the NATO bombing as a heinous act and praise the patriotic protesters while urging restraint.[61] At Huawei, executives held an internal meeting to discuss Hu's speech. "The United States' huge military budget is mainly funded by excessive high-tech profits," one employee declared.[62] Madam Chen Zhufang, the company's august party secretary, said that the US looked down on today's China but feared tomorrow's China. She said that by working hard at their jobs, they could help their nation: "Every bit of improvement of our products, and every bit of our development in the international market, is helpful for enhancing our nation's comprehensive national strength."[63]

Ren told staff that the bombing reflected how "the American empire's desire for the downfall of our nation always lingers." He continued: "This is not only for our generation to remember, but also for the next two or three generations to understand, until our nation's economic strength reaches international equilibrium."[64]

The incident would continue to loom large in the Chinese people's psyche. Just the previous year, at the Chinese embassy in Baghdad, they had thought they would be safe from American bombs as long as they marked themselves as Chinese bystanders. In a few years' time, Huawei would find itself squarely in the crosshairs.

10

Huawei's Basic Law

MANAGEMENT REFORMS:
1996-1999

I n August 1996, Huawei's vice-chairwoman, Sun Yafang, sat down to a meeting with Shenzhen's party secretary, Li Youwei, and several young business professors from Beijing.[1] They were there to discuss the thorny question of how a company should be owned. Not so long ago, this would have been a politically treacherous topic. People had been thrown into labor camps for expressing the wrong opinions on capitalism. Now Li encouraged everyone to speak their minds. He reassured them that they would not be punished. He quipped that some Marxist theory was "completely inapplicable" to modern China, drawing appreciative laughter from the room.

"I will listen to you today," Li said. "Today is just a discussion. There is no need to worry. We can talk casually."

One of the Beijing professors, who had been advising Huawei, began speaking.

"It is still difficult to determine what kind of company Huawei is," the professor said. "At present, there is no new theoretical guidance in the academic world."

Huawei had been on the cutting edge of China's economic reforms since its start. It was founded in 1987, months after Shenzhen legalized private tech startups under a pilot program. When Beijing had issued regulations for "collectively owned enterprises" in 1991, promising state support for these "red-cap" companies that operated under the socialist principle of workers owning the means of production, Huawei had decided to try it. Then, in 1994, China opened the option of setting up Western-style "limited liability companies" under the nation's new Company Law. Huawei's leadership was intrigued. But a lot remained unclear about if and how Huawei could make the shift, including how it could adapt its red-cap ownership structure of dispersed shareholdings by employees to meet the LLC requirements, which limited the number of shareholders to fifty. It was also unclear to what extent such a company should imitate a Western-style LLC, and to what extent it should hew to the tenets of Communism.

Ren Zhengfei had decided to seize his own fate instead of just waiting for instructions. He hired the team of professors to help him draft a unified theory for the successful operation of a modern Chinese company, which would cover not only day-to-day management strategy but also how the company should relate to the party, the state, and the world. The professors called it "the Huawei Basic Law."[2] The name echoed that of Hong Kong's mini-constitution, the Hong Kong Basic Law, a landmark document that carved out rights like freedom of speech within the city's limits, beyond what was enjoyed in other parts of China. It was an indication, perhaps, of Ren's ambitions: he was going to try to build something radically different, something separate from China even while a part of it.

Huang Weiwei, one of the professors involved in formulating the Huawei Basic Law, wrote that they were dismayed that China had failed to produce even a single world-class company over the past century.[3] "We have tried all the world's cutting-edge management theories and methods. America's Taylor method, Germany's lean production, Japan's just-in-time production . . . we've tried them all. And how have our crops grown as a result? Thin and short."

Huang had high hopes that Ren would accomplish what no one before him had done: "What the Huawei Basic Law was actually going to do was raise common problems faced by Chinese companies in management, and provide an answer."[4]

Ren had been meeting with other leading Chinese tech entrepreneurs to see how they structured their companies. Li Yuzhuo, head of Huawei's joint ventures during the 1990s, recalled in his memoir that he arranged meetings for Ren, at Ren's request, with Duan Yongji, the CEO of the Stone Group—China's star tech company in the 1980s—and Lenovo's founder, Liu Chuanzhi. In both meetings, Li wrote, Ren discussed the issue of employee shareholding with his counterparts.[5]

But Ren was also anxious to seek advice beyond China's shores. The week before Christmas in 1997, he traveled to the United States with several colleagues to visit the International Business Machines Corporation.[6] IBM had long been a role model for China's private tech industry, with the Stone Group declaring ambitions to become "China's IBM" in the 1980s. Now, just ahead of Ren's arrival in the

United States, IBM had achieved an even higher status: its supercomputer Deep Blue had recently beat a reigning world chess champion, Garry Kasparov, at the game, a landmark for artificial intelligence. IBM was offering pricy consulting packages to teach other companies its management moxie.

Ren was anxious to learn the secrets behind how to build a company that could last a century. There were no such examples in China, with everyone having started again from scratch after the Cultural Revolution. Silicon Valley entrepreneurs often grew through failure, launching one startup after another until they finally succeeded. But Ren was already fifty-three. His health was faltering. He knew he had only one shot to get it right. There were so many moving parts to master to turn a startup into a sturdy multinational. You needed to be able to develop new products on schedule and within budget, and the products had to work reliably. You needed supply chains that could deliver. You needed to manage far more people than you could ever learn the names of. You needed to pay taxes and follow the laws in countries around the world. You needed succession planning so that the company could survive beyond you. You needed guardrails so that a mistake by a single executive couldn't take down the entire company.

Ren was in poor health on the IBM visit, but he listened to the presentations with keen interest. The IBM representatives discussed how they screened investments, developed their product pipelines, kept projects on schedule, and organized their teams. The Huawei team furiously scribbled notes. Ren came out convinced that IBM's guidance could help Huawei save many years of trial and error in building a successful multinational company. IBM had developed this management know-how over a century. "Only by seriously learning from these large companies can we avoid taking a longer road,"

Ren told his staff. "IBM came to these conclusions by paying billions of dollars in direct costs."[7]

IBM's consultants started arriving at Huawei's headquarters in August 1998. They would remain in residence for a decade. Gary Garner, one of the early IBM consultants, recalled that his first impression of Huawei was that it was a vibrant but undisciplined company where things were sometimes just scrawled on sticky notes instead of being filed properly. "President Ren had a whole bunch of bright young PhDs," he said, "but it was disorganized. It wasn't ready to go to the international market."[8]

Guo Ping was in charge of the project, in which IBM would help Huawei map out a professional R&D workflow and global supply chain. This advice didn't come cheap. Ren later claimed the company paid $680 per IBM consultant per hour,[9] nearly the average monthly salary at Huawei, though some former IBM consultants said they didn't recall it being quite that high. Some of Huawei's managers protested the new systems, which they found burdensome. Ren insisted they follow the IBM way. If the shoes didn't fit, Ren told them, they had to "cut their feet to fit the shoes."[10]

IBM's output was fifty-five times Huawei's that first year, 1998. Ren set a goal of shrinking the difference to thirty-five to forty times greater by 1999. "We are making big strides forward," he told his staff. "We're narrowing the gap."[11]

As Huawei grappled with how to build a modern Chinese company, one of the biggest things that made it different from a Western company was the role of the party. In the Mao era, the Chinese Communist Party had governed all areas of life and work in the nation. The party was now ceding many decisions to private businesses, but it still expected to have a role.

The party's constitution had long required farms, people's communes, cooperatives, factories, and other work units to set up an internal party branch if they had at least three employees who were party members. In 1992, in recognition of the changing economy, the wording of this requirement was tweaked to specify that "companies" must also comply.[12]

The head of a company's party apparatus was called the party secretary, and this official was expected to keep the company in step with national priorities, as well as to provide ethical oversight of the staff.[13]

Huawei set up its internal party branch in May 1996, demarcating a formal role for the party within the company.[14] Ren himself was party secretary at first, with the company's main internal newspaper, *Huawei People*, reporting him in that role in September 1997.[15] Having the CEO double as the party secretary was common within smaller companies, ensuring that the two leadership roles would be in accord. Within Huawei, as in broader society, party members were an influential minority: the September 1997 article noted that a sixth of the company's R&D ranks, or 240 staffers, were party members.[16] Ren called on them to provide ideological leadership for the entire staff.[17] "In high-tech enterprises, more and more scientific and technological achievements must rely on collective efforts," the article said. "Therefore, how to correctly view the relationship between individuals and organizations has become a problem that every employee in the research system must face. In response to these circumstances, it was decided to establish a party branch in the research system to give full play to the exemplary role of party members and promote the formation of a good corporate culture."

Not long after, Huawei upgraded its party branch to a party committee, and Madam Chen Zhufang—the former Huazhong Institute of Technology administrator who had met Ren back when he was a manager at South Sea Oil—was appointed party secretary. It was still unclear how big of a role a party committee was supposed to be playing inside a private enterprise. Chen told the scholar Tian Tao that she asked around at other companies for advice, including at the American company Motorola, which had set up a party committee in its China outpost. "I thought a long time about how a party committee should work in a private company," she said.[18]

According to a bio published by Hubei provincial authorities, Chen was born in 1935, making her around nine years Ren's senior.[19] She'd grown up in a poor family in small-town Guangxi. "If I could avoid being hungry or cold my whole life, I would be fully satisfied," she recalled thinking as a girl. "This was my dream throughout my childhood."[20] As an engineering student at the Huazhong Institute, she had begun to show political chops: in 1958, she was selected to represent the university at a national convention for socialist youth.[21] After graduating from the Electrical Machinery Department in 1960,[22] she stayed on at the university to work on laser research and eventually rose through the management ranks to become party secretary of the Huazhong Institute's School of Economic Management. Chen spoke some English: in 1989, she had done an exchange stint in human-resources management at the University of Toronto.[23]

Ren had persuaded her to join Huawei in 1995, when she retired from her first career in academia at around the age of sixty.[24] Her academic network was valuable to Huawei's recruiting efforts, and

Ren named her Huawei's first human-resources manager. She also served briefly as editor in chief of *Huawei People* before becoming party secretary, the role she would retain for a decade.

With her halo of snowy hair, Chen served as something like a stern grandmother at Huawei. In a nation that was officially atheistic, the party took on the church's role of ethical guidance. Chen often lectured the young engineers on morality. She told them that they would suffer from karma if they stole intellectual property from the company or otherwise abused their positions. "This is justice, this is the law of the cosmos," she wrote to employees. "If you rely on unfair means to seek illegal gains, you will eventually vomit back up what you ate—indeed, more than you ate."[25] She reminded them of their broader patriotic mission. "You are shouldering the dream of becoming a strong nation that the Chinese people have carried for nearly a hundred years," she said.[26]

Chen played an important role in molding Huawei's company culture and infusing it with the Chinese Communist Party's themes of patriotism, struggle for the greater cause, and self-sacrifice. In 1996, she had helped organize the famous mass resignation of Huawei's sales team, where managers declared they were willing to give up their own jobs for the company's success.[27] Within Huawei, she also ran regular "democratic life meetings," a type of party meeting at which attendees criticized themselves and one another.[28]

Just how much power a party secretary should be wielding within a private company was a murky question mark. In Chen's case, her older age appeared to ease the potential of a power struggle with Ren. She had already retired once before she joined Huawei, and she seemed to be past some of the concerns of the younger staffers. Recalling how some Huawei executives fought against one another, she remarked to Tian, "At the time, the kids were fighting. It was pretty amusing." However, Chen also mentioned that she sometimes dealt with issues without consulting Ren, reflecting a certain confidence and autonomy in her role. Chen said that after once telling Ren about the suicide of a Huawei employee and seeing his terrified reaction, she resolved not to relate this sort of thing again unless necessary. "You really couldn't tell him," she said.[29]

In March 1998, after two years of drafting and redrafting, Huawei adopted its 103-article Basic Law.[30] The six professors had done their best to determine what kind of company Huawei was—and what kind of company Huawei was *not*.

The kind of company that Huawei was *not* was a Western-style, publicly listed company. The Basic Law declared that Huawei did not make its decisions based on the short-term maximization of shareholder value: "Profit maximization is by no means our only pursuit."

The purpose of Huawei was not to serve its shareholders but to achieve its goal, which was "to become a leading world-class enterprise" in telecom gear. Achieving this target would require focus and sacrifice. It meant that Huawei would plow much of its earnings back into strategic investments, seeking to maximize growth instead of profit. During economic downturns, employees would be expected to take an "automatic pay cut." Staffers could not expect a windfall from an IPO.

Ren was particularly wary about the temptation of a public stock-market listing. China was in the middle of a stock-market boom, with executives and casual investors alike starry-eyed at the prospect of instantaneous riches. But after a successful IPO, there was often a talent exodus, as employees cashed out their stock and retired early. The company was then stuck on the treadmill of keeping up its profit margin each quarter, giving executives a shortsighted and reactive mentality. "After going public, if the employees get rich overnight, will they still work?" rotating Huawei CEO Eric Xu remarked. "And if the employees don't work anymore, then why are we going public?"[31] The Basic Law declared that an IPO was not necessary for Huawei: "Our internal mechanism can be kept dynamic without relying on the stimulation from external market pressure."

The Basic Law also laid out other guidelines to prevent Huawei's management from losing focus. One was that the company would stick to its knitting of telecom gear and would not mindlessly diversify into other sectors, even if they looked alluring. A baseline of 10 percent of sales each year had to be plowed back into R&D. Huawei would narrowly pick its targets for intensive R&D, with an aim of matching or even surpassing its global rivals in strategic areas. "Once we decide to do a thing, we will go all out," the Basic Law said.

The document also warned against future successors straying from Huawei's mission: "We should make rules to prevent the third, fourth and future generations of successors from being corrupt, self-centered and indolent."

Huawei changed its registration in 1997 to a limited liability company, shedding the anachronistic "collectively owned enterprise" label and adopting an internationally recognized structure.[32] This change was not without complications.

For one thing, China's Company Law limited an LLC to fifty shareholders.[33] Huawei already had far more, due to Ren issuing shares to employees over the years as a central part of their compensation. According to one former executive, only 3 percent was held by Huawei's leadership and less than 1 percent held by Ren himself.[34] The Shenzhen government recognized this hurdle, and in September 1997, it suggested a workaround for local companies: collectively registering all their employee shareholders under a "trade union," which would serve as a single shareholder in the eyes of the law.[35] Huawei adopted this solution, an arrangement that would continue to the present day, causing much confusion and drawing accusations about the opacity of Huawei's ownership structure. On paper, Huawei would have just two shareholders: Ren himself, with around 1 percent of shares, and a trade union for the rest. Huawei executives would later say the ownership structure was a historical oddity that new companies in China weren't even allowed to use anymore. "Of course, according to the current law, it is illegal, but the special approval of the special district at the time was legal," Xu said in 2012.[36] He noted that there were about a thousand companies in the country with such special approval. The fact that Huawei was allowed to keep this structure perhaps reflects an acknowledgement by government officials that even if what the company was doing was unorthodox, it was working.

Huawei was seeking to buy out its five original investors as part of its efforts to reformat its shareholding structure, and it was running into problems. Professor Huang Weiwei, one of the professors who helped Huawei craft its Basic Law, wrote that under China's Company Law of 1994, profits converted into capital belonged to the original investors unless those investors agreed to let new ones be brought on board. "But Mr. Ren didn't think this way," Huang wrote. "He said other companies give too much consideration to entrepreneurs' profits, but Huawei gives more consideration to the interests of all those who have strived with us together. . . . If we insist on all the capital belonging to the original investors, we deny the workers ownership of the surplus value they created."[37] Ren had brought on many more investors through the shares he had issued to employees, and he'd promised them the profits as part of their compensation. Two of the investors sued—Chen Jinyang, the travel service manager, and Shen Dingxing, the inventor of the BH-01 switch, which Huawei had imitated.[38] By 1999, Huawei had succeeded in settling the lawsuits filed by the two early investors, paying them 70 to 300 percent of their original investments.

Huawei's chairwoman, Sun Yafang (center left), *gives a tour of Huawei's Latin America headquarters in Mexico City to China's vice-premier, Liu Yandong* (center right), *in 2016.*

Huawei made one more notable change to its management structure during this period. In 1999, Vice-Chairwoman Sun Yafang was promoted to Huawei's chairwoman.[39] It is unclear who had been Huawei's chairperson before her—if it had still been the company's founding chairman, Mei Zhongxing, or if someone else had since taken up the position. Sun would be very visible during her nineteen years as Huawei chairwoman, taking on many of the company's meetings with foreign dignitaries and gaining the nickname of "Huawei's Secretary of State" from the domestic press. She kept a jetsetting schedule, meeting with world leaders ranging from United Nations Secretary-General Kofi Annan to Prime Minister Theresa May.[40] She spoke with a hint of a British accent and had a fondness for maroon fingernail polish and brightly patterned scarves.

In September 1999, the year of her promotion, Sun had attended Harvard Business School's two-month Advanced Management Program for mid-career executives. As the program's "first class of the Internet," the roughly 170 students each got a PalmPilot and an email address.[41] They lived in groups of eight, attending lectures six days a week and meeting in small groups in the evenings to discuss case studies. "Yafang being on the program felt like it was part of China opening up to the world," said Graham Lovelace, a classmate in the program. Sun was affected by a lecture by the leadership scholar John Kotter. He told them that being a leader meant taking on personal risk to bring about change. He ended the lecture with a clip of Bobby Kennedy's improvised speech on civil rights in April 1968, delivered hours after the assassination of Martin Luther King Jr. and two months before he himself was assassinated. "It was communication from soul to soul," Sun wrote of Kotter's lecture. "I couldn't help the tears falling from my eyes."[42]

While Sun had a reputation as an able and tough manager at Huawei during her time leading the sales department, it was still a bit of a mystery what had separated her from the pack, catapulting her to the top of Huawei's pecking order. As the chairwoman of Huawei's board of directors, Sun steered the company's strategic direction and approved the selection, appraisal, and compensation of Ren as CEO, as well as the appointment and compensation of other senior managers.[43] She had all these powers on paper, at least. It was unclear how, exactly, power was shared between her and Ren in practice. Some in the industry believed that her background working for China's state security agency, the Ministry of State Security, was a source of her power, though this was the sort of thing that was difficult to prove or disprove. "As chairwoman at Huawei, Sun Yafang is representing certain government departments, that's my feeling," said Wan Runnan, founder of the early Chinese tech company Stone Group.[44]

The haziness in her history continued to be a source of intrigue. What Sun herself would write in a 2017 magazine essay was this: "I was born in 1957, graduated from the University of Electronic Science and Technology, served as a communication warrior, wore the army's green uniform, and later entered the Ministry of State Security to work in communications. In 1992, five years after Huawei was founded, I joined Huawei." Curiously, this account diverged from her official Huawei bio: Huawei's annual reports gave her birth year as 1955 and said she joined the company in 1989.[45] Such discrepancies were noted by the US director of national intelligence's Open Source Center in an unclassified report.[46]

James Lewis, a US Commerce Department officer during the 1990s, said that he once asked a Huawei representative about Sun's history in the MSS.[47]

"How did you know that?" the Huawei representative reportedly asked him.

"It's on your website," Lewis replied.

Within a week, Lewis said, the MSS mention had disappeared.

11

Winter

DOT-COM BUBBLE BURST:
1999-2001

I n the spring of 1999, the first mysterious letter surfaced.[1] It accused Huawei's stratospheric growth of being based on "debt" and "fraud," claiming that the company's vaunted stock for employees was just a number on paper. "No one is clear as to how much the stocks held by employees are actually worth? No one knows when employees can actually exchange the stocks in their hands for cash?" A second letter, around a year later, purported to "expose" Huawei's "illegal and fraudulent acts." It included allegations that Huawei Electric—Huawei's joint-venture company originally named Mobeco—was a pay-for-play tie-up with telecom operators.

It wasn't clear where the letters came from. One former Huawei executive alleged it was a smear campaign by Huawei's archrival, ZTE.[2] In any case, it spooked Huawei's customers. The second letter had come out just as the dot-com bubble was bursting, sending the entire industry into panic. Huawei's orders dried up. Worse, Beijing decided to investigate.

Ren Zhengfei appealed for help from local officials, saying that Huawei could not survive the pall of the rumors. Shenzhen's mayor, Li Zibin, went to Beijing and sought an audience with Vice-Premier Wu Bangguo. He told the vice-premier that if the rumors were true, Ren should be detained. But if he was innocent, the central government should publicly clear Huawei's name.[3]

Ren was terrified when he heard that some twenty staffers from the National Audit Office were coming to audit Huawei. Hao Chunmin, director of Shenzhen's Science and Technology Bureau, found Chairwoman Sun on his doorstep, pleading for help. Ren also phoned from South Africa in tears, saying that even if Huawei's name was eventually cleared, it could not afford such upheavals. "Director Hao, I love my country, but my country doesn't love me!"[4]

The audit would be only the first of a series of setbacks that Ren called Huawei's Winter. Trial followed tribulation for the next three years. Ren would later recall a period of six months when he often had nightmares and wept.[5]

The dot-com bubble burst in March 2000. The sky-high expectations for startups like Pets.com had come crashing back to Earth, erasing some $1.7 trillion in global wealth and laying low those who had built the internet's pipes. Huawei and its rivals all wondered if they could survive. More than two dozen companies in the global telecom industry would file for bankruptcy. Huawei and its competitors all slashed their prices as they struggled to stay afloat.

Amid the global tech winter, Huawei was feeling the pressure of skyrocketing expectations from Beijing. After Huawei's success in building an indigenous landline telephone system, China's leaders were pushing it to figure out how to build domestic mobile networks. In 1996, Vice-Premier Wu Bangguo had personally requested that Huawei take a stab at mobile,[6] saying the sector was dominated by foreign firms. Wu penned a calligraphy inscription for Huawei as encouragement.[7] Mastering the complicated radio technologies for cell towers would require enormous R&D expenditures, and it was far from a sure bet that Huawei could compete against America's Motorola, Finland's Nokia, Sweden's Ericsson, and Japan's Fujitsu. At the same time, it was being encouraged to go global in anticipation of China's entry into the World Trade Organization. Companies often collapsed at this juncture—as they tried to scale up from doing one thing successfully to juggling many things. Ren found his finances stretched to the breaking point.

Huawei would one day become the global king of mobile, number one in both consumer sales of smartphones and technical sales of cell tower gear. Yet its early days of mobile were anything but smooth. One problem was the lack of clarity in China's national mobile blueprint. In Beijing, there was bureaucratic gridlock over which mobile standard to base the country's networks on: Should they use the US's CDMA, opt for Europe's GSM, or try to strike out and develop a new standard altogether? The question was a little akin to asking whether you wanted to develop an app for iOS, develop an app for Android, or go down the entirely uncertain path of building your own app store. As Beijing officials debated the matter, companies like Huawei tried to hedge their bets by devoting some R&D funds to each of the technology standards, spreading their resources thin.

To add another wrinkle, it was unclear if China, once it picked CDMA or GSM, would go with the older 2G generation—traditional voice and text—or next-generation 3G, which was already being rolled out in countries like Japan and which allowed users to surf the web on a phone. Since Huawei's early days, Ren had been disinterested in lagging technology. He aspired to reach the cutting edge. Now he chose to focus Huawei's R&D efforts on 3G, in hopes of catching up with established rivals in the 3G generation. "Some people said this was a crazy idea," one Huawei executive later recalled in an essay. "After all, 99 percent of the market was 2G."[8] Some of his deputies warned him: "If you make the wrong choice, Huawei will collapse."[9]

Across town, Huawei's archrival, ZTE, had taken the opposite approach. ZTE's founder, Hou Weigui, had picked a slow-and-steady strategy, reasoning that 2G was good enough for many consumers in China, which was still a developing nation. ZTE put its R&D resources into 2G and, indeed, into an even lower-end technology, the Personal Handyphone, a rudimentary type of cell phone with a limited range and a price tag to match.

Unfortunately for Ren, China's 3G rollout proved to be a massive boondoggle, with the networks not up and running until 2009, more than a decade after the first trial 3G network was launched in Japan. "It turned out that we had made the wrong choice," Ren later admitted.[10] ZTE surged ahead in sales as China built out 2G networks year after year, with 3G nowhere in sight. ZTE's cheap and cheerful Personal Handyphones were such a smash success that Huawei was forced to reverse course a few years later and launch its own Personal Handyphones. Within Huawei, some executives wondered if Ren had lost his touch. A wave of early employees left.

The defection that stung the most for Ren was probably the departure of his "young prodigy," Li Yinan. Li had been promoted from a junior engineer to a senior executive at Huawei in record speed, and many felt that Ren had been grooming him as a potential successor. But Ren's succession plan was unclear, and to an ambitious young executive, it must have felt like there were greater opportunities beyond Huawei's gates. Soon after leaving Huawei, Li launched a rival company, Harbour Networks, that sold a line of routers and switches under the eye-catching brand PowerHammer. Unlike Huawei, with its clouded ownership structure, Harbour Networks raised international venture capital like a Western-style startup.[11] Li's team was soon aggressively poaching Huawei's engineers and customers. For the next few years, Ren would be preoccupied with defeating his former disciple.

During this period, Ren also lost his other close deputy, Zheng Baoyong, whom he had affectionately nicknamed "A-Bao," to illness. Zheng was diagnosed with a brain tumor that required emergency surgery.[12] Working at Huawei was not conducive to good health, given the grueling work hours, the psychological stress of the company's ferocious internal competition, and the outsize role of alcohol and cigarettes in China's business culture. The scholars Tian Tao and Wu Chunbo reported that two-thirds of Huawei's senior management suffered from stress-related diseases, including anxiety, hypertension, diabetes, and depression.[13] Ren himself was suffering from poor health. He had been diagnosed with diabetes and was once hospitalized on a trip to the US.[14] He had also plunged into a dark depression around the time of the audit. He later told a fellow industry executive that he had contemplated suicide more than once around the turn of the century, calling Chairwoman Sun each time for support.[15]

Ren gave a speech to his staff titled "Huawei's Winter." He warned that they were too complacent, that they had to be prepared for any potential crisis.

"Those who didn't predict it, who didn't prepare, will freeze to death," he said. "At that time, whoever has a warm coat will live."[16]

H uawei was cleared in the audit, giving Ren and his team a second lease on life. Now, at least, Ren knew he was not going to jail. Following the near-death experience, Huawei quietly sold off Mobeco, the subsidiary it had used to build a web of financial ties to telecom officials across the country. After giving Mobeco a new name, Avansys Power, Huawei unloaded it to Emerson Electric in the United States for $750 million.[17] "Avansys is an outstanding company with strong sales dynamics," Emerson CEO David N. Farr said in the announcement. Naturally, the press release didn't mention anything about an audit, allegations of pay for play, or a complicated tangle of financial connections.

There was another hopeful note: after China had negotiated for thirteen years to gain entry into the World Trade Organization, it looked like the country might finally be accepted. Once Beijing made a range of concessions, President Bill Clinton announced his support for China's WTO entry, making clear his hope that the liberalization of China's economy would lead to democratic reforms in the nation's political system. "Everything I have learned about human nature in over a half century of living now convinces me that we have a far greater chance of having a positive influence on China's actions if we welcome China into the world community instead of shutting it out," Clinton said in a March 2000 speech. "As Justice Earl Warren once said, liberty is the most contagious force in the world. In the new century, liberty will spread by cell phone and cable modem."[18]

The Clinton administration touted China's agreement to open up its telecommunications market for the first time as a key concession that made the deal palatable to Washington. "In opening China's telecommunications market, including to Internet and satellite services, the agreement will over time expose the Chinese people to information, ideas and debate from around the world," the administration announced. "As China's people become more mobile, prosperous, and aware of alternative ways of life, they will seek greater say in the decisions that affect their lives."[19]

With the world primed for greater integration with China, Huawei began opening offices around the world. One of Ren's star sales executives, Ken Hu, was sent to Latin America to establish a presence there. Declaring ambitions to grow, the company opened a ten-person office in Mexico in August 2000.[20] In the first year of the aughts, Huawei also set up an outpost in Kista, Sweden, the hometown of its established Swedish rival, Ericsson.[21] In January 2001, Huawei set up an office in Plano, Texas, called Futurewei Technologies, a stone's throw from the strip dubbed "Telecom Corridor," where telecom giants like AT&T and Lucent were based.

The growing visibility in the Western world had both rewards and risks. At the Hong Kong–based magazine *Far Eastern Economic Review*, editors had heard about an up-and-coming telecom gear supplier called Huawei. A thirty-four-year-old Canadian reporter named

Bruce Gilley was assigned to write a profile. Huawei allowed Gilley to visit and interview executives. "They didn't have their shields up. They were very open," Gilley recalled. "They thought of themselves as this great private-sector success story."[22]

But Gilley's profile—one of the first in-depth articles in English on the company and an influential one in Western policymaking circles—ended up focusing on Huawei's military and government links. Gilley opened the piece with a description of his visit to Huawei's headquarters, during which he saw several room-sized switching systems waiting to be shipped—with shipping labels that said they were headed for the People's Liberation Army.[23] "I will never forget standing there with these three big shrink-wrapped systems in front of me," he said.

Gilley's profile of Huawei would have curious staying power for an article in a regional magazine, continuing to be cited decades later in prominent Western government reports. Many of its details appear to be accurate, but one throwaway line would be contested and would generate controversy for years. In reviewing Ren's background, the piece gives his military title as "a former director of the Information Engineering Academy of the PLA's General Staff Department," which conducts telecoms research for China's military. US politicians seized on this title as proof of Ren's work in military telecommunications. Huawei would vigorously dispute that Ren had ever held that title, with one spokesman calling it "the most regularly trotted-out turd" about the company.[24] In retrospect, it looks likely to be a simple mix-up. Wu Jiangxing, inventor of the military's 04 switch and founder of Huawei rival Great Dragon, had held that exact title during his military years, and it is a standard part of his bio. Ren's time in the military is largely accounted for, and had he worked at the Information Engineering Academy, it's unclear why that tidbit would have been secret for him when it wasn't for Wu. "It may well be wrong," Gilley said when asked about the controversial title for Ren. "I don't think a lot hangs on that. We know he came out of the military. And we know his company was backed by the military. And then we know it was rapidly identified as the national champion."[25]

Even more than Gilley's profile, a report by *Forbes* caused consternation within Huawei in 2000. The magazine's second annual list of China's richest people placed fifty-six-year-old Ren at number three. According to *Forbes*, he was the third-richest man in all of China, behind only eighty-four-year-old Rong Yiren, the CITIC conglomerate's founder, and fifty-two-year-old Liu Yongxing, founder of animal-feed company East Hope Group.

Ren had not wanted to appear on the list. The *Financial Times* reported that Huawei had offered the list's author, Rupert Hoogewerf, a factory tour if Ren could be omitted.[26] Hoogewerf had estimated Ren's fortune at $500 million, based on his 5 percent stake in Huawei, using an estimated value of $10 billion for the company. Since Huawei wasn't publicly traded, it was hard to know how close or far this estimate was from the truth. Ren dismissed the list, telling staff that the foreign media had fabricated it out of ulterior motives.[27] He reminded them that he'd driven a humble Peugeot until quite recently, when he was persuaded to upgrade for safety considerations. He told them that he'd only just finished paying back the money he owed the company.

To be ostentatiously wealthy could be politically dangerous in China, and indeed, many of the executives on the rich list ended up being investigated for corruption in ensuing years. "My mother was constantly worried about the political implications of being called rich so publicly by *Forbes*," Ren later said. "She asked me where the money came from. Given the environment at the time, she was haunted by these fears."[28]

R en was one among a small group of executives invited to accompany Vice President Hu Jintao on a state visit to Iran in January 2001.[29] The two governments had agreed to deepen their ties, and now Hu told his Iranian counterpart that China wished to see more trade in the fields of transportation, energy, and telecommunications.[30]

Hu was already rumored to be China's next president, and it was valuable face time with the future leader. There was also little reason to believe that business in Iran would put Chinese companies in danger at the time: the United States had eased trade sanctions against Iran after the 1997 election of reformist president Mohammad Khatami. Bidding for a project in Iran in 2000, Huawei had competed against Finland's Nokia, Sweden's Ericsson, Italy's Italtel, and Germany's Siemens.[31] The greatest concern of a Huawei manager working on the bid had been his wife's fury that he was missing Chinese New Year for work.[32] But after the United States tightened sanctions on Iran—first under the George W. Bush administration, then further under Barack Obama's presidency—Huawei's relationships in Iran became dangerous. They would be the reason why Meng Wanzhou was detained in Vancouver.

On the trip, Ren was allotted a few minutes to give Hu a presentation on Huawei. Ren was thrilled that Hu seemed to know what Huawei was. But later on during the trip, Ren received a phone call.[33]

He was told that back in China, his seventy-seven-year-old mother had been struck by a car that morning after going to a market in Kunming. His sister had gone in search of her when she didn't return for lunch. Chairwoman Sun had already flown to her side.[34] Ren's daughter Meng Wanzhou had rushed there too.[35] When Ren arrived, he found his mother in worse shape than he had imagined. "Her heartbeat and breathing were being sustained by medication and machines," he wrote. "They didn't tell me over the telephone because they were afraid I might have a mishap on my trip back." She passed away soon after.

The death of Ren's mother prompted him to pen a long essay about his family titled "My Father and Mother." The piece offers the most that Ren has ever said about his family history, outlining his parents' early life, his own childhood, and the family's experiences through the Great Chinese Famine and the Cultural Revolution. Ren expressed regret that while immersed in the work of building Huawei, he had neglected to spend more time with his parents. His essay would be influential in the industry, with Liu Chuanzhi, founder of PC-making giant Lenovo, moved to write about his own early life.[36] Liu wrote that in 1966, his own father had refused to falsely accuse former comrades under coercion and, as a result, was expelled from the party. "The atmosphere then was tense, frightening," Liu recalled. "This is seared into my memory. My father taught me by example how to be a man. He taught me what integrity is!" Liu suggested that the successes of Huawei and Lenovo owed something to these early lessons: "Like Ren Zhengfei, we can lead by example and prioritize the interests of the company over personal gain. Going back to our roots, the earlier generations laid the foundation for how we should act."

———

Ren did not have long to grieve and contemplate. Weeks later, Huawei found itself in a shocking predicament. On February 16, 2001, under the orders of President George W. Bush, the United States and Britain launched a joint air strike on five targets outside the Iraqi capital of Baghdad.[37] When the dust cleared, the Pentagon announced that the target was a network of fiber-optic cables that Huawei was installing for Iraq's military.

The Pentagon gave few details publicly at the time, except to say that the fiber-optic cables were a threat and helped Iraq target allied jets. Behind closed doors, US officials acknowledged they were also trying to smoke out Iraqi troops by cutting off landline connections, which would force them to use radio communications that the NSA could intercept. "If the Iraqi air-defense communications were shifted to fiber, then interception of communication would be impossible and there would be increased risk to patrols," Charles Duelfer, former special adviser to the director of central intelligence, later wrote. "The attacks forced the Iraqis to use radio links or none at all."[38] An earlier classified CIA memo about the technology had noted that "fiber is immune to unauthorized intercept by conventional means," calling this "a unique feature not available from other modes of communications."[39] Matthew M. Aid, a former NSA analyst turned independent military historian, wrote that the NSA had persuaded US military officials to carry out the air strike.[40]

The controversy put Huawei in the diplomatic limelight at the highest levels in a way that Ren and his team were wholly unprepared for. Huawei denied having made any sales in Iraq that violated sanctions, but this did little to quell the controversy. US Secretary of State Colin Powell confronted China's ambassador to the United States, Yang Jiechi, directly.[41] *The Washington Post* reported that in 1999, Chinese diplomats had twice applied to a UN sanctions committee to obtain permission for Huawei to supply Baghdad with telecom equipment, reflecting that the Chinese government was aware of, and supported, Huawei's operations in Iraq.[42] *The Post* also reported that the Huawei contracts might have proceeded clandestinely after Britain and the US placed "holds" on Huawei's application with the UN sanctions committee. Pressed for comment, a spokeswoman for China's mission to the UN told *The Post* that if a company was found in violation of UN Security Council resolutions on Iraq, the Chinese government would investigate and prosecute. One former Huawei executive wrote that he'd only seen Ren scared out of his wits twice: "Once was when the central government's inspection group arrived, and the other was when Huawei exported equipment to Iraq and was facing US sanctions."[43]

Huawei ended up escaping more or less with a warning. Powell told reporters that China had ordered companies working on fiber-optic cable projects in Iraq to "cease and desist."[44] But the incident sparked broader scrutiny of Huawei in Washington, including calls for restriction of US technology sales to the company. At a Senate committee hearing on weapons of mass destruction in November 2001, Gary Milhollin, director of the Wisconsin Project on Nuclear Arms Control, criticized the Commerce Department for granting Huawei licenses to purchase advanced US components to build its products.[45] He said that Huawei had been allowed to purchase half a million dollars' worth of telecom gear from US tech giant Qualcomm, as well as high-performance computers from Digital Equipment Corporation, IBM, Hewlett-Packard, and Sun Microsystems. He added that Motorola had an export license application pending with the Commerce Department that, if approved, would help it build high-speed switching and routing equipment. Milhollin argued that this US technology had helped build Huawei "out of virtually nothing."

One former Huawei executive called the Iraq incident a pivotal moment in the company's history, even though few realized it at the time. Huawei had come onto the US radar screen as a potential national security threat, and it would never be able to fall off. "The Iraq incident was very important," he said. "The US strategy toward Huawei shifted. At that point, Huawei knew that something would happen eventually . . . though perhaps no one could have predicted that thing would turn out to be Trump."[46]

Days after the 9/11 terrorist attacks, Huawei again found itself under public scrutiny. The Western press was reporting that the company had a contract to install a twelve-thousand-line digital telephone exchange in Kabul, putting it—and China—on the wrong side of the war on terror. BEIJING IN QUANDARY OVER TRADE LINKS WITH TALIBAN, one headline blared. For the second time that year, China's Ministry of Foreign Affairs was forced to publicly defend Huawei. "The reports seriously deviated from the facts," a ministry spokesperson told reporters. "The accusations are groundless."[47]

The spat over Huawei's telephone lines for the Taliban came as Washington was broadly rethinking its China strategy as it focused on the war on terror.[48] The Bush administration decided to shelve the issue of containing Communism in order to concentrate on counterterrorism cooperation. China shared a border with Afghanistan and had close ties with Pakistan. Its suppliers, like Huawei, operated across the region. "People began to start thinking about how to work with China on the Afghanistan issue," Evan Feigenbaum, a State Department official at the time, recalled in an oral history. "This was something that really redefined the lines of debate. Instead of having a classic Cold War–like balance-of-power debate about how to deal with China as a challenge to American power, the orientation in foreign policy shifted."[49] A month after 9/11, Bush met with Jiang Zemin in Shanghai and sought China's help with intelligence sharing and cracking down on military technology proliferation. "China is a great power," Bush said. "And America wants a constructive relationship with China. We welcome a China that is a full member of [the] world community. . . . We welcome and support China's accession into the World Trade Organization."[50]

In December 2001, China was finally allowed into the WTO. While officials on both sides hailed it as a historic moment of China joining the international community, business executives in China and foreign countries alike were nervous about whether they could survive the flood of global competition. "After we enter the WTO, the number of unemployed people in our nation will rise, and it's unclear if things will still be politically stable," Ren remarked.[51]

Huawei's entry into the US market had created waves. Rumors were flying that the US networking giant Cisco was going to sue Huawei over its routers being too similar. A human-resources manager at Huawei's US division, Futurewei, asked an engineering colleague about the rumors.

"Don't worry," his colleague replied. "We are fixing the problems so we won't have to worry about that."[52]

12

Sudden and Acute

IRAQ, SARS, AND CISCO:
2003-2004

As the year 2003 began, the global telecom industry was excited by a tantalizing business opportunity: rumor had it that the US was going to invade Iraq and topple Saddam Hussein's regime. "Wireless vendors around the world are clamoring for a piece of this lucrative pie," one industry publication said.[1] Another reported that vendors were "salivating" at the prospect.[2]

The UN sanctions had prevented Iraq from modernizing: the nation still did not have a mobile phone network, and its landline networks, built by France's Alcatel in the 1980s,[3] were in dismal shape. But now the ouster of Hussein and the installation of a US-friendly regime pointed toward the lifting of sanctions—and a telephone network construction boom—on the horizon.

After the Pentagon had bombed Huawei-built installations in Iraq in 2001 and accused it of violating sanctions, Huawei had pulled back.[4] But with whispers of a US invasion circulating, Huawei quietly began sending employees back into Iraq. "At the start, we didn't have a clear mission in Iraq," recalled an employee who was sent in that January. "The task that the company's leadership gave us was to rebuild the cities after the war."[5]

In March 2003, President George W. Bush gave Hussein an ultimatum to leave the country or face an imminent influx of US troops. In hopes of sealing a contract, Huawei launched an urgent operation to whisk some employees from the Iraqi telecom operator Asiacell to Shenzhen, where they could attend a training session.[6] The company scrambled to sort out visas for the Iraqi engineers.

"The war was about to break out," a Huawei manager overseeing Middle East sales later wrote. "If the customer's engineers are not pulled out to the company for training at this time, then they will not be able to come out after the war breaks out, and even contact with the outside world will be interrupted."[7]

Meanwhile, the first pandemic of the twenty-first century had begun in southern China, with rumors that people were mysteriously struggling to breathe not too far from Shenzhen. Given little official information from the government, people were hoarding cold medicine as they tried to figure out how to protect themselves. The new disease was eventually called severe acute respiratory syndrome, or SARS. "This is the first time in our lives we have faced such a challenge," Huawei wrote to customers, acknowledging that the rapid spread of the disease had caused "psychological panic."[8]

As with other global disasters, Huawei's executives saw SARS as an opportunity to prove to customers that they had the bravery and chops to deliver on their contracts. As some of Huawei's foreign rivals paused business, Huawei ordered installations to continue in the field, with engineers arriving ten to fifteen days early so that they could self-isolate before meeting clients.[9] This was in line with Beijing's efforts to project calm: in a show of normalcy, the nation's leader, Hu Jintao, took a detour from his visit with local epidemiologists about containing the outbreak to drop by Huawei, with state media photos showing him chatting with Ren Zhengfei and his team, no face masks in sight.[10]

Huawei was also unwilling to let a pandemic foil its big plans for 3G. Network operators around the world had begun planning their 3G mobile networks, and Huawei was desperate to get its foot in the door after investing heavily in R&D for the technology. It was pushing especially hard in Hong Kong, where the company felt it had a shot at winning over Sunday Communications, the smallest mobile player in the city. "We pretty much pushed SARS to the back of our minds and forgot about it," a Huawei staffer working on the Sunday account later wrote. "We met almost every day, ate together, talked. Except for necessary precautions, no one mentioned SARS."[11]

The Iraqi engineers arrived in Shenzhen with SARS raging. Huawei staffers took them to halal restaurants around town and brought them to the company for the training course.

In February 2003, on the eve of the Lunar New Year, Ren learned that US rival Cisco was suing Huawei. He couldn't quite believe it at first. "He was saying, 'No, I've had very friendly discussions with them. I can't believe they would actually sue us,'" recalled one person involved in the deliberations at Huawei.[12]

Cisco's general counsel, Mark Chandler, had traveled to Shenzhen a couple months earlier to personally deliver the warning, saying Cisco had "determined definitively" that Huawei had copied Cisco's routers.[13] And now Cisco had followed through.

Founded in 1984 by Stanford University computer scientists, Cisco Systems was the builder of the internet's pipes and the world's most valuable company, with a market capitalization of more than half a trillion dollars. Cisco's CEO, John Chambers, was the industry's blond-haired, blue-eyed golden boy. The press fawned over him as "King of the Internet," "world's greatest CEO," and "best boss in America." There was even speculation that he would run for president. But then came the dot-com bust. In 2001, Chambers reported Cisco's first loss in its seventeen-year history. When Huawei came bursting into the US market with routers that were suspiciously similar to Cisco's, Chambers was in no mood to let it slide.

Ren told his trusted deputy, Guo Ping, who was now Huawei's executive vice president, to get to the US as quickly as he could. Ren invoked the fable of ancient Chinese military general Han Xin, who had accepted the humiliation of crawling between another man's legs to prevent a deadly fight.[14] They could take some blows to their pride as long as the company survived.

Guo met with a series of expensive lawyers, each time asking, "If we lose, how much will we have to pay?"[15] Cisco's message made it back to Guo through one of Huawei's consultants: "You guys will be facing astronomical fines. Huawei will go bankrupt."[16]

he case looked rough for Huawei. Cisco's lawsuit alleged that certain bugs from Cisco's source code were repeated in the software for Huawei's Quidway line of routers, a telltale sign of copying. It said that Huawei had infringed on at least five Cisco patents and had copied sections of its user manuals verbatim. The lawsuit also revealed that Cisco had hired a sting operator, a California consultant named Scott McElroy, to surreptitiously gather evidence against Huawei, including by chatting up Huawei staffers at a trade show and purchasing a Huawei router to turn over to Cisco for forensic analysis.[17] In an early win, the court granted Cisco a temporary restraining order that required Huawei to preserve evidence.

Cisco had also taken political care by making a trip to Beijing ahead of filing the lawsuit. It was the number-one router vendor in China, and it didn't want to lose that position by stirring up a nationalistic backlash. Its executives impressed upon Chinese officials that Cisco's gripe was with a single company, not with the government or the nation. Cisco CEO John Chambers, who had grown up duck hunting in West Virginia, instructed his team to carefully weigh the pros and cons of a lawsuit ahead of time, likening the exercise to studying a duck's habits before a hunt.[18] "We looked at everything, from the family background of CEO Ren Zhengfei to China's handling of unrelated but similar cases," Chambers later wrote. He concluded that Cisco could come out ahead by suing, so long as it took pains not to embarrass the Chinese government or the company.

Within Huawei, the mood was tense. When some Huawei employees circulated a satirical piece that mentioned the Cisco lawsuit in a mocking way, the 225 staffers who forwarded the email had their pay docked. "Anyone who participates in circulating chain emails unrelated to work will have their pay cut!" management warned.[19]

Huawei was frantically seeking to shore up its intellectual-property standing, striking IP-sharing agreements with Nokia and Siemens. It even considered the drastic move of selling itself to Motorola. Ren met with Motorola's COO, Mike Zafirovski, on a beach in Hainan, where the two sketched out a $7.5 billion deal. "Ren and the management, they were very excited," one person with knowledge of the talks recalled. The deal never firmed up, and it was unclear if it even could have passed regulatory approval, with both companies being military suppliers in their home nations. But word of the talks trickled back to Chambers at Cisco.[20] Perhaps that was the point.

Huawei's savior turned out to be 3Com, a Cisco rival. Founded in 1979 by the inventor of Ethernet, Robert Metcalfe, 3Com was an industry forefather. It was now struggling to keep up. Its CEO, Bruce Claflin, a bespectacled IBM veteran with salt-and-pepper hair, admitted to a personal rivalry with Cisco's Chambers. "My wife said she loved me, but that John Chambers knew a lot more than I did," Claflin told *The New York Times*. "Then it was personal."[21]

An alliance between 3Com and Huawei was attractive to both sides. Huawei would get the immediate legal protection of 3Com's deep patent portfolio; 3Com would get Huawei's lower production costs and its connections to the vast China market. Soon after the two announced their joint venture, called H3C, 3Com's lawyers filed a motion to intervene in the Cisco case, calling 3Com an interested party.[22] Cisco's lawyers tried to argue that 3Com had no interest in the case, since its prospective joint venture with Huawei was still awaiting regulatory approval. Counsel for 3Com fired back,[23] contending that 3Com had been so "eager to consummate [its] business relationship" with Huawei that the two companies had struck a separate side deal by which Huawei had already begun manufacturing some products for the 3Com brand. Claflin told the court: "3Com and the JV are committed to not releasing any products into the marketplace that they believe infringe the intellectual-property rights of third parties, including Cisco."

Shielded by 3Com's patent umbrella for any current and future products, Huawei saw its legal problem shrink to the much smaller one of whether it had previously infringed on Cisco patents. It was now harder for Cisco to argue that the court needed to block Huawei from pursuing any new sales into the US market.

As for the question of how sections of Cisco's code got into Huawei products, some would find Huawei's explanation extraordinarily implausible, though it was difficult to prove one way or another what had really transpired. Huawei told the court that in 1999, a third party who was not employed by Cisco had given a Huawei employee a disk containing source code for a router protocol, and that employee had given it to a colleague, who'd then proceeded to use it without doing much checking into its provenance.[24] Huawei called it a one-off act by a rogue employee that violated company policy. "The conduct that Cisco seeks to enjoin was stopped and will not resume," Huawei's lawyers wrote to the court.

After Saddam Hussein was overthrown in April 2003, the global telecom industry went into a frenzy. Iraq would be able to build a mobile phone network for the first time—a project worth up to $900 million. Iraq was on the agenda of Huawei's top management, and Huawei was far from alone.[25] It was on everyone's agenda.

The World Health Organization declared SARS contained in July 2003, and soon after, a tender conference was held in Amman, Jordan, to pick the telecom operators who would get the licenses to set up Iraq's mobile networks. A Huawei engineer stationed in Iraq traveled to Amman for the tender, passing a bombed-out landscape along the way. "If not for war and tyranny, what a rich and happy land this nation would be," the engineer wrote.[26] Huawei's customer Asiacell emerged as one of the three winners.[27]

By December 2003, streams of Huawei engineers in sturdy SUVs were making the seventeen-hour drive from Amman to Sulaymaniyah, in northern Iraq, to work on Asiacell's 2G wireless network. Meeting some friendly US soldiers patrolling in Hummers, one managed to get an incongruous snapshot as a souvenir: a smiling Chinese man in a black suit and tie, hands clasped, standing amid a bunch of American troops toting machine guns.[28]

With the SARS threat contained, mobile operators around the world were proceeding with selecting vendors for next-generation 3G networks. The tireless efforts of Huawei's sales teams during the pandemic paid off. Hong Kong's Sunday Communications and the United Arab Emirates' Etisalat both announced Huawei as their pick for 3G.

Huawei even landed its first small US mobile operator during this period. Ironically, it got its foot in the door thanks to an effort by the FBI to expand the agency's wiretapping capabilities. The 1994 Communications Assistance for Law Enforcement Act, or CALEA, had required telecom operators to have a technical side door through which the FBI or other US authorities could wiretap phone calls. But with more and more communications taking place via the internet,

US regulators were pushing for an update to CALEA. The FCC ordered operators to retrofit their equipment so that web traffic could also be tapped.[29]

For small mobile operators, the cost of buying the new gear on sudden notice was prohibitive. Huawei offered a generous financing package in which an operator could pay the cost over time. Based on this financing option, ClearTalk, which served some twenty thousand residents around El Centro, California, and Yuma, Arizona, chose Huawei. Eric Steinmann, ClearTalk's owner, recalled the US supplier Lucent quoting around $30 million for the CALEA upgrade and two other new technical requirements by the FCC, "which, for a small company, was more than we had spent building out all our networks, and certainly nothing we had. . . . So that's why we had to go with Huawei."[30]

Cisco dropped its lawsuit against Huawei in July 2004. The two sides did not announce financial terms, except to say that each company had to pay its own legal fees. Each side put its own spin on the outcome. Cisco's Mark Chandler declared it a "victory for the protection of intellectual property rights." Huawei said the company was very satisfied with the result.[31]

Huawei would continue to be trailed by intellectual-property lawsuits in the ensuing years. While Huawei largely disputed the claims, Ren has acknowledged that the Chinese market was wild and lawless in its infancy.

"Everyone knows about this thing, Facebook," he once quipped. "If it had arisen in China, it might have been copied many times. Not only would the original inventor have been cast aside, but the early copycats would have been as well."[32]

13

The Roads to Empire

GLOBAL EXPANSION:
2004-2008

D uring Ren Zhengfei's childhood, traveling outside the country was almost unheard of. Now Huawei employees were seeing the world in style, for work and for amusement. One popular destination was Australia: Ren appealed personally to the Australian consul general in Guangzhou in 2005 for help with visas that would enable Huawei employees to go on holiday in Australia.[1] Those who went on work trips to the United States arrived with shopping lists of designer bags, brand-name sneakers, and other desirable gifts for friends and family back in Shenzhen. On their return, employees sometimes picked up a few tins of imported baby formula in Hong Kong, prized by colleagues with infants who preferred the foreign brands.[2] Ren even amassed a collection of oil paintings, which Huawei staffers helped him tote home from abroad.[3]

Huawei was becoming a frequent host to foreign dignitaries and international executives, with the company often offering to cover travel expenses for visitors. And it now boasted a gleaming new campus that was so large it had its own highway exit.[4] Gone were the hot and humid old offices, where staffers had ducked beneath nets to try to escape the mosquitoes. The new employee dorms had air-conditioning and televisions. Across 350 acres, there were tree-lined boulevards, soccer fields (four in all), tennis courts, and swimming pools.[5] For visitors, there was an upscale hotel operated by Huawei and a palatial white hall, filled with product demos, that some waggish staffers had nicknamed "Saddam's Palace."[6] Chefs cooked food from around the world with attention to detail: both northern- and southern-style Indian dishes were served so that Indian software engineers from either part of the country could feel at home. There were hostesses trained in the art of traditional tea ceremonies.[7] The statuesque receptionists and waiters had been screened for height, weight, and posture, their hands and arms checked for scars.[8]

Some employees thought all the pomp was wasteful. Ren told them it was just good business. "When customers come to see it, they'll say this company looks beautiful, it doesn't look like it will collapse, let's give them the contract!" he said. "You must understand this point. We serve the customer. So if the customer likes the look of it, we'll build it for them."[9]

In the early days, Ren had told his engineers they would get so rich that they'd have to air out their cash on balconies so it didn't get moldy.[10] They'd all laughed. But Huawei's employees were indeed getting wealthy. Foreign employees too. Huawei's representative in India, Lu Ke, got the nickname "Mr. Double," due to his willingness to double Indian engineers' salaries to get them to join Huawei.[11] Robert Read, who was working at Huawei's office in Sweden, recalled his boss sending him out on recruiting missions whenever Ericsson was doing layoffs. "He'd give me a big stack of money and send me down to the train station," he said. "And he'd say, 'Be friendly with them; buy them drinks. Buy the whole place drinks.'"[12]

Ren thought of Huawei's staff as more than just dumb money. He pushed them to cultivate themselves. He felt that the Huawei man should be a Renaissance man, learned in history, literature, philosophy, and global cultures. He set the example himself, penning wide-ranging essays to staff that recounted his own personal experiences, interspersed with musings on historic battles, poetry, and geopolitics. His engineers scrambled to follow suit, to prove themselves sophisticated and philosophical men and women, not just cogs in a router-making machine.

The cash was flooding in faster than ever before, and much of it was from Beijing. In 2005, the China Development Bank, a Beijing-controlled policy bank, allocated a whopping $10 billion to fund Huawei's overseas expansion.[13] This was a staggering sum—twice Huawei's 2004 revenue. It meant that telecom operators around the globe could buy Huawei equipment with little cash down, paying back the loans bit by bit. It was clear encouragement from Beijing to go forth as quickly as possible. In quick succession, Huawei announced deals in South Africa, Jordan, Argentina, Thailand, and a string of other countries.

Hu Jintao had succeeded Jiang Zemin as the nation's leader, and he showed up personally for Huawei's deal-signing ceremonies in countries ranging from Nigeria to the Philippines to Germany. Some of these projects were being negotiated at the diplomatic level. During a visit to Huawei's headquarters in August 2005, Indonesian president Susilo Bambang Yudhoyano said: "Chinese president Hu Jintao and I have reached agreement on expanding the scope of our cooperation, in particular in the areas of information, telecommunications, and national defense."[14]

As Huawei went global, Ren and his team considered changing the company's name to something catchier to foreign ears. Ren wasn't fully satisfied with the name Huawei, which he thought had too soft a sound, even if it had the nice meaning of "China is great." They decided it was too late to change Huawei's name, but they did revamp the logo. Up until then, it had been a red sunburst with fifteen thin rays. Now, in May 2006, the company streamlined it into eight wider red petals reminiscent of a chrysanthemum.[15] The domestic press nicknamed Huawei "the Chrysanthemum Factory."

Ren appeared in the ranks of *Time*'s "100 Most Influential People of 2005." Ren was "a former soldier who fashions himself after Chairman Mao," *Time* said. "Like China's former leader, Ren Zhengfei is known for spouting folk witticisms, purging associates and challenging U.S. power."[16]

I n London, there was hushed discussion among officials. British Telecom, or BT, Britain's biggest phone and internet company, had flagged to British authorities that Huawei was vying for a spot in BT's £10 billion network upgrade from dial-up internet to speedy broadband. Ren and his team were hoping this would be their breakthrough into the West. Officials at the UK's National Security Information Exchange considered banning Huawei from the bid but ultimately allowed it to proceed.[17] They were wary of the possibility of a lawsuit if they barred a single vendor. And there was certainly the risk of political retaliation from China.

Huawei sent more than a hundred employees to the UK to work on its bid.[18] The company had been wooing BT's CTO, Matt Bross, for months, and while Bross had responded positively, it was hard to know if Huawei really had a shot. Huawei's staffers had never worked with a major Western operator, and they scrambled to meet BT's strict supplier requirements and to answer all the technical questions in the bidding process. "We were sleeping on the floor for a couple hours and then continuing with the work," one Huawei employee recalled. "We went for seven days nonstop."

BT's decision to pick Huawei in April 2005 broke open the dam into the West. With BT's seal of approval, Huawei quickly landed contracts with the UK's Vodafone, France's Orange SA, and Spain's Telefónica. These deals plugged Huawei into not just individual countries but entire continents. Vodafone ran mobile networks across Europe and the developing world. Orange SA spanned France and Francophone Africa. Telefónica dominated Spanish-speaking nations. If these operators' footprints had echoes of the European empires of old, it wasn't entirely a coincidence. Building out telephone networks across their empires had been a priority for European governments as a way to connect to and manage their territories. This telephone infrastructure had gradually come into the ownership of privatized companies. Ken Zita, former strategic adviser on telecommunications to the US Pacific Command, said that a lot about geopolitics could be explained by the layout of telecommunications networks. "If you understand how information flows in a system, then you can understand how the whole thing works," he said.[19]

Huawei's entry into Europe with Vodafone began humbly: it started out supplying 3G "dongles"—USB sticks that could project a Wi-Fi hotspot when plugged into a laptop—then advanced to making Vodafone-brand cell phones.[20] Pretty soon, Huawei was supplying the whole kit and caboodle: routers, servers, fiber-optic networks, mobile base stations. Telecom operators around the world couldn't get enough of Huawei's gear or, especially, its bargain prices.

It was the beginning of the end for several of Huawei's Western rivals. After losing the BT contract, Britain's Marconi and Canada's Nortel considered the possibility of a Huawei takeover or merger, with Ren's trusted deputy, Guo Ping, having discussions with both.[21] Nortel's CEO, Bill Owens, said he tried for several months to get the Canadian and US governments to agree to a merger between Huawei and Nortel, which he said would have been "a wonderful thing for the relationship of China, Canada, and the United States."[22] (Nortel's significant US operations meant that Washington regulators would involve themselves in any deal.) "I thought that Mr. Ren Zhengfei was going to be willing to share all the source code of Huawei with the National Security Agency," Owens said. "I had talked to the National Security Council about this." It quickly became clear, however, that any such deal would be viewed as a security risk by Western regulators.

As Beijing opened the financing taps for Huawei's overseas expansion, the company's challenge was now keeping up with orders. It was grievously delayed on some of its contracts and struggled to pacify irate customers. "At the time, people would joke that 'even if you are able to find a project manager on the moon, they still won't be able to deliver a Huawei project,'" Guo Ping recalled.[23]

In Kenya in 2004, Huawei held a grand signing ceremony with mobile operator Safaricom, and the Chinese Communist Party elder Wu Bangguo even flew over for the occasion.[24] Three years later, Safaricom was still waiting on the billing system. Safaricom's CEO, Michael Joseph, was beside himself. "I had lots and lots of meetings, quite upset meetings," he recalled.[25]

Finally, Joseph flew to Hong Kong. "I want to cancel this contract," he remembered telling Huawei executives. "And if you don't give me my money back, I'm going to sue you in London."

Huawei agreed to refund the money, and the problem seemed resolved. But when Joseph returned home, Kenya's information and communication minister summoned him. According to a WikiLeaks-leaked cable from the US embassy in Nairobi, Joseph was told that canceling the Huawei contract had put all Chinese foreign assistance to Kenya at risk. Other ministers also telephoned Joseph to ask him to reconsider. The minister of immigration insinuated that as a foreigner, he might have work-permit problems if he went through with the cancellation.[26]

Asked about the incident years later, Joseph acknowledged it had taken place, but he came to Huawei's defense. He said that the company had succeeded in winning back Safaricom and had gone on to become a key partner. Huawei had provided the engineering resources that Safaricom needed to build a mobile payment system called M-PESA (*pesa* is Swahili for "money"), which became a smash success, with people signing up for Safaricom service just to use it.

A Safaricom shop in Siaya County, Kenya, advertises M-PESA, the mobile payment service developed by Huawei in 2016.

This was not something Safaricom could have done without Huawei's help. In any case, Safaricom had few options beyond making up with Huawei. Only a handful of companies in the world still made cell tower systems, and at budget price points, it was either Huawei or ZTE.

When Joseph stepped down as Safaricom's CEO in 2011, Huawei threw him a lavish party in Shenzhen, true to its tradition of remembering old friends. "They knew I liked classical music, and they brought in a classical orchestra," Joseph recalled. "They brought in an opera singer. They gave me a bottle of wine that was made in the year that I was born."

On a Sunday morning in January 2006, North Korea's leader, Kim Jong Il, emerged from his hotel in Shenzhen, stepped into a car, and rode by motorcade to Huawei Technologies.[27] He stayed for only twenty minutes. But the visit opened the door to a contract for Huawei to construct North Korea's first 3G mobile phone network, Koryolink.[28]

Huawei's experience in Iraq had perhaps left the company's executives with the lesson that they could successfully work in countries sanctioned by the United States so long as they proceeded carefully. While Huawei had suffered a setback in 2001, when the Pentagon blew up its fiber-optic network in Iraq and the company had faced the prospect of penalties for violating UN sanctions, it had made it through. Indeed, Huawei had been rewarded in the end for going where others shied away. When the sanctions were lifted in 2003, Huawei was positioned to quickly win a place in Iraq's new mobile network.

Now, in North Korea, which was under US technology sanctions, Huawei approached the project carefully, using the code name "A9" in internal records. Huawei sold its antennae and other gear to an intermediary Chinese company, Panda International, which shipped the equipment by rail across China's far-northeast border, as later reported by *The Washington Post*.[29] (Asked by *The Post*, Huawei said it had "no business presence" in North Korea.) Due to his own childhood experience of famine, Ren sympathized with the nation's plight. "I can truly understand the difficulties faced by the North Korean people in recent years," he once remarked.[30]

Huawei was also staying in the Afghanistan market, even though the US war against the Taliban made the business prospects unclear. "We were just spending money," one Afghanistan-based Huawei engineer recalled. "After one year, I didn't see any returns." He said that management told him it was okay. They were taking the long view. "This is how they grow from country to country," he said. "They are long-term thinkers." The engineer recalled that he received a daily "war allowance" stipend of one hundred dollars.[31] Workers often had to hunker down at the company's secure villa in Kabul, where they lived and worked. "There were bombs, and during a blast, we used to get the message 'Okay, today we just stay home.'" Another Huawei staffer stationed in Afghanistan wrote that a local colleague was once held hostage but fortunately released unharmed.[32] Huawei sent over a chef from Chongqing to ease homesickness, and Ren went to visit the Afghanistan office to shore up morale. "I promise that as long as I can fly, I'll come to visit you in hardship zones," Ren said. "If I fear death myself, how can I ask you to fight heroically?"[33]

Huawei's business in Iran also carried on, though the political environment had grown increasingly fraught. In the late 1990s, the US had eased sanctions on Iran under the reformist president Mohammad Khatami, but the revelation that the country had covertly built nuclear facilities in 2002 sparked an international crisis. After being elected president in 2005, hard-liner Mahmoud Ahmadinejad pushed the nuclear program more forcefully, with Iran announcing in 2006 that it had succeeded in enriching uranium for the first time.[34] President George W. Bush's administration instituted new sanctions against individuals connected with Iran's nuclear industry, though other trade was allowed to continue. Iran was a frequent pit stop for Huawei employees in the region, partly because they had at some point discovered that it was a convenient route for renewing their visas for the United Arab Emirates. Huawei employees who were posted to the UAE often worked on tourist visas, but they had to leave the country each month to renew them.[35] The quickest round trip out of Dubai was the short flight across the Persian Gulf to Iran and back again, an arrangement that the employees were largely okay with until a plane on the route crashed, killing forty-three of the forty-six people on board. In a complaint to Huawei's leadership, they wrote that only by luck had none of them been aboard the doomed flight. "Perhaps it is for convenience, or considerations from the cost perspective, but tourist visas are used for work in many countries, bringing great inconvenience to employees," their grievance read.

During this period, Huawei was also selling products to Iran Electronics Industries, an Iranian military contractor owned by the Ministry of Defense. As with the North Korea project, it was making sales through an intermediary. In the October 2006 issue of *Management Optimization*, one of Huawei's internal newspapers, an article berating staffers for sloppily pasting shipping labels included, by way of illustration, a photo of a box being shipped from the China National Technical Import and Export Corp., a state-owned Chinese company, to "Iran Electronic Industries."[36] The shipping label gave no indication that the package had any relation to Huawei, but the author of the article, a Huawei employee working on the company's Middle East supply chains, wrote that their business partner had complained about the label peeling off the box due to not being glued on securely enough. "It was really embarrassing to be a Huawei employee in that moment!" the employee wrote. Weeks later, this very same Iranian company was sanctioned by the US State Department, which accused it of being involved in the development of missiles and weapons of mass destruction.[37]

I n 2007, Huawei leveled up into the big leagues when it launched two exotic offerings: submarine cables and managed services. These product areas might have been obscure to the general consumer, but they reflected that Huawei had arrived at an elite level in the networking world.

Submarine cables, the pipes that carry some 99 percent of the world's internet traffic, form the backbone of the global telecommunication network. While people tend to imagine data being beamed to their devices by satellite from the other side of the earth, it almost always travels under the sea. The industry is viewed by governments as a critical one, since a severed cable can temporarily knock an entire country off-line. For obvious reasons, the sector has also been of high interest to intelligence agencies.[38] In a famous case, Operation Ivy Bells, the US Navy, CIA, and NSA put a tap on a Soviet subsea cable in the early 1970s, with divers swapping in a new set of tapes each month for a decade until the operation was compromised.[39] Since then, these networks have been built with more secure fiber-optic cables, which transport the information through beams of light. In 2001, *The Wall Street Journal* reported that the NSA was keenly interested in developing technologies to tap subsea fiber-optic cables, calling such operations "technologically daunting, physically dangerous and potentially illegal."[40] *The Journal* added that missions to intercept signals were among the most highly classified US government operations, and leaking information about them was a federal crime punishable by imprisonment.

The cloak-and-dagger stuff aside, building the cables was big business. With global internet traffic growing exponentially, the world was in a subsea cable building spree. Traditional networking vendors like Cisco and Nokia were involved. Newer companies like Google, Microsoft, and Facebook were also jumping in. Huawei made its entry through a joint-venture company set up in 2007 with the UK's Global Marine Systems.[41] Guo Ping, who was now Huawei's chief strategic officer, was named the chairman of the new submarine cable venture,[42] called Huawei Submarine Networks. The joint-venture company was soon bidding for projects like an undersea fiber-optic cable to connect Kenya and the United Arab Emirates. Huawei lost that project, which was awarded to Alcatel-Lucent—the French networking giant that had absorbed the strongest US player, Lucent, a year earlier amid a wave of industry consolidation. But Huawei kept bidding, and pretty soon it began winning submarine cable projects.

In 2007, Huawei also began selling managed services, a comprehensive service offering pioneered by Western companies like Ericsson. If a customer opted for managed services, Huawei helped run its networks for a fee.[43] This bland-sounding part of Huawei's business was often entirely overlooked by outside observers. But in terms of the company's geopolitical importance, it was one of the most critical. It put Huawei's engineers at the controls of customers' networks. In ensuing years, many of the controversies that would arise over Huawei's participation in government surveillance would involve contracts whereby Huawei was providing managed services for the customer. The scope of such deals was outlined in corporate press releases. For example, Huawei announced in 2008 that Saudi Arabia's Mobily was contracting it to administer Mobily's "network operations, back office, field operations, network optimization and spare parts management." Huawei would also maintain equipment from third-party companies in Mobily's network. "This managed services agreement will enable Mobily to reduce operations costs," a press release said.[44]

With Huawei increasingly integrated into global networks, it was being watched closely by spy agencies. Several industry executives recalled Western intelligence officers reaching out with questions. In July 2007, FBI agents interviewed Ren at a New York hotel. Not much is known about the circumstances, except that Ren told them Huawei had not dealt directly with any Iranian company, having only sold some equipment to a third party, "possibly in Egypt." When Ren and his deputies applied for visas to travel to the US for business trips, they were frustrated to find that they were limited to single-entry visas.[45] The State Department had flagged all Huawei employees as a technology-transfer risk, prohibiting them from multiple-entry visas under the Visas Mantis program.

Charles Clancy, who was a research leader with the National Security Agency, recalled visiting Asiacell's headquarters in Sulaymaniyah, Iraq, in 2009 or 2010 and seeing a lot of Huawei engineers posted there to support a managed services contract. "The Huawei engineers and the Asiacell engineers were playing soccer," he said. "They were the ones that were really running a lot of the infrastructure."[46] Clancy later told a Senate committee that Huawei's managed services gave the company's employees broad access to overseas networks without any hacks having to take place. "A back door is not needed if you already have a key to the front door," he explained to the committee.[47]

Western spy agencies were also meeting with domestic networking companies, not all of which were receptive to the visits. Michel Juneau-Katsuya, a former senior Canadian intelligence officer, recalled warning Nortel executives that their company was being targeted by China's intelligence services. "We were disregarded," he said. "Like, 'What's the problem? . . . Everything's fine. We don't need you guys. Go play James Bond somewhere else.'"[48]

I n September 2007, Huawei found itself at the center of a political maelstrom in Washington. News had broken that Huawei and Bain Capital—the Boston-based private equity company cofounded by former Massachusetts governor Mitt Romney—had struck a deal to take over the US networking company 3Com. US politicians were up in arms, denouncing it as a threat to national security and calling for the Bush administration to block the deal.

From a purely financial perspective, the transaction made sense. Bain knew that 3Com's success depended on Huawei's blessing. What few people on the outside understood was that practically the only thing keeping 3Com afloat in those days was sales from its China unit, H3C, which Huawei had helped set up as a joint venture in 2003. In line with the agreement between Huawei and 3Com, Huawei had sold its H3C shares back to 3Com in 2006, promising not to compete head-to-head with H3C for eighteen months. But they all knew that after the eighteen months were up, Huawei could crush

H3C if Ren felt inclined. Bain had made Huawei a peace offering of a 16.5 percent stake in the $2.2 billion deal.

In Washington, folks did not see things that way. US politicians pointed out that 3Com was a Pentagon contractor. Congressman Peter Hoekstra of Michigan warned that China might be able to learn what systems the US government had put in place to block hackers. Thaddeus McCotter, chairman of the House Republican Policy Committee, called it a "stealth assault on America's national security." Huawei's executives were taken aback by the vitriol. Asked by a *Financial Times* reporter if the deal would endanger US national security, Huawei's chief marketing officer, Eric Xu—a serious, bespectacled PhD known within the company for his plainspokenness—exclaimed: "That would be bullshit."[49]

The fate of the deal came down to a cloistered US regulatory panel called the Committee on Foreign Investment in the United States, or CFIUS. People called it "Sif-ee-us," the pronunciation giving it an ancient Grecian ring of authority and intrigue. The Treasury secretary usually chaired the twelve-agency committee, but Secretary Henry Paulson had recused himself due to a potential conflict: he was a former chairman of Goldman Sachs, which had advised 3Com on the deal with Bain and Huawei.[50] Paulson passed review of the case to Deputy Treasury Secretary Robert M. Kimmitt.

CFIUS was powerful, and its workings were mysterious. The members made closed-door decisions on which foreign investments in US companies would be blocked for national security reasons. Due to their work touching on classified information, they did not feel able or obligated to explain their decisions. Such was their power that they often didn't even have to reject a deal outright. They just had to intimate that it would not pass, and a deal would be stopped cold.

A first exchange with CFIUS was often a small, private meeting with a few lawyers. But when Huawei representatives turned up to begin the review process, they found themselves in a packed hall with senior Pentagon officials in uniform. "It means they've already decided you're done," said one person with knowledge of the meeting. "They just want to see how much information they can get out of you before they tell you to go screw yourself."

Huawei, 3Com, and Bain persisted for a few months in trying to find a risk-mitigation plan that could appease CFIUS. But by February 2008, they knew the deal was dead.

14

Separation of Powers

MANAGEMENT EVOLUTION:
2006-2008

In 2007, Huawei's management told staff of a change: the company's Communist Party committee now had veto power over executive appointments.[1] The move was controversial. Some employees had chosen to work at a private company like Huawei precisely because they liked having some distance between themselves and the state apparatus. There were worries, too, that closer involvement of the party in Huawei's operations would be detrimental to the company's international expansion. Foreign governments were wary of the party's role in Chinese companies: by having a say in promotion decisions, a party committee could theoretically assist in embedding intelligence agents across a company's operations.

There was enough discomfiture among the rank and file that Huawei's management felt the need to defend the new policy in a two-page explainer that December. It said that executives had considered the move carefully, with discussions beginning in 2005. Huawei had drafted the new rule in autumn 2006, with senior management and party officials holding several days of meetings in March 2007 to debate the details of implementation. "The entire period of discussion and decision-making for this system took more than a year and a half," the company told employees.

Huawei's leadership said that this new "separation of powers" was meant to stem nepotism and corruption, and that it was inspired by the checks and balances among the three branches of the US government. Executives could no longer unilaterally make the decision to promote a subordinate. They had to seek a green light from the human-resources department and party committee. The party committee could veto planned promotions or even "impeach" unfit executives after the fact.

It was unclear who had suggested this idea of giving the party committee a say in Huawei's executive appointments—whether it had originated from Ren Zhengfei's team or been imposed upon Huawei by external party authorities. In any event, the move aligned with a push from Beijing in the mid-2000s to give the party a larger role in private enterprise, with China's leader, Hu Jintao, calling for it personally.

As the party committee prepared to take on a greater role within Huawei, Ren told committee members that he hoped they would use the power well. "This 'veto power' and 'impeachment power' are very powerful," he said.[2]

The party's push to institute heavier oversight of Huawei came during a period of domestic outcry against the company. Huawei had fetishized long work hours as part of its culture, with engineers keeping mats at their desks so that they could nap on the floor while pulling all-nighters. Reflective of the self-flagellating culture, Huawei titled a volume of essays about its R&D *Purgatory*, alluding to a Karl Marx quote about the struggles of scientific research.[3] When an employee complained about excessive overtime at a town hall, Chairwoman Sun Yafang dismissed it, saying that extended work hours were unavoidable. "The resource we most lack is time," she said. "It's impossible for us to sleep more if we are to catch up."[4]

But then, in 2006, Huawei employees began dying. And as much as Ren tried, he could not make it stop. The local press cast the deaths at Huawei as emblematic of the unspoken human costs behind the nation's economic boom. The nation's GDP was at 11.1 percent, a twelve-year high. Many had attained wealth beyond their wildest dreams. But the skies were smog-choked, historic neighborhoods had been flattened to make room for skyscrapers, and factory bosses pushed their workers beyond the boundaries of safety and humaneness.

The first was a twenty-five-year-old engineer named Hu Xinyu, who had an open face and dimples.[5] In March 2006, Hu started a high-priority project at Huawei, his girlfriend told the local press. She claimed that over the next month, he returned home only four times, spending the other nights at the office, stealing brief naps atop a mattress on the floor. In late April, Hu went to the hospital and was diagnosed with a severe brain infection. He fell into a coma and never woke up. As Huawei struggled to quell a nationwide backlash, a spokesperson told reporters that Hu Xinyu had died from an illness, not overwork.

The string of "unnatural" deaths at Huawei continued for two years. One Huawei employee jumped to his death at an R&D center.

Another leaped over the railing of a third-floor cafeteria. A third hanged himself. It was hard to say afterward if work pressures played a role in their demise. The local press counted no fewer than six deaths. A posthumously discovered blog post from one of the engineers hinted at the heavy financial pressures he had felt.

> With tears in my eyes, I have left my wife and seven-month-old daughter.... I have no alternative but to come back to Shenzhen.... I've returned to this city I've come to love and hate.

In June 2007, Ren published an open letter in *Management Optimization,* one of Huawei's internal newspapers, appealing to the party secretary, Madam Chen Zhufang, for help. He wrote that he was at his wit's end about stopping the deaths among his employees. "Huawei continues to have employees committing suicide and self-harm," Ren said. "And the number of employees suffering from depression and anxiety is increasing, which is very worrying. Is there any way to help employees face life positively, openly, and uprightly? I've thought about it again and again, and I can't solve it."[6] In the letter, Ren revealed that he himself had suffered from clinical depression in the past, but he claimed to have made a full recovery with medical treatment. He suggested that employees spend more time relaxing outside of work, drinking tea together or strolling through a park. "As long as these activities do not involve discussing politics, violating the law, or violating ethics, we will not interfere."

But some external critics thought it was clear that Ren himself had created this crisis through Huawei's pressure-cooker work culture. Huawei had long cultivated a Wall Street–esque ethos that saw employees pitted against one another, the winners showered with riches and the losers weeded out. "Humanistic concern for individual employees is not part of this corporate culture," one Shanghai sociologist, Zhang Youde, told a domestic magazine. "Huawei not only treats its employees as a means to maximize its profits, but it also encourages a dark side of human nature, namely that everyone is competing with everyone else."[7]

Even as Huawei was in the thick of the suicides scandal, another labor controversy erupted. China had just adopted its landmark Labor Contract Law, which would provide some protections for workers who had put in a decade of work at the same company. Huawei had long had a reputation for laying off older engineers to keep its salary costs lower with a younger staff. Now, in late 2007, Huawei rushed to get ahead of the new law. With Ren taking the lead himself, some sixty-five hundred Huawei employees resigned and rejoined the company, wiping out their seniority.[8] Huawei called the resignations voluntary,[9] and it gave the resignees buyout compensation, but the local press reported that employees felt forced to go along with the move. The local government launched an investigation, and though it later announced that the mass resignations were not illegal,[10] the incident was yet another blemish on Huawei's domestic reputation.

China was changing, and Huawei would have to keep up. In the past, the company had repeatedly pressured its staff into mass resignations, most famously the 1996 culling of its sales team, an effort led by Madam Sun Yafang. But now the new generation of workers had legal protections, and they increasingly knew their rights. "Workers born in the 1980s are different than those of us born in the 1960s and

'70s in their values and way of thinking," Ren's younger brother, Steven Ren, once remarked. "They have a stronger sense of independence, and they have a strong sense of self."[11]

Huawei stopped boasting that it had a "wolf culture." Ren ordered overtime hours to be cut. The company stopped telling visitors that employees worked so hard they slept on mats on the ground overnight; instead, it explained that the engineers' mats were there for taking daytime naps, thanks to considerate management.

For a few years, Ren, who turned sixty-three in 2007, had been delegating more management tasks to a group of eight executives he called Huawei's "executive management team," or EMT. This EMT included Chairwoman Sun Yafang, William Xu, Ji Ping, Fei Min, Hong Tianfeng, the early engineer Guo Ping, and the early salesmen Eric Xu and Ken Hu.[12]

Ren quipped internally that he had become number two in the company and that Chairwoman Sun was now the one aging quickly from all the stress. "When I was number one, there were a lot of annoyances, and you get older faster as number one," Ren said at a staff meeting in 2004. "I'm radiant and vigorous now as second-in-command, because I don't have as much pressure or inner pain."[13]

His daughter Meng Wanzhou was also stepping into a larger role. In November 2006, the Mauritian press reported that a new Huawei finance office had opened in the Indian Ocean's island nation, and it was headed by "a woman, Meng Wanzhou, 34."[14] She had been tasked with opening the center, which would take advantage of Mauritius's favorable tax environment to handle Huawei's finances across sub-

Saharan Africa. Due to the low level of public disclosures required for companies in Mauritius, Meng's team would also channel business operations that Huawei wanted to keep out of the public eye through the island nation.

It had taken Meng a while to learn the ropes of finance. By her own admission, when she'd first joined the department, she'd struggled to balance the ledgers, and her work had needed to be checked by others. "Thanks to the tolerance and guidance of others, I was able to pick up my lost financial knowledge, bit by bit," she later wrote. Huawei's finance department was also disorganized and chaotic, with Meng recalling that she and her departmental colleagues were often beset by criticism from Huawei's other departments, the company's customers, and her father. It sometimes took Huawei employees five months to get reimbursements.[15] "We were like a headless chicken, running around aimlessly," Meng wrote.[16]

In 2007, Ren put Meng in charge of an IBM consulting project meant to overhaul Huawei's finance operations. Conversing with the IBM consultants was a challenge for Meng due to her rudimentary English, but she kept at it. Her project wasn't widely popular within the company either, as some salespeople felt that the strict new rules made their work more difficult. "In the early days of promoting internal controls, finance was viewed as being in opposition to the business side of our operations," Meng wrote.

In Hong Kong in February 2007, Meng remarried, tying the knot with Huawei's former Mexico representative, Liu Xiaozong, also known as Carlos.[17] Meng had three sons from previous marriages; it was Liu's first marriage. Liu, three years younger, was a tall southerner who sometimes styled his hair in a wavy pompadour. Like Meng, he was born in the Sichuan provincial capital of Chengdu, giving them some common childhood experiences.[18] Liu had joined Huawei in 1996 after graduating from college, and by the early 2000s, he'd worked his way up to head of sales for Liaoning Province. As part of Ren's first big international push, Liu was sent abroad to Mexico. While he didn't make major headlines during his posting there, he was noted once by the Mexican press as representing Huawei at a 2005 meeting of senior telecommunications officials from Mexico and China.[19]

Huawei had a rule against couples working for the company, an effort to prevent nepotism and conflict. The rule was only sometimes enforced. But as Liu's relationship with Meng became serious, he left Huawei for an MBA program, with local media attributing the decision to his desire to earn his own professional achievements outside Ren's shadow. After their marriage, Meng changed the name on her passport to Wanzhou Meng Liu in the Hong Kong custom of adding her husband's surname to her own. But when this created complications, since her passport no longer matched other IDs, she ended up changing it back.[20]

Meng and her husband bought a house in Vancouver, where they would start spending their summers. It was a sturdy two-story house on a sunny corner lot, a block from a neighborhood park with baseball diamonds. The two soon had a daughter, adding to Meng's three sons from previous marriages. Liu's parents stayed with them sometimes, helping to look after the children. The pink and blue hydrangeas bloomed riotously each year.

Around the time Meng set up the Huawei unit in Mauritius, another company, Canicula Holdings Limited, was also registered in the island nation. From the outside, it wasn't possible to tell that Canicula was controlled by Huawei. In 2007, Canicula purchased a Hong

Kong–incorporated company called Skycom Tech Co. Ltd. from a Huawei subsidiary. Few people knew it at the time, but Skycom was a shell company that Huawei had been using to obscure its business in Iran.

In early 2008, Meng, who was now president of the financial management department at Huawei, registered as a director of Skycom.[21] It's unclear why she created a paper trail linking herself to Huawei's dealings in Iran. It very well might have been the worst mistake of her life. *Cathy Meng,* she signed on the Hong Kong disclosure form, the English letters slanting optimistically upward.

After Huawei set up its party committee in 1996, its number of party members grew apace with the company. In 2000, Huawei had eighteen hundred party members. In 2007, this number was up to twelve thousand out of more than sixty-one thousand employees.[22] As was common in Chinese companies, there was sometimes grumbling among Huawei employees about how the patriotic and moralistic activities organized by the party committee were a waste of time. Madam Chen Zhufang, the party secretary, once remarked that some executives seemed to be just going through the motions in their self-criticisms.

One of the roles of the party committee within Huawei was ethical oversight. Employees were encouraged to report misbehaving managers for investigation. "Certain managers are even engaging in corruption, participating in gambling and visiting unhealthy establishments," the committee said in an alert to staff. During a crackdown on gambling, it warned that party members found in violation would be punished by both the company and the party.[23] The committee fielded internal complaints of all sorts, including an anonymous letter from an employee alleging that the company's overseas offices were grossly inflating their earnings by booking projects as revenue before they were installed.[24] In the internal publication *Management Optimization*, party officials chided employees for infractions ranging from falsifying receipts at hotels, to being disrespectful to the Special Economic Zone's border checkpoint officers, to leaving their desks a few minutes early for lunch.

Party organization leaders signed pledges to provide moral leadership to colleagues and steer clear of graft. "If large-scale corruption and party member corruption occurs in the area that I oversee, then I agree to take on joint liability for my poor supervision," read one pledge that Huawei party members signed.[25]

There was sustained interest from outsiders in the role of Huawei's Communist Party committee. At a 2005 meeting, when an Australian diplomat asked Ren about the party secretary's role, he replied that the party secretary helped align business with national goals. "Business works best when private business and state coordinate," a person at the meeting recalled Ren saying.[26]

The party committee also oversaw internal "democratic life meetings," at which executives criticized themselves and received criticism from staff.[27] Many of the complaints were common enough for a company town hall in any nation: employees griped that managers were too distant, that the bosses only emerged for chats when something went wrong, that lower-level staff were reluctant to volunteer for tasks because they knew they would be punished if there was a mishap.[28] Ren cautioned staffers against criticizing one another too harshly at the meetings. "I believe people fear pain," he said. "If it's too painful, that's not too good either."[29]

The self-criticism sessions for senior executives were occasionally recounted internally in *Management Optimization*. In one session, Steven Ren, who was overseeing construction projects as head of Huawei's Capital Construction Management Department, confessed before the party committee that he was not a good listener, that he was too quick to lose his temper, and that he let personal feelings interfere with his decisions. "My personality is relatively confident and stubborn," he said. "So when an issue arises, my first instinct is to think I am right. In fact, for some things, there is no absolute right or wrong."[30]

In a December 2006 criticism session for global sales chief Ken Hu—a rising star at Huawei who was increasingly representing the company at overseas events—Party Secretary Chen Zhufang upbraided him for not being enthusiastic enough about party work, and for staying at arm's length from the committee.[31]

"To be honest, it's quite hard to find you," she said, according to an internally circulated account of the meeting.

"It's true," Hu acknowledged. "We've known each other for many years, but we haven't talked a lot."

Madam Chen expressed her hope that Hu would encourage the party committee to organize activities at Huawei's overseas offices. She said that they'd taken three trips to Huawei's overseas offices the previous year but hadn't dared make any further visits after receiving feedback that they'd "interfered" with sales work.

"If Mr. Hu doesn't say the word, we don't even dare to go," she said.

Hu apparently obliged. Not long after, Chen visited Huawei staff in Latin America, where she encouraged them to learn to sing local songs as a way of better adapting to the culture around them.[32]

P arty Secretary Chen retired quietly in 2007 or 2008. Huawei's internal publications began to refer to a new party secretary, Zhou Daiqi, as early as March 2008.[33]

Zhou would keep a low profile, lower than that of Madam Chen. While she had been a prolific writer of moralistic and patriotic essays and speeches, Zhou rarely put pen to paper for public consumption. Perhaps during Huawei's international era, it seemed prudent to downplay the role of the company's party officials. Huawei's annual reports would leave out Zhou's party secretary title—the more powerful of his positions—referring to him only as a member of the company's supervisory board, or as the chief ethics and compliance officer.[34]

Three years younger than Ren,[35] Zhou had been a telephone switching researcher in Xi'an at the State Key Laboratory of Integrated Service Networks at Xidian University, a lab funded by the central government. He appeared to have kept this affiliation after joining Huawei in 1994 as an engineer, continuing to publish academic papers under both his Huawei and Xidian titles for years. One colleague recalled that in 1996, Zhou tapped a group of Xidian University researchers in their twenties to help Huawei work on a switching technology project funded by Beijing's 863 high-tech research program.[36] At Huawei, he worked his way up through positions such as chief engineer and director of the hardware department. In

2002, some six years before his promotion to the powerful party secretary position, Zhou still seemed to be somewhat outside Ren's inner circle. In *Management Optimization*, he was quoted as head of Huawei's Xi'an Research Center and praised a recent Huawei training session for bringing his team closer to the company.[37]

Huawei's senior executives tended to be those whom Ren had trained from a young age, true believers who had spent nearly their entire careers at the company. In the case of Huawei's party secretaries—first Madam Chen, then Zhou—they had reached senior levels at academic institutions before joining Huawei. This suggested, perhaps, that having high-level connections in China's academic and official realms was valued for the position.

Huawei executives stipulated internally that party members would be treated differently in some respects, that they would have higher expectations of patriotism, and that they would be seen as suitable for leadership positions. "Our requirements for party members must be stricter, and in various types of work, we should encourage party members to take the lead," Ren said in March 2005 while visiting Huawei finance staff in Europe. Ren claimed that the company kept personnel records on each party member employee to better "encourage and supervise" them, and he acknowledged that the interests of the nation must supersede all else: "Ahead of the individual and the organization, party members should first of all comply with the big picture and understand the big picture."[38]

15

The Torch

Huawei's engineers began work on Mount Everest in the latter part of 2007.[1] China would be hosting the Olympics in the summer, and authorities were planning an epic torch relay spanning the globe, with a dramatic ascent up the world's highest mountain. Huawei had been hired to rig up cell service on Mount Everest so that the images could be beamed out to the world in real time.

By the time Huawei's team reached base camp at Mount Everest, all five members had altitude sickness, with headaches and dizziness. They were more than seventeen thousand feet above sea level. With each breath, they were getting only half as much oxygen as what they were used to. The air was so thin that it was even difficult to cook their food, which had been hauled up by yaks. "Even though there was a pressure cooker, the rice always felt undercooked," one engineer recalled. In the morning, they'd wake in their tents with ice crystals clinging to their hair. They swaddled the antennae and radios in waterproof packs and continued to climb from base camp. A bit past twenty-one thousand feet, they stopped and installed the highest base station in the world. It looked small and frail: a few white boxes lashed to a tripod, sparkling in the cold sunlight.

The year 2008 would be a landmark one for Huawei—and for China. With the Summer Olympics, a modern China would come out onto the world stage. Huawei would achieve new heights in R&D, reaching number one worldwide in the total number of patent applications filed, the first time a Chinese company had held the honor.[2] The company would also launch a popular cell tower technology called SingleRAN (RAN stands for "radio access network"), codeveloped with the major European operator Vodafone, which would help secure Vodafone as a longtime partner.

China had been attempting to host the Games for well over a decade. Ren Zhengfei recalled the disappointment in 1993 when China lost its bid—to Australia by two votes—to host the 2000 Games.[3] After Beijing won its bid for 2008, officials were so proud that they started a countdown clock in Tiananmen Square as soon as the Athens 2004 Games had concluded.[4] As the date finally approached, people were excited. Under the direction of a low-profile but ambitious vice president named Xi Jinping, Beijing had undergone a complete transformation, with shiny, futuristic-looking buildings anchoring the skyline. Li Yinan—Ren's "young prodigy" from Huawei's early days—had since returned to the company and was spotted by a Chinese reporter on a flight to the US to attend a conference. "Look, I'm wearing a Beijing Olympics T-shirt," Li told him. "I'm going to show off our Olympics in America."[5]

A s the Olympics drew closer, China was now the world's largest internet market. With 253 million people online, it had surged past the United States in number of users.[6] For Beijing authorities, tightening control over this explosion of internet use was a high priority. A major international event like the Olympics meant soaring phone and internet demand. It also meant security risks ranging from cyberattacks to political protests to the potential for stampedes and terrorist plots. Chinese authorities called their project to shore up the police's cyber capabilities "Golden Shield." Overseas, it took on the nickname "the Great Firewall."

Much of the Great Firewall had come from the US company Cisco, which was a leading supplier for a technology called "deep-packet inspection," or DPI. DPI allowed authorities to peek into packets of internet data in transit. If the data was deemed objectionable, the system could stop a website from loading or an email from arriving in the receiver's inbox. With the Olympics approaching, Huawei had developed its own version and had struck a deal to sell it to the capital's network operator, Beijing Netcom. "For the '08 Olympics, Beijing Netcom will adopt this solution to inspect abnormal traffic," a Huawei cyber expert wrote in a technical journal. "This is primarily aimed at defending against network attacks during the Olympic Games."[7]

Huawei's overview of the product highlighted its capability to sniff out viruses and cyberattacks with names like Smurf, Fraggle, and Ping of Death. There was more in the fine print: the product could also monitor VoIP traffic (internet phone calls over services like Skype) and P2P file-sharing networks (which many young people used for downloading foreign TV shows, circumventing Beijing's censors), as well as analyze user behavior. Chinese authorities in the city of Shenyang had successfully used Huawei's DPI system to hunt down illegal VoIP calls and disrupt them with high-decibel noise.[8]

China was also ramping up physical security. Huawei was helping set up a citywide surveillance-camera system in Beijing that state media said would help prevent accidents and public security incidents. At the Beijing city government's command center, a big screen let authorities see the traffic on every street connecting to the Games venues. The city would have some three hundred thousand surveillance cameras by the time the Games began. A telecom expert who visited China that year recalled getting a peek at one of the video display rooms for surveillance cameras and finding them surprisingly advanced. "They had an AI on all those screens," he said. "Any movement, any anomalies on all those cameras, would get flagged automatically with alarms."[9] A domestic technology journal observed that the Olympics had accelerated China's adoption of new surveillance-camera features like facial recognition and thermal imaging. "The shared feature of these technologies is that they are rarely used in ordinary security systems," the journal reported. "But driven by the security needs of the Olympics, these technologies will be popularized rapidly."[10]

The surveillance-camera boom was good news for Huawei's chip unit, HiSilicon, which had become a major supplier of chips for both Huawei's own surveillance cameras and those of other companies. Founded in 1991 as Huawei's in-house chip design center, HiSilicon was formalized as a subsidiary in 2004. In 2006, it launched its first surveillance camera chip, which it used in Huawei's own systems and also sold to other camera makers.[11] HiSilicon ranked number one in China in revenue among integrated-circuit design companies for 2008, with $452.47 million in sales, according to the China Semiconductor Industry Association.[12] This was more than twice the sales of the number-two company, China Huada Integrated Circuit Design. By 2009, HiSilicon would capture 40 percent of the surveillance-camera chip market, with more than two million units in shipments to mainland China, Taiwan, and South Korea.

"Before HiSilicon entered security, the entire semiconductor industry had not developed chips specifically for security," HiSilicon executive Ai Wei told *China Public Security* magazine. "It can be said that HiSilicon is the first semiconductor company with a close interest in security."[13]

Chinese officials were tense in May 2008 when the torch arrived in Tibet. Despite Beijing's years of tightening security, the run-up to the Olympics had been marred by the breakout of deadly protests in Tibet. The first riot had left 22 dead according to the official count, or more than 140 dead according to human-rights groups. The wave of clashes that followed brought the worst unrest that the region had seen in decades. Chinese officials blamed supporters of the Dalai Lama, the exiled Tibetan spiritual leader, for fanning separatism to undermine the nation. Overseas, many were sympathetic to the Tibetans, who had endured oppressive assimilation by the party for decades. As the Olympic torch wended its way from country to country, anti-China protesters showed up in droves to yell "Free Tibet!" and "Shame on China!"

Huawei had been rolling out phone service across Tibet for years, including in rugged rural areas only accessible by foot.[14] Indeed, Beijing viewed the rollout of these utilities as an important part of assimilation efforts to connect Tibetans to the rest of the nation. Ren had previously criticized the United States for attempts to intervene in Tibet. "America wears the human-rights hat to attack China with all its might, using the Taiwan issue, the Tibet issue," Ren said.[15] Another time, he denounced President Clinton's decision to meet with the Dalai Lama as "an instigation to subvert China."[16]

Early in the morning on May 8, 2008, a team of Tibetan mountaineers in thick red parkas lit a red torch and began their frigid climb.[17] The climbers were carrying mobile phones outfitted to easily shoot and upload photos.

The Chinese side of Mount Everest had been closed off to climbers. China had secured Nepal's cooperation for the other half, with Nepali soldiers warning that any anti-China protesters might be shot.[18] At base camp, Huawei's engineers were ready to make sure that the ascent went off without a hitch.

At 9:23 a.m., the first photo went live on the website of the official state news agency, Xinhua.

A Huawei engineer excitedly texted colleagues back home: "The sacred Mount Everest fire has successfully reached the summit and been set aflame. It was all Huawei's equipment that broadcast and safeguarded it."[19]

On the morning of the Olympics' opening ceremony, Huawei engineers arrived early at Beijing Netcom's office for their sixteen-hour shift. They reviewed their checklists.[20]

The streets were quiet. Most Beijing businesses were closed for the day, the roads blocked to all but official Games traffic. In an effort to avoid smoggy skies, factories surrounding the capital had been ordered to suspend production. For two months beforehand, cars were only allowed to drive on alternating days, with restrictions based on whether the last digit of a license plate was odd or even. Prominent political dissidents were under house arrest to eliminate the risk of disruption.[21] Near the main stadium, two surface-to-air missile launchers sat at the ready.

There had been talk of elevated online surveillance for the Games, though it could not be proved to just what extent authorities were monitoring the traffic, or if Huawei's staff were involved. A US senator warned that Beijing hotels had been required to install monitoring systems so that all of the guests' emails and web activity would be viewable by local authorities.[22] A Huawei employee separately recalled, without elaborating, that all international roaming on mobile phones had to pass through a special switching office in Beijing during the Olympics.[23]

That wasn't something visitors could see, though. What Olympics spectators could see when they arrived in Beijing was gleaming futuristic buildings, a sea of flowers, and cheerful English-speaking university student volunteers at every turn.[24] Huawei had helped China Mobile roll out an automated hotline to help visitors with any questions about hotels or transportation. Huawei's internal hospitality arm, Smartcom, prepared a lavish dinner party for VIP customers visiting to watch the Games.[25]

Now, four hours before the opening ceremony, rockets containing silver iodide began to fire into the air. They seeded rain in the clouds to Beijing's south to ensure that the skies stayed dry over the stadium to the north. The city had left nothing to chance.

Just after 8:00 p.m. on August 8, 2008—eight was an auspicious number—2,008 drummers began pounding in unison on rows of bronze drums. Fireworks shaped like twenty-nine enormous footprints exploded overhead, walking across the city's sky, an incredible feat of pyrotechnics. To ensure that each footprint was launched at the right choreographic moment, a telephone system had been set up, with the help of Huawei gear, to connect the twenty-nine sites so that each fireworks team knew when to launch.[26] Just to make sure it was perfect, the state TV broadcaster played a digitally rendered version of the firework footprints instead of a live feed. The meticulous Olympics preparations of the low-key Vice President Xi Jinping had paid off, and would help pave his rise to become the nation's most powerful leader in a generation.

Later, some Huawei engineers wistfully remarked that they had missed seeing the historic opening ceremony despite being right there in Beijing. They hadn't been allowed to turn on the TVs at their desks, lest it distract them from their important job of guarding the networks.

16

The Western Front

I n November 2010, Dan Hesse got a phone call.[1] Hesse was the CEO of Sprint Nextel, the third-largest wireless provider in the US behind Verizon and AT&T. The man on the line was Gary Locke, the US commerce secretary. Locke told Hesse that he and his colleagues knew Sprint was considering a bid from Huawei to expand its 4G network upgrade. He said they had concerns.

"It wasn't heavy-handed in any way—he actually made it clear this was Sprint's decision," Hesse recalled. "He wasn't telling me as a member of the government not to choose Huawei equipment. But they wanted to make sure I knew that they had security concerns with Huawei equipment going into our network."

China had only just rolled out 3G, but many nations, like the US, were moving on to 4G. The arrival of a new generation of mobile technology meant that telecom operators around the world were doing a once-in-a-decade overhaul of their networks. Contracts were open. Operators were entertaining offers.

Huawei was bidding vigorously for 4G projects around the world—including for the Sprint expansion in the US. The news raised alarms in Washington. "If Huawei builds the components for our cell towers in the U.S. 4G network, then every cell tower is a potential listening post for Beijing," Edward Timperlake, former director of technology assessment for the Pentagon, was quoted as saying in *The Washington Times*.[2] Sprint's previous 3G supplier, the Canadian networking giant Nortel, had gone bankrupt in 2009, driven out of business in part by its inability to match Huawei's low prices.

There were also murmurs over who was now representing Huawei: Admiral Bill Owens, the former Nortel CEO. Before he landed at Nortel, Owens had been the vice-chairman of the Joint Chiefs of Staff, the number-two officer in the US military.[3]

Now Secretary Locke told Hesse that if Sprint picked Huawei, there was a possibility that some US government agencies might no longer use Sprint due to network security concerns.

"It was a friendly call," Hesse said. "It wasn't threatening in any way. But he wanted to make sure that I knew."

I n August 2010, as talk of Huawei's Sprint bid circulated, eight Republican lawmakers sent an urgent letter to top officials in the Obama administration.[4] "Sprint Nextel supplies important equipment to the U.S. military and law enforcement agencies," they wrote.

"We are concerned that Huawei's position as a supplier of Sprint Nextel could create substantial risk for U.S. companies and possibly undermine U.S. national security."

This was followed by a letter from four lawmakers to the FCC requesting that the agency take measures to block Huawei from conducting business in the US. "The sensitivity of information transmitted in communications systems, as well as the potential for foreign espionage, requires that the U.S. government take decisive action," the letter said.

Huawei had been allowed to pick up some small contracts in the US, such as with ClearTalk in December 2004 to supply small patches of California and Arizona. But there was a lot more concern in Washington about Huawei being plugged into a major network. Would China's government potentially be able to listen in to calls through Huawei's equipment? Could the gear be hacked to disrupt the network? There was also considerable intrigue about why Owens was now on Team Huawei.

Intellectual-property infringement allegations also continued to dog Huawei. Fujitsu had written a stern letter to Ren Zhengfei in 2004, decrying that a Huawei employee had been caught at an industry conference removing the casing of a Fujitsu optical networking device and examining the circuit boards inside.[5] Fujitsu called this unlawful and said that it had turned the matter over to the FBI. In July 2010, Motorola sued Huawei, alleging that in the early aughts, the company had sought out proprietary details about Motorola's mobile base stations, with Ren himself allegedly involved in the meetings. Huawei called the lawsuit groundless, and it was quietly settled without the terms being disclosed.

When he was CEO of Nortel, Owens had explored the idea of a

Nortel-Huawei merger, meeting with Ren and Guo Ping, but ultimately abandoned it due to the likely hurdles of getting such a deal past Western regulators. But he had come away from the experience with a deep respect for Ren's management and vision. "As a military man I have known many clever and truly outstanding strategists," he'd later write. "I have rarely come across an individual more strategically oriented than Ren."[6]

After spending years in senior military leadership, Owens should have had no illusions about the potential for telecommunications equipment to be tapped and infiltrated by governments. But there were different schools of thought on just how sensitive the information traversing consumer networks was. In any event, government secrets and military data were kept not on public networks but on specialized systems with heightened security. And Owens often said that he felt the gravest risk facing the United States in his lifetime was a war with China. Each country getting a certain degree of visibility into the other's workings could help prevent a paranoid downward spiral into war. To this end, Owens had started something called the Sanya Initiative in 2008, an annual dialogue between retired American and Chinese generals and admirals.

Now Owens proposed to US officials that Huawei's equipment could be safely integrated into Sprint's network via a new US-based company called Amerilink that would oversee the security vetting of the gear, with the US government's close involvement. The chairman of Amerilink was Owens. "Huawei would not be involved in any way in Amerilink," Owens wrote. "Equipment and services would be delivered to Amerilink, tested, quality-controlled and delivered to Sprint. There would be no direct Huawei-to-Sprint interface."[7] Owens said that Amerilink was offering to open its board and all deliberations to the National Security Agency, and that such a deal would save Sprint hundreds of millions of dollars, as well as give Washington a new level of insight into Huawei as a company.

Huawei had other supporters too. Texas governor Rick Perry praised Ren in October 2010 for creating local jobs through Huawei's expanded North American headquarters in Plano and said Ren's straight-talking style reminded him of residents of the Lone Star State. "If you didn't know any better, you'd say he grew up out in West Texas," Perry said. "He wasn't sugarcoatin' it a lot."[8] Matt Bross, the BT CTO who had helped select Huawei for that crucial first contract, was named Huawei's global chief technology officer and one of two copresidents of Huawei USA.[9] At Amerilink, a former Sprint Nextel vice president, Kevin Packingham, had signed on as CEO. Amerilink's board included Gordon England, former US deputy secretary of defense and homeland security; former House majority leader Richard Gephardt; and former World Bank president James Wolfensohn. "It is doable," England told the *Financial Times*, in reference to Amerilink's ability to ensure that Huawei's technology was secure.[10]

Behind closed doors, Ren was skeptical about Huawei's chances, and he told Owens that he thought the company's bid would fail because of political opposition in Washington.[11]

A cross the Atlantic, British government officials were grappling with the same questions that Hesse faced at Sprint. Was having Huawei's gear in the network a security risk? If so, could the risk be mitigated?

Huawei had already been in major UK networks for years, having won a spot in BT's nationwide broadband upgrade in 2005, but London had been reconsidering its stance. "The British government said, 'Look, we don't want you to put any more Huawei equipment into UK networks,'" a Huawei executive recalled. "They said, 'It's not possible. It's a security risk for the UK.'"[12] After intensive efforts by Huawei to find a solution, British officials were convinced that the risk could be mitigated. Huawei's solution was something called "the Cell."

The Cell was located in a nondescript office complex[13] on the outskirts of Banbury, a quiet English town known for its spiced currant cakes. The Huawei facility featured all manner of security precautions. "It had a door that was bombproof," recalled one person who worked there and spoke on condition of anonymity. "There were no phones inside the secure area. . . . All the servers that contained the source code were in locked cages, and only one person had the key to the cages."[14]

The official name, the Huawei Cyber Security Evaluation Centre, was a mouthful, as was the acronym, HCSEC, so people had taken to calling it "the Cell." It was a center where UK officials could look under the hood of Huawei's gear to see for themselves if it was safe, the first such center that Huawei had opened in the world. In November 2010, Ken Hu, the early star salesman who was now the company's senior vice president and chairman of Huawei's Global Network Security Committee, flew over for the launch.[15] Huawei's executives were proud to have such a sophisticated facility in the UK. "They felt they were finally coming of age on the international scene, that they were being taken seriously as a supplier," recalled Gary Garner, an IBM consultant working with Huawei.[16]

The Cell wasn't too far from Cheltenham, where Britain's signals-intelligence agency, GCHQ, the British equivalent to the NSA, was based. This was convenient. What Huawei's press release about the Cell didn't mention, however, was just how deeply involved GCHQ was in the operation. "It was more like an arm of the British intelligence agencies, as opposed to being Huawei itself," said Chris Powell, a former UK government cybersecurity researcher who began working at the Cell in 2016. "People would say, 'Oh, you're trusting Huawei to check its own code.' And I just thought to myself, *If only you knew.*"[17]

Huawei technically owned the Cell and supplied the funding, but GCHQ ran the show. Without clearance, Huawei executives couldn't even access the center. The intelligence agency vetted prospective employees, requiring all staffers to have "Developed Vetting" security clearance, the level required for members of the British intelligence services.[18] It meant that they were cleared for frequent, uncontrolled access to classified information. GCHQ gave new staffers a security briefing and ensured that they signed the Official Secrets Act.

The first managing director of the Cell was Andrew Hopkins, a former deputy director for GCHQ and a forty-year veteran of British intelligence.[19] Other former GCHQ agents were the Cell's researchers. Some in London argued that the Cell's staff should be employed directly by GCHQ, not put on Huawei's payroll. At any rate, according to Powell, there was no contest when it came to loyalties: "People were, like, infinitely more loyal to the British government than they were to Huawei."

The Cell was soon finding vulnerabilities and pushing Huawei to fix them. One team looked at each product, one by one, while another looked for weaknesses in the broader systems. The Cell's researchers could find problems in the code, but they had little visibility into *why* these aberrations were there. "It's very difficult to tell the difference between a back door and a mistake," Powell said. "Every organization has bugs. And Huawei, at least at the beginning, had a significant amount of bugs—beyond anyone else." One such issue, according to someone who spoke on condition of anonymity, was devices all being set to the same default password. This person said that UK authorities received the Cell's reports before Huawei did.

There was more than a little dispute among UK officials about just how effective the Cell was at guaranteeing cybersecurity. But the existence of the center did a lot to reassure customers anyhow, and not only in the UK. "Since we set up this security center, I think it's a great help for our business growing not only in the UK but also the European market and other countries," Huawei's chairwoman, Sun Yafang, said in a speech during a visit to Britain.[20] Vince Cable, UK secretary of state for business, innovation, and skills during this time, later recalled that the government largely felt that any risks from Huawei's gear were containable. "There was some discussion, mainly from one or two conservative backbenchers who said that we were taking too many risks. But it wasn't very loud," he said.[21]

Huawei would continue to make extra efforts to win over the UK, seeing the market as its key foothold in the West. It would pour funds into hosting British politicians, seeking their favor. In late 2012, the British TV news program *Dispatches*, which airs on Channel 4, would report that Huawei had spent more than £90,000 ($144,000) over nearly two years on trips for British members of Parliament, according to the politicians' public filings of financial interests.[22] That included a £12,000 trip to Hong Kong and Shanghai for MP Mark

Hendrick and his wife in January 2011, a trip that Hendrick said he took "to consider the implications of Chinese technological investment in the UK."[23]

F or decades, Ren had looked askance at the vulgarity of hawking gizmos and gadgets to lay consumers. He was a discreet tradesman selling specialized products to specialized buyers. Ren also suspected that this buzzy new thing called a smartphone was overhyped. "We believe that the internet has not changed the essence of things," he told staff. "A car must be a car first, and tofu must be tofu."[24]

But amid Huawei's challenges in the West, Ren came around to the idea of a pivot into consumer electronics. Consumer gadgets could help Huawei soften its image overseas and gain acceptance in markets that were otherwise hard to crack. Smartphones were more innocuous than radio antennae, surveillance cameras, and submarine cables. Even as US officials were sounding the alarm over Huawei's Sprint bid, Best Buy outlets across America began carrying Huawei-branded Android tablets.[25] Consumers around the world began to see ads for a new brand called Huawei.

Due to years of bureaucratic delays, China was very late to the smartphone revolution. The country finally launched 3G networks in 2009, making it possible to use smartphones like iPhones domestically, a decade after the first 3G network was launched in Japan. But smartphones had been made in China since long before they could be used there. Indeed, the manufacturing center of Taiwan's Foxconn, the world's largest contract manufacturer of smartphones and the primary assembler of Apple's iPhone, coincidentally sat just across the road from Huawei's Shenzhen offices.

It took a while for Huawei's own executives to come around to the idea that Huawei was now a consumer brand and that they had to like its phones—or at least pretend to like them. When Ken Hu, Huawei's deputy chairman, opened an account on Weibo, China's answer to Twitter, netizens were amused to see that each of his posts carried the telltale auto-stamp showing that it had been posted from an iPhone.

In the end, Huawei wasn't able to convince the doubters. Soon after Secretary Locke's phone call to Hesse, Sprint rejected Huawei's bid.

Hesse maintains that he didn't tell his team members about Locke's call, as he wanted them to make their recommendations independently. Huawei was "very strong on price," he said, but what it lacked was "reference accounts."[26] The company did not have a track record of successfully building other large networks in the US, which Hesse said was the biggest thing they were looking for. "We would have been their first big account," he said. "You're taking a big risk. You're kind of their first marquee customer in North America."

Hesse said that Huawei's inclusion on the bidding shortlist probably helped Sprint get a better deal from the winning vendors: Ericsson, Alcatel-Lucent, and Samsung. "It caused them to sharpen their pencils and be more aggressive on price than they would have been," he said. "They knew they had to be competitive."

On the Huawei side, executives felt that it had simply been a political call. "We came face-to-face with the political reality of Washington, and the fact that it was an election year," Owens told a journalist.[27]

Hu texted Ren the news of the loss of the contract, reporting that Huawei's US team was in tears.[28] Ren read it and laughed. It was a shame, he said, but there was also an upside. He no longer harbored any illusions.

"I can finally put down that mental burden," Ren told his staff. "We no longer have to have so many worries, no longer have to compromise with them. . . . The result of America's arrogance and bias is that we are pushing out our chests and competing directly."[29]

17

Revolution

THE ARAB SPRING: 2011

R en Zhengfei was in Iraq in early 2011 when Huawei's Middle East chief, Yi Xiang, who was traveling with him, got a phone call. The Chinese embassy in Bahrain was urging Huawei to pull out of the country.[1] A wave of unrest that people were calling the Arab Spring was intensifying. Bahrain, where Huawei's Middle East headquarters were based, was no longer safe.[2] The Chinese embassy in Turkey was also appealing to Huawei and other Chinese companies for help with organizing an emergency evacuation of tens of thousands of Chinese nationals from Libya.[3] One of Ren's contacts in Iraq, a prominent businessman, urged him to make haste in departing, telling him that Iraq's roads were about to be sealed off. The window for safe passage out was closing.

The Middle East was the beating heart of Huawei's global empire. This was, in part, due to Huawei's struggles to make progress in the

United States and other Western countries. Many of the governments in the Middle East had complicated relationships with Washington and were interested in forging closer ties with China. "In the Middle East, the decisions are not taken just because of some news in the West," said one former Huawei manager in Saudi Arabia. Huawei's first 3G network customer overseas was Etisalat in the United Arab Emirates. It now had some four thousand employees across the region.[4] Since 2007, Huawei had sold not only networking gear itself but also managed services, or outsourced tech support, to operators around the world. This meant that Huawei's engineers were contractually obligated to be available if a network operator was experiencing problems. With the Arab Spring turning violent, Ren set off across the Middle East to steel his staff's nerves.

During his visits to Iraq, Afghanistan, Libya, and Mali, Ren told Huawei employees that while he sympathized with family members' concerns over their safety, they couldn't leave their posts without properly handing off their work. "You can't flee unconditionally," he said. "Our professional ethos is to maintain the stability of the network." He reminded them that theirs was a special vocation. "Tofu shops, fried dough stands, and the like can be shut down at any time, but we cannot."[5] Ren advised his staff that they should "never" interfere in the politics of any country. "If we give up the network's stability, then even more people will be sacrificed."[6]

Huawei helped the Chinese embassy in Turkey facilitate the evacuation of Chinese nationals from Libya, but some of Huawei's own engineers stayed behind. The company had mobile and landline networks across Libya and also had an ongoing contract for a submarine cable.[7] "Huawei might be the only foreign company remaining there," a Chinese newspaper reported.[8] Interviewed by local press in late

February, the wife of one Huawei staffer reported that her husband was still there, and that Huawei had stocked lots of food and water. "You could hear the sound of machine guns all the time," she said after getting off an evacuation flight.[9]

Ren and his team also decided to stay put in Bahrain, despite the Chinese embassy urging them to withdraw.[10] They had a fledgling business relationship with mobile operator Viva Bahrain, owned by the Saudi Telecommunications Company, and wanted to honor their commitments. Huawei set up a fourteen-person emergency response team to monitor its customer's network, which was nearly at a standstill at times as protesters thronged the streets.[11] In mid-March, Bahrain's king declared a state of emergency and sent thousands of security forces out to crush the protests. In the chaos, network sites were at risk of losing power. The Huawei team raced out to hook up gasoline generators to keep the network running.[12]

Ren ended his visit to Iraq abruptly. His contact arranged a series of armed cars to shuttle him out of the country. Ren was apparently worse for wear after his trip. Meeting him weeks later in Shenzhen, *Financial Times* editor Lionel Barber found that Ren was ill but still anxious to keep the appointment. As Ren sat down, an assistant placed a silver spittoon at his feet while another prepared acupuncture.[13]

M uch remains unclear about Huawei's role during those chaotic months in the Middle East, with Huawei employees having mentioned only fragments here and there. What is known is that Huawei made a push to sell its surveillance solutions in the region during this period. Four days after Tunisia's president, Zine el-Abidine Ben Ali, fled to Saudi Arabia—the first leader to fall in the Arab Spring—Huawei announced it was launching a Middle East enterprise business unit that would sell "Safe City" surveillance solutions to governments.[14] Huawei sent a truck equipped with demo Safe City gear on a tour through the region, and it wended its way from the UAE to Saudi Arabia.

It is still unknown whether Huawei received requests from Middle East customers to help track protesters, censor online content, or otherwise help regimes stay in power during the Arab Spring. However, *The Wall Street Journal* reported that Huawei had earlier pitched such services to Iranian officials.[15] The paper noted that Huawei had signed a contract to provide Iran's largest mobile operator with technology that would allow police to track people based on their cell-phone locations. "Many of the technologies Huawei supports in Iran—such as location services—are available on Western networks as well," the paper said. "The difference is that, in the hands of repressive regimes, it can be a critical tool in helping to quash dissent." *The Journal* added that Huawei had contracts for managed services in Iran—by which it carried out the operation of the network for telecom operators—and that during the 2009 protests, it had carried out government orders to suspend text messaging and block Skype, which was used by dissidents to communicate. Huawei disputed having blocked the services. *The Journal* said it had interviewed three Iranian student activists who said they were arrested shortly after turning on their phones.

Huawei executives have confirmed over the years that the gear they build tracks users' locations for their customers, which they say is a standard function of all telecommunications networks, regardless of the brand. "If you think about what telecommunications does, it tries to connect you with a base station, wherever you are, in order to connect you to the network," Huawei's global cybersecurity officer, John Suffolk, once said in a UK parliamentary hearing. "It therefore does know where you are, because it knows where the information is coming from. In that context, telecommunications networks from all vendors know where you are, so as to connect you to those networks. Huawei's equipment is no different from anyone else's equipment."[16]

Pushed by parliamentarians to confirm whether Huawei would follow even "wicked" laws in third countries, Suffolk replied, "Our starting point and our end point—I am sorry to repeat this—is that we understand the laws in the country. That can be a difficult thing to do, but once we understand the law, we will operate within the law. We do not make judgments."

By this point, Huawei had been hawking its Safe City video-surveillance solutions for several years, to mixed success, landing one of its earliest contracts in Pakistan in 2009.[17] The Middle East now gave this fledgling unit a boost. In the first half of 2011, Huawei's Enterprise Business Group saw its global sales soar by 80 percent from a year earlier.

The idea of a Safe City had been dreamed up by IBM as it sought to drum up sales in the wake of the 2008 financial crisis.[18] IBM touted its "Smarter Cities" as being able to streamline paperwork, save energy, and prevent pollution through the use of video cameras and other sensors hooked up to big data algorithms. But what made officials really sit up was the prospect of a new, omniscient sort of crime fighting.

IBM had a long history as a supplier of technologies to police, and now it had helped the NYPD build the Real Time Crime Center, an $11 million state-of-the-art facility with a two-story video wall, satellite imaging, and integration with databases holding more than thirty-three billion public records.[19] IBM executives went around the world selling this next-generation policing vision in which crimes could conceivably be predicted before they took place. "Ensuring public safety is crucial to cities' quality of life," IBM CEO Sam Palmisano said in Shanghai during a speech about Smarter Cities. "This no longer appears to be a losing battle. New York and other cities are using advanced data analysis to achieve historic reductions in crime."[20]

Later on, during the Black Lives Matter protests and amid scrutiny over ingrained racial bias in policing, IBM would walk back its marketing about its technology's ability to predict crimes. But at the time, the idea was alluring to many governments. As IBM traveled around China promoting Smarter Cities in 2009, China's premier, Wen Jiabao, also gave the concept his seal of approval.[21] That year, Huawei launched its own versions, which it called "Smart Cities" and "Safe Cities."

In December 2011, Ren, sixty-seven, announced he was stepping back to allow younger hands to steer the company. "I increasingly don't understand the technology, increasingly don't understand finance, and only half understand management," he told his staff. "If I can't treat our group kindly and democratically, and fully unleash the talents of all our heroes, I will have achieved nothing."[22] Without offering details, Ren also disclosed that he'd had two cancer surgeries over the years.[23] He blamed it in part on overwork: "I was too tired. My body just collapsed from fatigue."

People had wondered for years who Ren's successor might be. Now Ren revealed there would be not one successor but three: Guo Ping, Eric Xu, and Ken Hu would serve as "rotating CEOs," with each taking a six-month stint at the helm. Such a management setup was a curiosity. It brought with it the risk of the company's strategy swinging back and forth every few months if the three rotating CEOs could not work in unison. Ren also risked the rotating CEOs quitting for full-fledged CEO positions at other companies. But the benefits of such an arrangement were also clear. Ren could delay fully handing over the reins to any one person while training several executives to be up to the task. Huawei was now the number-three vendor of wireless gear globally, behind only Sweden's Ericsson and Finland's Nokia. It had surpassed the French-US giant Alcatel-Lucent and the US's Motorola. In 2010, Huawei's annual revenue of $27 billion was higher than that of Google, McDonald's, or Coca-Cola.

The three successors had all been faithful Huawei employees for more than eighteen years, and each had played a pivotal role. Guo Ping had been Huawei's early face to the West, spearheading Huawei's defense against Cisco's lawsuit and negotiating the potential takeovers of Marconi and Nortel. He'd overseen the company's early entry into the European consumer sector with its 3G Wi-Fi dongles. More recently, in 2011, Guo had been overseeing Huawei's settlement of a legal dispute with Motorola over intellectual property, as well as Symantec's exit from a joint venture with the company. Guo had been so devoted to his work that he'd missed the births of both his children while on Huawei business, which he told colleagues was something his family members continued to hold over his head.[24] Sometime around the year 2010, Guo was diagnosed with lung cancer.[25] The doctor told him he had six months to live. "They said that around 80 percent of people with cancer die from the fear," Guo told colleagues. "So I said I would believe in myself, and I would not give up easily." Guo recovered and resumed his work, although going forward, he would spend a little more time on rest and exercise.

Eric Xu, the only PhD of the three, had steered Huawei's fledgling wireless business in the early 2000s—the company had landed its first 3G contracts in Hong Kong and the United Arab Emirates under his watch—and its early foray into cell phones. Xu had managed some of Huawei's international partnerships, such as the setup of a joint venture with Germany's Siemens and, in 2010, negotiations with India's government involving the setup of a factory in the country to try to allay security concerns over its equipment. Before becoming one of the rotating CEOs, he'd worked his way up to global president of R&D. Some of Huawei's foreign executives found him to be the most distant of the three. "Eric was a cipher to me," one recalled, adding that Ken Hu and Guo Ping were "always on my calendar, but Eric, never."

Ken Hu had risen through the ranks of Huawei's domestic sales team, then served as president of Huawei Latin America and later chairman of the board of Huawei USA. He'd represented Huawei when it launched "the Cell," the center where UK officials could check Huawei's software code for security vulnerabilities. He would increasingly become Huawei's designated spokesperson at international conferences. His account on Weibo, China's equivalent to Twitter, reflected his jet-setting schedule—oysters one day, Japanese ramen the next—as he traveled the world on Huawei business. "Ken Hu is perhaps the most well-rounded of the three," a former Huawei executive said. "He's strong in many areas, though there isn't one area where he is particularly outstanding. When a company is that large, perhaps that's the kind of person needed."

After the announcement of the rotating CEOs, many thought that Ren had abandoned the idea of a family succession. His son, Ren Ping, remained in a lower post running Smartcom, Huawei's in-house hospitality arm, which encompassed Huawei's banquets, hotels, receptionists, and chauffeur services for guests.[26] Smartcom operated a five-star hotel near Huawei's campus for visiting executives. The wow factor of Huawei's elaborate hospitality was a crucial ingredient in its efforts to win over global customers. Ren wanted foreign executives who arrived in China with preconceived notions of the nation's technological level and manufacturing standards to be bowled over by the perfection they experienced from Smartcom's service staff. Yet Smartcom was far afield from Huawei's core technical business, and wasn't seen as a stepping stone for higher leadership. "The longer you work in this industry, the more you will feel inadequate," Ren Ping wrote of his work at Smartcom. "You must constantly study and spend all your time honing your skill, and still you may not make a big name for yourself."[27] Ren's brother, Steven Ren, was also still at Huawei as a vice president but did not appear to be groomed for succession.[28] Steven Ren once called his career at Huawei "just ordinary, without any grand achievements to show for it."[29]

Out of Ren's family, his daughter Meng Wanzhou had risen the highest at Huawei, getting promoted to CFO and becoming a member of the board of directors as part of the management overhaul.[30] Meng had told colleagues that the CFO position was one with upward potential. "In the vast majority of companies, the CFO becomes an assistant to the CEO, helping the CEO achieve business targets," she said. "CFO is a good position for training executives. It's both specialized and comprehensive."[31] But Meng lacked the engineering chops that Huawei's staff widely believed their leader needed. And it was unclear if she had the temperament for leadership. Ren roused his staff with sweeping speeches about historic battles, but Meng's essays for Huawei's internal publications were not quite as inspiring and often detailed her vacations. In one essay, she wrote that the lavender fields of France's Provençal countryside were her favorite place in the world. "That day my dream came true," she wrote of her visit to the lavender fields. "Long in servitude, I had finally returned to nature."[32]

E arlier in 2011, an open letter under Ken Hu's name had been issued to the US government. In it, he pushed back against accusations of security risks inherent in Huawei's equipment and suggested that the US government conduct an investigation to clear the company's name. "We sincerely hope that the United States government will carry out a formal investigation on any concerns it may have about Huawei," the letter said. "We believe the results of any thorough government investigation will prove that Huawei is a normal commercial institution and nothing more."[33]

If the missive was meant to be just a literary flourish, it backfired. US lawmakers decided to take Hu at his word. "I appreciate that invitation, and I gladly accepted," Mike Rogers, chair of the House Permanent Select Committee on Intelligence (HPSCI), told a Huawei representative. "We decided to give Huawei that investigation."[34]

The hearing was set for September 2012. The probe also covered other Chinese companies, including ZTE. But Rogers declared from the outset that Huawei was the "800-pound gorilla in the room."[35]

A chill came over Huawei's DC office. The company's senior leadership felt that the aggressive public relations campaign the DC office had orchestrated had boomeranged. The American managers felt that headquarters now viewed them as double agents and kept them out of the loop. This was not just paranoia: in July 2012, a leaked FBI affidavit had revealed that ZTE USA's general counsel, Ashley Yablon, who had previously worked at Huawei, was serving as an informant. It was hard to know what Yablon or others were telling the feds.[36]

"People in the industry often say Ren Zhengfei is as mysterious as he is great," Ren told his staff in a speech. "This is actually not true. I understand myself better. I keep a low profile, not because I'm attempting to build myself up but because I am scared."[37]

18

The Hearing

HOUSE INVESTIGATION: 2012

hortly before 10:00 a.m. on September 13, 2012, Charles Ding sat down at a gleaming wooden desk in room HVC-210 at the US Capitol Visitors Center. He had a fresh haircut,[1] a pale-blue tie, and a stiff black suit. There was a microphone, several black binders filled with notes, and bottled water. Behind him, the room was packed with spectators, sitting claustrophobically close. In front, two rows of grim Americans in suits stared him down from an elevated platform.

In the middle of the platform were two solid, squarish men: one light-haired with a touch of white coming in at his temples, one dark-haired with heavy eyebrows. The blond one was Rep. Mike Rogers (R-MI), a former army officer and FBI special agent. The dark-haired one was Rep. Charles "Dutch" Ruppersberger (D-MD), a former assistant state's attorney in Baltimore. The two cochairs of the House

Permanent Select Committee on Intelligence were from different parties, but they worked well together and liked to joke about divine approval of their partnership: the first time they shook hands over a deal, an earthquake happened to shake the Capitol Building at that very moment.[2] Their staff had spent nearly a year preparing for this hearing, talking to Huawei's customers and rivals and sending letter after question-filled letter to Huawei itself. They had flown to Hong Kong to interview Ren Zhengfei. They had declared that they'd use the full scope of the committee's powers to uncover the truth.

Round-faced, bespectacled, and soft-spoken, Ding was now the face of Huawei in America. He was a seventeen-year Huawei veteran.[3] In 2010, he'd been appointed Huawei's chief US representative after spending much of his career in the Middle East, where he'd worked his way up to regional president. Many would have considered such a Washington posting a reward. He'd moved into a comfortable house in Bethesda with his wife and children. But now, as he looked out at the stern faces, it was unclear if it was a reward or a punishment. "They are planning a massacre," a contact had said in an email to one of Ding's deputies.[4]

The gavel sounded.

"Call the committee to order today for the purposes of an investigative hearing into the possible threat posed by telecommunication companies influenced by a foreign nation."[5]

Rogers told the room that Ding—along with his counterpart from ZTE—had been called there to answer the committee's questions. He said there were rumors of "back doors." There were questions about how closely Huawei was associated with China's government. There were reports of trade-secret theft.

Charles Ding, Huawei's senior vice president and chief representative in the US, at the House Permanent Select Committee on Intelligence's hearing in September 2012.

"We must get to the truth and see if these companies are tied to or influenced by the Chinese government," Rogers said.

Now Ding was asked to stand and raise his right hand.

"Mr. Ding, do you swear or affirm that the statements you will make to this committee will be the truth, the whole truth, and nothing but the truth?"

Ding swore they would be.

C hairman Rogers, Ranking Member Ruppersberger, members of the committee, my name is Charles Ding. I have been with Huawei since 1995."[6] Ding began his prepared remarks in English.

He gave only a slight introduction of himself. He didn't tell them that he had been one of Huawei's earliest staffers in the Middle East. He and his team had landed their first contract in Saudi Arabia in the early days and, later on, their first international 3G contract outside Greater China—with Etisalat in the UAE.[7] Etisalat's executives had been skeptical of Huawei, but Ding and his team had methodically eliminated their objections, one by one, until Etisalat could no longer find a reason to reject Huawei's bid. When Huawei was declared the winner, Ding told his team, "We did each task perfectly, so the customer could no longer find a reason to reject us."

Ding had met with US officials as early as 2006, when he briefed the US consulate in Guangzhou about Huawei's university recruiting programs.[8] When he was transferred to Washington, he started going by Charles instead of his Chinese name, Ding Shaohua. The going was much harder in America, but they still made progress. They'd won 4G bids with smaller operators: SpeedConnect in Michigan, United Wireless in rural Kansas. They'd opened R&D centers in Santa Clara, California, and Bridgewater, New Jersey, and upgraded their headquarters in Plano, Texas.

Ding was not the only one being grilled that day. There was another man sitting to his left: ZTE's senior vice president, Zhu Jinyun. He wore a jet-black suit, his hair slicked with gel. Behind closed doors, Huawei executives liked to protest how unfair it was that Huawei was always lumped in with its crosstown rival, ZTE; after all, ZTE was state-owned, and Huawei was not, so it shouldn't have been in the same boat. By the same token, ZTE didn't like being lumped in with Huawei. It might be state-owned, but it also had a publicly listed unit, which entailed opening the company's books more transparently than Huawei ever had.

Now ZTE's Zhu seemed intent on drawing a distinction between the two, and one had to admit that some of his lines were snappier. "I'm pleased to appear today to represent ZTE, one of the world's remarkable companies," he said. "We believe that ZTE is the *most* transparent publicly owned telecom company in China," he went on, "and that ZTE is the *best* choice to work in concert with the Congress and the United States government."[9]

As for Ding, he declared in his opening statement that Huawei had not engaged in any of the improper behavior of which it was accused and that, indeed, it would not be willing to risk ruining its reputation. "Our customers throughout the world trust Huawei. We would never do *anything* that undermines that trust. It would be immensely foolish for Huawei to risk involvement in national security or economic espionage."[10]

N

ow the questioning began. Furrowing his brow, Rogers asked Ding about "unauthorized beaconing" in Huawei's equipment, cases where overseas Huawei gear was allegedly found chattering back to China. He said there were also reports of "anomalies" in the code that would allow unauthorized access. "Can you explain to me, sir, why that might be?"[11]

"Mr. Chairman, there are no back doors in any of Huawei's equipment," Ding said. "I'm also not aware of the issues you've mentioned just now. . . . Huawei has never and will never harm any country or any of our customers." He shook his head emphatically and waited for the translator to repeat his words in English.[12]

Rogers did not look convinced. The Huawei team had earlier discussed whether it was better for Ding to reply in English or Chinese. Ding had settled on Chinese, followed by English translation, to avoid slipups. But there was the risk of looking like they were dithering, like they were trying to run out the clock by answering each question twice.

Rogers turned to the question of Huawei's Communist Party committee. The party committees within private companies were an object of fascination and concern for Westerners. There was haziness around what kind of powers they had—if they were like a sort of book club for employees to discuss Marxism after hours, or if they were actually meddling in major business decisions. Rogers noted that they had so far failed to get details on the compositions of those committees at Huawei and ZTE and their internal scope of influence.

Ding acknowledged that Americans might find it strange for a private company to have a party committee but said it was a requirement under Chinese law. Even Walmart and General Motors had them in their China operations. "In Huawei, however, I have not seen the party committee participating in any business management or decision-making," he said.[13]

His answer perhaps understated the role of the party committee at Huawei. It operated as a second, arguably more powerful human-resources department. Since 2006, the party committee had been vested with the power to reject managerial appointments or to fire managers. The company's top executives were sometimes called in to make self-criticisms before the committee. In 2009, Huawei's party organizations had ordered two managers fired after determining that they retaliated against a software engineer who was planning to quit.[14] The party organizations had also reviewed three thousand proposed managerial promotions, vetoing thirty-five and stipulating improvements for fifty-one of them.[15]

By late 2011, Huawei had more than 30,000 party members,[16] out of some 140,000 employees. The company's party cell leaders pledged that they would not "say or do anything that will cause negative effects for the company or for society" and that they would help maintain stability.[17]

"The party committee in Huawei is focusing on promoting professional ethics and also employee caring," Ding said. "Thank you."[18]

Rogers asked him to name the members of the committee. Ding coughed up the name of the party secretary, Zhou Daiqi—who had succeeded the founding party secretary, Madam Chen Zhufang—but Rogers wasn't satisfied. He wanted a full list, past members included. "I don't think there would be a problem," Ding said. "I think we can contact Professor Zhou Daiqi for that list off-line."[19]

Rogers turned the floor over to Ruppersberger. The former Baltimore prosecutor came out with guns blazing. "If you want to do business in the United States," he told Ding and Zhu, "then you have to tell your Chinese government to stop cyberattacking our businesses." Ruppersberger expressed concern that the two companies had declined to answer some of the earlier written questions by citing China's state-secret law. He asked Ding what Huawei would do if the party asked it for information from its customers. "And I want a direct answer to that."

Ding replied that Huawei would not be instigated by any third-party government, including China's, into harming any other country. "We believe business is business, and this is very sure."

"Even if that meant by denying your government, you would go to jail?"

"Huawei operates complying to laws and regulations. If Huawei had not . . . violated any law, how can the government—or why will they put us in jail?"[20]

Ruppersberger did not seem satisfied by this response, but he allowed the questioning to move on to Iran.

"We've heard that your companies sell equipment to Iran, perhaps in violation of US sanctions," Rep. Sue Myrick (R-NC) asked. "So, Mr. Ding, does your company sell equipment to Iran?"

"Congresswoman, Huawei, just like other Western vendors in Iran, we just perform our normal business in that country. And while we do that, we abide by all the applicable laws and regulations."

"I also want to ask you: Has your company sold equipment to the Iranian government?"

"We have never provided any equipment to the Iranian government. All of—we provided are only for commercial, civilian use."[21]

Now Rep. Adam Schiff (D-CA) circled back to a variation on Ruppersberger's question. He read aloud a line from Article 11 of China's State Security Law: "'A state security organ may inspect the electronic communication instruments and appliances and other similar equipment and installations belonging to any organization or individual.'"

"If the Chinese government or the Chinese Communist Party were to come to you, Mr. Ding . . . are you not required to give them access?"

"Thank you for your question, and it's nice to see you again, Congressman. I personally do not know clearly about such law in China. And if Huawei is put into that situation, I think we would say no."

"Would you agree, though, Mr. Ding, that the plain language of Article 11 provides that the state may inspect your communications equipment?"

"As to the specific article you mentioned, I have not seen that, and I would not be able to explain or comment on that."

Schiff was not willing for this to be the last word. "I think you are too well-informed . . . to be unfamiliar with the laws that directly apply to your industry," he said. "The plain language of Chinese law would require you to make your equipment available to the Chinese government upon their request. And I see no opportunity for you to fight that in the Chinese court system. And I yield back, Mr. Chairman."[22]

The questions continued, fast and thick: *How many of the banks that finance Huawei are state-owned? Does the party influence those banks? Was Cisco's code in Huawei's equipment? Who determines the price of shares in the company's employee ownership program? Does Huawei plan to continue purchasing US companies?* Ding fielded them as best he could. He spoke softly, sometimes tapping his hand emphatically as he spoke. At one point, he held up a three-ring binder to illustrate the wealth of detail that Huawei had shared with the committee.

Ding had almost survived the gauntlet. Now there was time for just one more question. Rep. Luis Gutiérrez (D-IL) asked Ding why Huawei was more welcome in the UK than in the US. It was a good question. The answer was not obvious. Washington and London shared intelligence, so it stood to reason that they would have a similar evaluation of Huawei. Yet they didn't.

Over the summer, Huawei's chairwoman, Sun Yafang, had chit-chatted with Prince Charles at a London trade event, with the prince asking her what she thought of investing in the UK.[23] Just two days before the hearing, Ren had met with Prime Minister David Cameron at Ten Downing Street, with Cameron declaring that Britain was "open for business." Indeed, Huawei was the largest Chinese investor in the UK.[24]

"In all of those countries Huawei operates in," Ding said, "we always hope we can have booming development in these markets."

"Well, you didn't answer the question," Gutiérrez pressed. "I asked specifically why was it that the challenges that you have in the United States—you overcame them in the United Kingdom, and I didn't hear an answer to that."

"I think the United Kingdom's government also values cybersecurity a lot," Ding ventured. "We communicated with the British government about what would be good solutions to cybersecurity issues."[25]

The UK and US's divergence in opinion on Huawei was not something that policymakers had ever explained clearly. It might have had something to do with each country's deep-seated view of its relationship to the rest of the world. "I think it might be because the Americans and the Chinese are more equal in terms of competition, perhaps," ventured one British national who worked at Huawei's cybersecurity center in the UK. "I don't think the UK could ever compete with China in terms of its economy. Politically, I've always seen America as being much more anti-Chinese than in Europe."[26]

Sitting before the US lawmakers, Ding dodged the question of why the Americans were more hostile than the Brits. And then the clock ran out.

"I can say I'm a little disappointed today," Rogers said as he wrapped up. "I was hoping for more transparency, more directness."

It was "very concerning," he added, that Ding had claimed not to be aware of certain details of Chinese law on disclosing information to authorities. He said that various inconsistencies in the statements worried him.

"So with that, this meeting is adjourned."[27] Rogers hammered the gavel, the corners of his mouth turned downward. He stood up, gathered his papers, and walked out.

The House Permanent Select Committee on Intelligence issued its report in October. The committee expressed dissatisfaction with Huawei's evasion of questions, including queries about the five original investors and how Ren had come to know them. It recommended that Huawei and ZTE be shut out of US government systems, particularly sensitive ones. It further recommended that US companies stop buying from Huawei and ZTE. It also suggested that US regulators block the two companies from acquiring US firms. "Huawei and ZTE cannot be trusted to be free of foreign state influence and thus pose a security threat to the United States and to our systems," it said.[28]

The committee was also irked by Huawei's reticence about Ren's work during his years in the military. "Huawei refused to describe Mr. Ren's full military background," the committee's report groused. "Huawei refused to state to whom he reported when he was in the military."

The report would immediately become political fodder. President Barack Obama's reelection campaign seized on it the day it was published, using it to blast the incumbent's Republican challenger, Mitt Romney, by reminding voters that Romney's company, Bain Capital, had been a part of Huawei's ill-fated bid to purchase 3Com in 2007. "The House Intelligence Committee concluded that a Chinese tech firm that previously partnered with Bain Capital on an attempted deal from which Romney stood to profit poses such a threat to our national security that it should be banned from doing business in the United States," an Obama campaign spokesman told *Politico.* "But Romney refused, despite requests from his fellow Republicans, to oppose the deal that could have put our security at risk."[29]

The report would prove to have lasting influence beyond the political moment, and it would be cited repeatedly by US officials and foreign governments over the years. "It was the first US government entity to put on paper what a lot of folks already knew was happening in the national security space," said Andy Keiser, former chief of staff for Congressman Mike Rogers. "This was an official report. It was no longer being conveyed in a hushed tone."[30]

Australia had joined the United States, citing cybersecurity concerns when it banned Huawei from bidding for its next-generation broadband network in March 2012. But the anti-Huawei camp was a small minority in the world. Even some other members of the Five Eyes intelligence alliance—comprising Australia, Canada, New Zealand, the United Kingdom, and the United States—were reluctant to follow suit.

Shortly after the ban by Australia, New Zealand prime minister John Key was asked by a domestic lawmaker whether Huawei should continue to be allowed in the nation's broadband infrastructure. "We are comfortable with the current arrangements," Key said. He pointed out that Huawei wasn't banned from all business in Australia, only from next-generation broadband contracts. "If it is so unwelcome in Australia, I was amazed to find out that it has just become the official sponsor of the Canberra Raiders."[31]

As 2012 drew to a close, Huawei was the world's top telecom vendor, having deployed more than five hundred mobile networks, including in sixty-eight capital cities around the world. The company's fixed-line switches and routers were being used by forty-five of the fifty top carriers in the world. Its fledgling smartphone business was number three in the world in sales, just behind Samsung and Apple. Huawei's products now reached three billion people: two-fifths of humanity.

19

Low Visibility

THE IRAN AFFAIR: 2013

Meng Wanzhou traveled to Beijing in January 2013 to hold her first press conference amid China's worst smog in years. The haze was so thick that it had shut down schools and grounded planes; years of careless industrialization had caught up with the nation. The reporters were intrigued by forty-year-old Cathy Meng appearing from behind the curtain at such a moment. Hardly anyone in the press had seen a member of the Ren family in the flesh, rain or shine (or fog).

The appearance seemed to be at least partly in response to the criticism of opacity that had been leveled against Huawei at the House hearing the previous year. Meng told the gathered reporters that her father owned a 1.4 percent stake in Huawei, with the remaining shares divided among some sixty thousand employees, and she promised that Huawei was going to be sharing more information about its ownership and operations going forward. She said that the company had distributed $2 billion in dividends to employee shareholders the previous year.

In an effort to soften the company's image, Meng even shared a few personal details. The *Financial Times* reported that she was a mother of two who liked to go on power walks along the Shenzhen shoreline on weekends, and the business daily also described her as a fast talker with an agreeable smile.[1] "He was a forbearing father when I was little, and he has been a strict father ever since I entered Huawei," she was quoted as saying about Ren Zhengfei. A local reporter even ventured to ask an impertinent question about whether there was any truth to the rumor that she had married William Xu, the early chip engineer who was now head of Huawei's enterprise business division.[2] Meng acknowledged that the rumor was widespread, but she said it was untrue. She noted that her husband wasn't in the telecom industry and that they had a ten-year-old boy and a four-year-old girl together. This was the truth but not entirely the whole truth—Carlos Liu, whom she had married in 2007, had been Huawei's representative in Mexico before leaving the company to work in the investment field.

Meng's appearance garnered largely favorable reviews, even as reporters pointed out that many questions about exactly how Huawei was controlled and how it operated remained a mystery. There were enough whispers about her being groomed for succession that Ren felt the need to clear the air. A couple months later, he told a meeting of shareholding employees that none of his four relatives working at Huawei would be his successors. "I am saying this clearly to everyone to reduce suspicions, and so you will not waste your energy," he said. Ren said his successor must have vision, a deep understanding of customer needs, the ability to manage such a sprawling company, and the disposition not to rest on their laurels. "None of my family members have these abilities, and as a result, they will never enter the succession sequence," he said.[3]

M eng barely had a few days to enjoy the glow of her soft launch to the press before she was in the headlines again, this time for a much more unflattering reason.

For months, a Reuters investigative reporter named Steve Stecklow had been steadily digging into the Iran businesses of Huawei and its crosstown rival, ZTE. Indeed, Stecklow's reporting on ZTE's shipment of US technology to Iran the previous year had prompted the Commerce Department to launch an investigation into the company.[4] Late in 2012, Stecklow had revealed that a company called Skycom had offered to sell nearly 1.3 billion euros' worth of embargoed Hewlett-Packard equipment to Iran's leading mobile operator in 2010, which would have violated US sanctions on Iran. Skycom appeared to have very close ties to Huawei, Stecklow wrote, with staffers at the Skycom office in Tehran carrying Huawei badges and some employees' résumés saying they worked at "Skycom-Huawei."

Now, as Stecklow and his team scrutinized Skycom's corporate filings in Hong Kong, they came across Meng Wanzhou's name in Skycom's list of board members. There was a panicked scramble at Skycom and Huawei when they learned of Reuters' inquiries, an employee later recalled to US prosecutors.

"We are in trouble," the employee recalled a colleague saying at Skycom's office in Iran.[5]

"They found out about the daughter of the chairman," another said.

As Stecklow reported, Skycom's corporate filings showed that Huawei's CFO, Meng Wanzhou, had served on the company's board from 2008 to 2009.[6] This meant that Huawei's dealings in Iran could not be dismissed as the errancy of a few lower-level employees working beyond the purview of top management. Ren's daughter would have known about the business, and by extension, Ren himself likely would have too. Stecklow's article quoted Huawei as saying that its business in Iran was in compliance with all applicable laws.

Ren and his team were beginning to realize just how different doing business outside China really was. The country's entire economic boom had been based on entrepreneurs pushing the bounds of what they could legally do—"crossing the river by feeling the stones." As the nation emerged from total state control under Maoism, there were many capitalist practices that officials could not officially endorse, due to the apparent conflict with socialist theory, but that they would tacitly approve by turning a blind eye. As a result, the most fearless entrepreneurs—the roguish ones who erred on the side of asking for forgiveness instead of permission—had been the ones who'd reaped the biggest rewards of the market. Huawei fit such a profile. It had been founded in 1987 as a private company under a Shenzhen pilot program, without anyone knowing if such companies would be allowed in the long term or if they would be a brief experiment. In a nascent market free of conflict-of-interest restrictions, it had conquered the domestic landscape through a series of tie-ups with local telecom bureaus.

Such a fearlessness had served Huawei well in its early years, but this trait was now getting the company into trouble. In a memoir,

Ashley Yablon, the assistant general counsel for Huawei's US division from 2010 to 2011, recalled being taken aback when his boss remarked that the law was only a suggestion.[7]

Within the British multinational bank HSBC, a news article was being passed from banker to banker: "Please see below Reuters article on Huawei, self-explanatory. Most grateful if you could obtain an update from the company."[8]

The Reuters Skycom exposé now sent HSBC's bankers racing to check their books. One staffer confirmed to colleagues that an entity called Skycom Tech Co. Ltd., which shared an address with Huawei, had maintained an account with HSBC for over a year. Worse, Huawei had sent over Skycom's annual report at the time, a sheaf of papers stamped CONFIDENTIAL. It was typed right there in black and white: Skycom's purpose was "investment holding and acting as a contractor for contracts undertaking [sic] in Iran."

Founded in 1865 as the Hongkong and Shanghai Banking Corporation, HSBC had deep business ties with China and was keen to grow them. Huawei was a key account. An HSBC staffer reached out to the company to ask it to confirm if the Skycom in the HSBC account was the same one that appeared in the Reuters article, and to find out what Skycom's relationship was to Huawei. Huawei defensively responded that Skycom was its local business partner and insisted that it was fully compliant with all applicable laws. To be safe, HSBC closed the Skycom account on February 23, 2013.[9]

Meng had declined to comment for the Reuters piece. While it was unclear exactly what her thoughts were on the Skycom incident, that summer she was visibly preoccupied with reducing risks in the finance department. She wrote to colleagues that what was scary about risk was that one didn't know where it was or what the effects would be. "Should we manage it?" she wrote. "And how do we manage it?"[10]

H SBC's bankers debated internally whether or not they should continue doing business with Huawei. They commissioned an internal report to evaluate the reputational risks.[11] On the one hand, there were reports of sanctions violations in Iran, concerns from US officials that Huawei's equipment might pose security risks, and bribery allegations in countries like Algeria. On the other hand, Huawei was "an absolute global powerhouse" with "high earnings potential," and it banked with HSBC across forty-two countries, according to the report, which laid out mitigating factors for each of the concerns. US lawmakers had failed to provide clear evidence substantiating their security concerns about the company. Huawei had said that its deals in Iran were of a civilian, not military, nature and that it was pulling back. The company denied the Algerian bribery allegations.

"Clearly this would have a very real impact on the franchise should the decision be made to withdraw," an HSBC employee wrote in an email.[12]

HSBC wanted to continue working with Huawei. But to settle the dust, a meeting was arranged between Meng and Alan Thomas, HSBC's deputy head of global banking for Asia-Pacific, on August 22, 2013, in a back room of a Hong Kong restaurant.[13]

Meng spoke in Chinese through an interpreter, saying that she wanted to be precise. She showed a PowerPoint presentation titled "Trust, Compliance & Cooperation."

"Huawei operates in Iran in strict compliance with applicable laws, regulations and sanctions of UN, US and EU," the PowerPoint said. "Huawei's engagement with Skycom is normal business cooperation."

The PowerPoint acknowledged that Huawei was once a Skycom shareholder but said that the company had since sold off its shares and that Meng had quit her board position. It also pointed out that Huawei was far from alone in the Iran market, with Ericsson, Nokia Siemens Networks, and ZTE also hawking their wares in the country.

The PowerPoint presentation would end up being the linchpin in the US prosecutors' case alleging that she had committed bank fraud by misleading HSBC about Huawei's Iran business. But in the moment, the meeting appeared to be a success. Thomas dashed off an email to HSBC colleagues. "No new issues—which was a relief to me," he wrote. "No new contracts, very high scrutiny of end customers, careful product and supply chain control, so everything appears to be above board."[14]

That same day, Huawei announced it had secured a $1.5 billion five-year loan from a consortium of banks that included HSBC, as well as Citibank, ANZ, DBS, and Standard Chartered, in the largest overseas loan that Huawei had raised to date.[15]

"We are pleased by the strong support received from leading international banks," Meng said in a press release.[16] "This highlights the trust and confidence that the financial community has in Huawei's sustainable growth."

M eanwhile, Huawei's crosstown rival, ZTE, was feeling the heat from the FBI probe into its Iran business. Reuters had reported that ZTE had sold Iran's largest telecom firm a powerful surveillance system containing US technology and capable of monitoring landline, mobile, and internet communications.[17] This was in apparent violation of US restrictions on the sale of US technology to the country, and it pushed ZTE's reclusive founder, Hou Weigui, to do something unprecedented.

In April 2013, Hou appeared in Beijing for an interview with Reuters.[18] Hou had kept an even lower profile than Ren over the years. Now, wearing a simple dark-blue collared coat zipped over a gray sweater, he sat with one leg crossed over the other as he spoke to Reuters' Greater China bureau chief, Jason Subler.

Hou told Subler he felt aggrieved that ZTE had been singled out for practices that were common in the industry. He said that ZTE had by now "basically stopped" doing business in Iran, and that the compensation the company had had to pay Iranian clients for breaking off contracts contributed to ZTE's first-ever annual loss in 2012.

"I think we've really been treated unjustly on this issue. Others are selling the same things, and we weren't even selling the most," Hou said. "Now we face these restrictions, and others in the industry aren't facing any restrictions—they're still selling. This is a bit unfair."

Hou said Huawei was still doing business in Iran: "We are not in a position to comment on what Huawei and others in the industry are doing. But in any case, they are still involved in the market. But we have stopped."

20

Shotgiant

THE SNOWDEN LEAKS:
2013-2014

In March 2014, *The New York Times* and German magazine *Der Spiegel* published startling news. Citing classified documents provided by the NSA contractor turned whistleblower Edward Snowden, they reported that the NSA had infiltrated Huawei years ago through a program code-named "Shotgiant."[1]

American spies had hacked into Huawei's central email system in 2009 and had been reading the company's emails ever since—including the communications of Chairwoman Sun and Ren Zhengfei himself, *The Times* and *Der Spiegel* reported. The NSA had accessed Huawei's product source code, its most valuable intellectual property. And that was not all. The spy agency was using Huawei's infrastructure to listen in on targets around the globe.

"Many of our targets communicate over Huawei produced products," one of the leaked NSA PowerPoint slides read. "We want to make sure that we know how to exploit these products—we also want to ensure that we retain access to these communication lines, etc."[2]

Another leaked PowerPoint slide showed a web around Ren's and Sun's names, suggesting that the NSA had analyzed their social networks based on their emails. Another slide stated, "This is what we are hoping to accomplish: Determine if Huawei is doing SIGINT [signal intelligence] for PRC [the People's Republic of China]. . . . Leverage Huawei presence to gain access to networks of interest. . . . Obtaining actionable intelligence of Huawei's (and potentially PRC's) leadership plans and intentions."

It was now clear why Washington had been so confident that Beijing could use Huawei's gear for snooping: the NSA had been doing exactly that for years.

Ren was restrained in public comments, calling the disclosure of the NSA hack "within expectations." Huawei's US spokesman William Plummer declared: "The irony is that exactly what they are doing to us is what they have always charged that the Chinese are doing through us."[3]

Snowden's path to becoming an exiled whistleblower had run through China. During his time at the NSA, he had been stationed in Tokyo under cover of being an employee for the US computer company Dell. In Tokyo, he was assigned to brief US defense officials on China's surveillance capabilities.[4]

As he'd studied classified NSA and CIA reports to try to understand China's capacity to electronically track US officials and informants, Snowden had been overwhelmed by the gargantuan amount of phone and internet data that China was gathering each day. As he later recalled in a memoir, it sparked the question in his mind of just how the US government could know so much about what China was doing without using some of the same tactics itself.

Snowden had found his answers, and he was now sharing them with the world. He alleged that US spies had hacked Chinese mobile operators and stolen millions of text messages. He shared documents with the press that showed the NSA was collecting nearly five billion records pertaining to global cell-phone location data every day. He revealed that with the help of telecommunications operators, the NSA and its British counterpart, GCHQ, were tapping undersea cables carrying intercontinental phone calls and internet traffic. He alleged that the NSA had monitored phone conversations of dozens of world leaders and bugged Cisco routers sent to overseas targets.

In the wake of Snowden's leaks, a pall of fear fell over China: a fear of Western technology.[5] "He's Watching You," warned a Chinese magazine cover, the line superimposed over an illustration of a shadowy figure in a helmet. China's national broadcaster, CCTV, cautioned that the iPhone could pose national security risks due to its ability to track and time-stamp user locations. "This is extremely sensitive data," a researcher told the broadcaster, adding that it could potentially expose state secrets. CCTV also advised against government institutions running Microsoft's Windows 8 operating system, saying it could be used to gather information on Chinese citizens. "Your identity, account, contact book, phone numbers—all this data can be put together for big-data analysis," a Chinese expert said on CCTV. Beijing security hawks called for a broad rip-and-replace program to remove American components from key infrastructure. China accelerated its programs to develop domestic technologies in key fields.

There was also public backlash in countries around the world. The controversy pushed some major Western telecommunications operators to begin to pull back the curtain for the first time. Vodafone, the European mobile network giant, revealed that in around six countries, governments maintained "direct access" links to their networks, allowing authorities to access network data whenever they wanted, without having to produce a warrant or notify Vodafone. "These pipes exist, the direct access model exists," Stephen Deadman, then Vodafone's group privacy officer, was quoted as saying in *The Guardian*.[6] Privacy advocates called it a "nightmare scenario."

Vodafone's transparency report said the company's networks were designed so that a government authority could only access communications in their own country. It noted, however, that "a number of governments have legal powers to order an operator to enable lawful interception of communications that leave or enter a country without targeting a specific individual or set of premises."[7] Vodafone reported receiving tens of thousands of lawful intercept requests from governments around the world, including 7,677 from Czech authorities and 24,212 from Spain. In addition, Vodafone reported that it was unable to disclose statistics of lawful interception requests from Albania, Egypt, Hungary, India, Ireland, Malta, the Netherlands, Qatar, Romania, Turkey, and the United Kingdom due to those countries' legal requirements around maintaining secrecy.[8] In many cases, this wiretapping was being done with the help of specialized mass-surveillance technology developed by companies like Narus and Verint.[9]

These wiretapping requests were generally sent to operators like Vodafone, not to hardware makers like Huawei. But Huawei and its rivals were aware that such requests took place; indeed, they were required by governments around the world to design their products to have a standardized side door that authorities could use to access data. They also sometimes received requests for next-level help. In 2014, Ericsson told the London-based Institute for Human Rights and Business (IHRB) that an unnamed customer had once sought the company's help in making major changes to its telephone and internet network that "would have enabled the surveillance of a large number of people and allowed the government in question to collect and store much more data on citizens across all methods of digital communications than was otherwise possible." Ericsson said it had turned down the contract.[10]

Hardware makers like Huawei and Ericsson also sold managed services, or outsourced IT support to operators, which sometimes put them in the path of wiretapping requests. Ericsson employees acknowledged that they could be involved in lawful interception: "Ericsson personnel would only carry out lawful interception under requests from the operator, as part of their Managed Services," the IHRB reported.[11] Huawei's global cybersecurity officer, John Suffolk, confirmed during a UK parliamentary hearing that Huawei would comply with government requests for lawful interception. "Lawful intercept is lawful," he said. "Yes, of course we comply with lawful intercept."[12]

Evidence was also emerging that the NSA had successfully exploited Cisco routers for spying. The journalist James Bamford had reported in 2009 that the NSA had targeted Cisco for years. "I really need somebody today and for the next couple of years who knows Cisco routers inside and out and can help me understand how they're being used in target networks," Terry Thompson, then the NSA's deputy director for services, had said at a 1999 internal meeting, according to a recording reviewed by Bamford.[13] Now Snowden's leaked files suggested that the NSA had succeeded. In a book based on Snowden's files, the reporter Glenn Greenwald revealed that the NSA routinely intercepted routers and other networking devices being exported from the United States and implanted them with bugs before sending them onward to their intended recipients. He included a photo from an NSA document that showed three people carefully opening a Cisco box. "It is quite possible that Chinese firms are implanting surveillance mechanisms in their network devices. But the United States is certainly doing the same," Greenwald concluded.[14]

US vendors like Cisco were now in the same boat as Huawei, facing shadowy allegations that by their very nature could not be disproven. As Cisco's sales in China plunged, there was not much it could do beyond issue a denial to Chinese media that it had ever been a knowing participant in NSA spying operations. Cisco's CEO, John Chambers, wrote a letter to President Obama pleading for "rules of the road." "We simply cannot operate this way," Chambers wrote. "Our customers trust us to be able to deliver to their doorsteps products that meet the highest standards of integrity and security."[15]

After so many years of defending their company against similar allegations, Huawei's executives couldn't resist throwing a jab or two. "PRISM, PRISM on the wall, who's the most trustworthy of them all?" Guo Ping said in a speech at the Mobile World Congress. "If you don't understand this question, go ask Edward Snowden."[16]

R en was now sixty-eight, the gray coming in at his temples, lines etched across his forehead and around the corners of his eyes. For two years now, Huawei had been the world's largest telecom gear vendor by sales. In 2014, Huawei would book $46.6 billion in revenue—half of Microsoft's revenue that year but almost four times Facebook's. Huawei had also catapulted itself into the place of world's third-biggest smartphone maker, behind only Apple and Samsung, shipping seventy-five million smartphones in 2014. Huawei was filing more patent applications per annum than any other company in the world. Global operators like Spain's Telefónica, the UK's BT, and Germany's Deutsche Telekom were not only its customers but also its research partners. Its Safe City surveillance solutions had been deployed to more than one hundred cities around the world. Not bad for a boy from the Guizhou hills who had grown up in a famine, without enough food or shirts.

For most of Huawei's history, just catching up to its rivals had seemed an impossible goal. When Ren had told his staff in the 1990s that Huawei would become one of the world's biggest telecom vendors, they had thought he was tilting at windmills. But the company had indeed become the biggest, and Ren was now setting his sights higher.

Ren told Teresa He, a serious and discreet woman in charge of Huawei's chips research, that she had $400 million at her disposal each year to advance the fundamental building blocks of Huawei's technology. He told her he wanted twenty thousand staffers working on chip design.[17] Huawei also launched a Hong Kong–based lab for artificial-intelligence research that bore the evocative name Noah's Ark Lab, and it set up branch offices from Moscow to Paris to Montreal so that it could recruit the brightest minds from around the world. As it sought to reach the global technological cutting edge, Huawei was now hiring not just engineers but also mathematicians and quantum physicists.

Ren observed that the most powerful tech companies in the world—Microsoft, Google, Apple, and IBM, for instance—sold not a stand-alone product but a technological platform that served as a springboard for hundreds or thousands of other companies' technology. He said that was Huawei's goal. It would seek to be a global technological force, and that meant building the company's chips, servers, and algorithms into platforms and getting partners and allies on board around the world. "If we only seek to dominate the world without learning to share the cake with our allies," he told staff in late 2013, "we are like Genghis Khan, like Hitler, and our own demise will be the ultimate outcome."[18]

When Huawei's staffers had begun to go overseas in the late 1990s, they'd gotten doors slammed in their faces left and right. Against all likelihood, they had broken into the market in nearly every corner of the world. Huawei's overseas sales teams continued to push. Guy Saint-Jacques, Canada's ambassador from 2012 to 2016, recalled Huawei landing a meeting with him by winning a charity auction whose prize was a dinner at the ambassador's residence. "I noticed that there was one table that was always bidding higher," Saint-Jacques said. "It was a Huawei table. And they won."[19] Chairwoman Sun Yafang was also doing much of the diplomacy personally. The world leaders she met in 2014 included Egyptian president Abdel Fattah el-Sisi, Sri Lankan president Mahinda Rajapaksa, Kazakh president Nursultan Nazarbayev, and UK business secretary Vince Cable. *Forbes* ranked Sun as the most powerful woman in China for 2014.

Huawei had been using the rotating CEO system for several years now, with Guo Ping, Ken Hu, and Eric Xu taking six-month turns at the helm under the direction of Ren and Chairwoman Sun. It was an unorthodox succession approach, but it seemed to be working for the time being. But when Ren might retire and what would happen then remained the subject of much public speciation. At the company's annual analyst conference in March 2014, Eric Xu remarked that Ren's successor would likely be a team instead of a single person. "How we get there, only time will tell," Xu said. A surprising number of Ren's early team members had stuck with him for two decades, a testament to the success of Huawei's employee shareholder business model. Zheng Baoyong, Ren's early right-hand man, whom he had nicknamed "A-Bao," even made a return to Huawei around this time, after recovering from a brain tumor that had unexpectedly sidelined him in the early 2000s.

Several of Ren's family members remained involved in Huawei's management. Ren's son, Ren Ping, was still at Smartcom, the Huawei hospitality division that ran its restaurants and hotels. Ren's younger brother, Steven Ren, held seats in powerful internal oversight units such as the audit committee and the supervisory board, and Ren's daughter Meng Wanzhou was on the board of directors as the company's chief financial officer. For now, the question of succession was anybody's guess.

In June 2014, Meng arrived in New York for the latest Huawei ICT Finance Forum, an annual conference that the company organized for Huawei executives to hobnob with prominent global financiers. It wasn't the most comfortable time to travel to the United States: US-China tensions had spiked after Snowden's revelations. Beijing had just announced a security review of imported technology equipment, with state media calling US companies like Google and

Apple a threat to the nation. Western executives were anxious that they were about to be shut out of China's lucrative market. Meanwhile, Washington was adamant that the US was the more aggrieved party when it came to hacking.

Despite the controversies that swirled around Huawei, many banks were eager to do business with it. "All the political nonsense aside, the bankers were like, 'This is real business, this is real money. And we want a piece of it,'" said former Huawei spokesman William Plummer, who noted that he helped make preparations for the conferences.

For this year's conference, they had landed Alan Greenspan, former Federal Reserve chairman, as a keynote speaker. Meng had also prepared an address, an upbeat speech that praised US innovation and called Apple founder Steve Jobs a hero and visionary.[20]

But as Meng arrived at New York's John F. Kennedy International Airport, Department of Homeland Security agents took her in for secondary questioning, telling her the stop had something to do with her visa. They confiscated her electronics.

Plummer received a frantic call from a colleague on Meng's team.[21]

"You used to be a diplomat. You need to get her out."

Plummer replied that this wasn't quite how it worked.

"They held her for three or four hours, and during that time they had her tablet, PC, and phone," Plummer said.

Meng was allowed to enter the US after the search, and she continued her business trip.

Afterward, Plummer says, he told other Huawei executives that Meng's devices had likely been copied by the US authorities. He suggested that they discard them.

"I told her people, 'Burn them all. You can't use them. Have them burned. They're done.'"

PART III

We are like a small sesame seed, stuck in the middle of conflict between two great powers.[1]

—Ren Zhengfei, January 15, 2019

21

Sharp Eyes

On an overcast Wednesday afternoon in October 2015, London security officers in neon-yellow vests stopped traffic outside a glassy office tower on Wormwood Street.[1] Curious onlookers stood across the street outside a barber's shop and an Indian restaurant, craning their necks. A dark-haired Chinese man in a suit and red tie got out of a car amid flashing cameras, accepted a bouquet of flowers, and walked into the global finance center of Huawei Technologies. The staff clapped and cheered: "We warmly welcome Chairman Xi!"

China's leader, Xi Jinping, was making time on his state visit to the UK to stop by one Chinese company, according to his public schedule, and the company he was bestowing this honor upon was Huawei.[2] It was a reflection of Huawei's place in Beijing's global ambitions. Here was a Chinese company that was not only a major seller to the UK but also an R&D partner in cutting-edge fields. This was a rare and precious thing for the nation. Timed to Xi's visit, Huawei was set to announce a new partnership with the University of Manchester to research graphene, a next-generation material two hundred times stronger than steel, and Xi planned to tour the university's graphene research center.[3]

Wearing a whimsical pink-and-blue tie, Ren Zhengfei showed the Chinese leader around Huawei's offices, energetically pointing a small baton at a robotic arm, smartwatches, and other gadgets. A gaggle of Huawei executives in black suits followed them around. So did Meng Wanzhou, who stood out in her burgundy-colored dress. Despite her scare at the JFK Airport the previous year, she had resumed her work travels. And a meeting with China's leader was too important to miss.

Ren had reason to be proud. After a decade and a half of bloody competition, Huawei was one of the last ones standing. America's Lucent had disappeared into France's Alcatel, which had in turn been absorbed into Finland's Nokia. Canada's Nortel had gone under. Britain's Marconi was subsumed into Sweden's Ericsson. In quick succession, the United States, France, Canada, and the United Kingdom had all fallen by the wayside. China's Huawei and ZTE now rounded out the Big Four along with Ericsson and Nokia.

Xi had now been in power for three years out of the standard ten-year tenure for a Chinese president. He had proved more aggressive than anyone had predicted. Xi had declared ambitions for China's global renaissance, launching the trillion-dollar Belt and Road Initiative to build roads, dams, and telephone networks across developing nations. He had also kicked off a bold, decade-long industrial program called "Made in China 2025," its goal being to make the country a world leader in critical technologies like semiconductors, robotics, and artificial intelligence. Huawei was now stepping up into a key role in Belt and Road, Made in China 2025, and other Beijing flagship programs. Ren had once again successfully anticipated the policy winds and maneuvered Huawei to catch them.

Having come to power amid the aftershocks of the Arab Spring, Xi was preoccupied with security. He had immediately launched a sweeping anti-corruption campaign, which was putting hundreds of thousands of officials and executives behind bars across the nation. It was a savvy move, providing cover for Xi to take down potential rivals, even as the campaign played well with the grassroots population. The crackdown had begun in the Ren family's stronghold, Sichuan Province, which had a reputation for trying to go in its own direction far from the nation's capital. Beijing's anti-graft investigators were now scrutinizing officials' business links at all levels, making it a tense time to be, like Huawei, in a line of work that was deeply intertwined with the government. Who *hadn't* crossed paths with Huawei over the years? Its business interests were in every province, every city, possibly even every village. Everyone's fortunes were now twisting in the wind. Back in 2000, Sichuan's party secretary, Zhou Yongkang, a son of impoverished eel farmers, had toured Huawei's Sichuan factory for caller ID–enabled telephones and had endeavored to persuade Ren to deepen his business investment in the province.[4] In 2001, Liaoning Province's governor, a charismatic man named Bo Xilai, had come to visit Huawei, where he'd exclaimed in admiration that these comrades down south were building things they hadn't even thought of yet in the far north.[5] Zhou had risen to become the nation's security czar, and Bo tipped as a candidate for president, and now they had both been sentenced to life in prison for corruption.

At Huawei, executives had scrambled to ensure that their house was clean. Ren, Chairwoman Sun, Meng Wanzhou, and Huawei's other board members had appeared onstage before staff in a solemn ceremony, raising their right hands and swearing that they would not embezzle or take bribes.[6] "Actually, there's still quite a bit of corruption at Huawei," Ren warned. "In the future, if you've been in prison, your children will always say, 'My dad's been in prison.'"[7]

Huawei did not escape the crackdown unscathed. Teng Hongfei, sales head of Huawei's smartphone division, was detained for investigation on allegations of "accepting bribes as a non-state functionary."[8] Another Huawei sales executive, Tian Qingjun, admitted to giving a senior executive at China Unicom a string of bribes, including thousands of dollars' worth of gift cards to restaurants, department stores, and a foot massage parlor, as well as plane tickets to Toronto.[9] The Unicom official was sentenced to four and a half years in prison; Tian, it appeared, was granted clemency for cooperating with prosecutors. Ren's early "young prodigy" and onetime succession contender, Li Yinan, was arrested during this period and sentenced to two and a half years in prison for insider trading in a case that involved his work after he left Huawei.

Xi was also bolstering Beijing's legal powers. A slew of new laws governing national security, counterterrorism, and cybersecurity—which began rolling out in 2015—ordered individuals and companies to cooperate with government investigations. It was a thorn in Huawei's side: foreign officials would repeatedly cite them as a reason why they couldn't trust Huawei. But Huawei's executives, who jet-

setted around the world and saw all different kinds of political unrest, would have appreciated the reasoning behind Beijing's tight
controls. In 2016, after witnessing mass protests in South Korea's
capital, Seoul, to demand the removal of impeached president Park
Geun-hye, rotating CEO Guo Ping posted a scared-face emoji on
Facebook. "There are thousands of people gathering here to protest
the step-down president," he wrote. Park was deposed and sentenced
to twenty-five years in prison.

In 2015, Xi's administration also launched a program called
"Sharp Eyes" that was aimed at blanketing the country with a network of security cameras, a lucrative new business opportunity for
vendors like Huawei. The target was 100 percent coverage of China's
public spaces by 2020. As Xi set out on his UK trip, Beijing police
announced that there were no more blind spots in China's capital.
Electronic eyes were watching over 100 percent of Beijing.[10]

R en had grown up without computers.[11] Now everything was
becoming a computer. Everything was becoming smart: smartphones, smartwatches, smart thermostats, smart vacuums, smart refrigerators. The gadgeteers called it the big-data era or the Internet
of Things and touted a Jetsons-esque life of incredible convenience.
But it also meant that companies and governments could track individuals to a far greater degree than ever before. Years earlier, the US
big-box store Target had drawn backlash after an attempt to predict
which women were pregnant by analyzing their buying habits.[12] Now
this act of peering into customers' shopping baskets seemed quaintly
innocent. In this new day of big data, major tech companies and

governments could quite plausibly track not only an individual's shopping cart but also their location twenty-four hours a day, their conversations and texts, their social contacts, and even their thoughts before they spoke them aloud, as extrapolated through their internet search history and notes jotted in their phone's note-taking apps. Even their sleep patterns and heartbeat could no longer be said to be personal and private.

"The era of big-data traffic should be quite terrifying," Ren told his executives. "Because we don't really know what big data is. The sheer volume of traffic is also unimaginable."[13]

This flood of data was turning the wheels of Huawei's Safe City surveillance systems, which were gaining traction at home and abroad. Huawei and its partners touted their systems as being able to help police combine real-time facial-recognition streams from surveillance cameras with users' mobile data and social media to produce sophisticated automated tracking. They landed contracts across the nation, from Beijing's elite Tsinghua University to Duyun No. 1 Middle School, where Ren's father had been principal, in a sleepy Guizhou town.[14] One district in the city of Tianjin was rolling out a Huawei database that an official said could begin tracking residents even before they were born. "Beginning in utero, individual profiles are created for each person," an official wrote about the system. "Additional information is added as residents progress through their lives."[15]

Other countries were also signing on. Huawei touted its Safe City in Kenya, which it claimed had reduced crime rates in the covered areas by 46 percent from 2014 to 2015; the company said the system had even helped ensure a safe visit for Pope Francis in November 2015.[16] One of the most detailed overviews of such a system emerged as part of a lawsuit that a Huawei partner filed against it.[17] In 2016,

the two companies had worked together to build a Safe City in La-
hore, Pakistan, with the deal later souring. According to the filing by
Huawei's partner, Business Efficiency Solutions, the system they developed included a data warehouse that stored sensitive records from
Pakistan's government agencies and other parties, including national
ID card information, data from cellular companies, land records, tax
records, and immigration information. There was a "digital media
forensic center" where captured video and still images could be en-
hanced and analyzed. A media monitoring system tracked platforms
like Facebook and Twitter, as well as print and broadcast media.
There were video feeds from surveillance cameras installed across
the city, in addition to body-wearable cameras and covert miniatur-
ized cameras for police. There were also "industrial-strength" drones
that could broadcast real-time video to a control room and had thermal vision for nighttime surveillance.

I n 2014, Ren made a trip to Xinjiang.[18] Some of Huawei's staffers
posted to the region were unsettled. There had been a deadly
blast at a train station in Ürümqi after Xi had declared a "People's
War on Terror." Huawei employees' family members pushed them to
leave for safer assignments.

Xinjiang is China's largest region, bigger than Alaska or Texas,
covering a full sixth of the nation's land, with some twenty million
people. It might be a borderland, but it is vital to the nation. Amid its
steppes and deserts are China's borders with key neighbors: Russia,
Afghanistan, Pakistan, India. Many of China's oil fields are in Xinjiang. The region produces the vast majority of China's cotton crop

and much of its tomatoes, nuts, and fruits. The military has used re-mote stretches of Xinjiang for nuclear and military tests.

Huawei's engineers on the eastern coast saw Xinjiang as a distant hardship posting with the promise of adventure and danger. A Hua-wei employee was once stuck for two days in the desert when a rock-slide blocked their train's passage from Kashgar to Hotan.[19] Outside major cities, many of the native Turkic Uyghur residents didn't speak Mandarin Chinese, or resented having to do so, and viewed Han Chi-nese workers as colonial invaders who were trying to dominate their economy and erase their cultural heritage. The ethnic tension peri-odically erupted into violence. Authorities saw the phone and inter-net networks that Huawei had helped build as a tool for controlling the region. After deadly ethnic riots broke out in Ürümqi in 2009, authorities cut off internet access to Xinjiang for ten months.[20]

Now, despite the uncertainties, it was clear that new business op-portunities were opening up in Xinjiang. The People's War on Terror was in large part a technological war, an effort to build a digital net that no suspected Uyghur separatist could slip through. That meant potential big sales of Huawei's Safe City solutions. Huawei had never been a company to shrink from danger. Indeed, it was the Huawei ethos to bravely push forward when others fled. In the autumn of 2014, Ren announced internally that employees who went to work in the region would receive accelerated promotions in line with war-zone postings. "In this way, people will go to difficult areas," he said. "Otherwise, no one will go."[21] Ren further told his staff: "The current approach is to use unique incentive schemes in Afghanistan, Iraq, or the Xinjiang region to draw people to go."[22] These incentive initia-tives would ensure that Huawei remained robustly staffed in the re-gion as the repression intensified over the next few years.

At the time, few could have predicted the full extent of the brutal crackdown that would take place—the vast detention camps, the forced labor, the allegations of torture. In the ensuing years, there must have been a moment when it dawned on Ren that his team would go down in the history books not for heroically helping to secure the peace in Xinjiang but for abetting what international human-rights experts were calling crimes against humanity.

One morning in March 2016, Huawei's brass woke to shocking news out of Washington: after years of investigating Huawei's crosstown rival, ZTE, the US Commerce Department had put the company on its sanctions list for violating Iran export controls. ZTE was now blocked from buying US technology, which was all but a death knell. Everyone knew that ZTE could not make its products without US chips and software, because no high-tech company could. If the sanctions weren't quickly lifted, ZTE's remaining lifespan would be measured not in years but in months.

To justify the sanctions, the US Commerce Department had published several incriminating internal ZTE records that it had somehow acquired. These records outlined how ZTE had set up shell companies to obscure its business dealings in Iran and North Korea. Incredibly, one of the documents laid out the penalties that ZTE executives might face if they were caught skirting sanctions:

1. Company will be subject to a large amount of civil penalty;

2. High-level managers will face prison sentences in a criminal case;

3. Company will be placed on the Blacklist and be banned from purchasing U.S. products directly or indirectly for a period of time.[23]

ZTE's plight set off alarm bells across China. Security hawks in Beijing saw it as proof that the country needed to reduce its reliance on US technology as fast as possible. For years, the idea that Washington could assassinate Chinese tech companies by severing their supply chains had floated in the realm of conspiracy theory. Few in Beijing believed that such a thing was possible in an age of globalized supply chains. But now it was real.

At Huawei, there were more specific reasons for panic. Whispers swirled that Huawei was the top prize, the big fish that US investigators were actually seeking to bring down. Ashley Yablon, the ZTE whistleblower, had previously worked as a senior lawyer for Huawei in the United States. And one of the internal corporate documents published by the Commerce Department mentioned a ZTE rival, codenamed "F7," that was using similar tactics to get around US sanctions. Based on the descriptions, there was no ambiguity: F7 was Huawei.[24]

The company had played fast and loose for years. Now Ren warned his staff that they must avoid violating US law in sensitive regions. "We must strictly stay within bounds," he said. "We are only businesspeople. We only do business."[25]

22

A Thing of Beauty

Back when he had visited the United States in the 1990s, Ren Zhengfei had been struck by the grand architecture of Las Vegas, modeled after Roman palaces. He'd remarked that Las Vegas might be the most beautiful city in America. Now in the hinterland to the north of Shenzhen, he began building his own version. Huawei had outgrown its Shenzhen headquarters by 2016, with 180,000 employees globally and counting, and Ren's team was searching for more space. This was hard to find in Shenzhen, which was a thicket of skyscrapers by now, with soaring property prices. They found what they were looking for in Dongguan, Shenzhen's up-and-coming northern neighbor, which still had stretches of undeveloped land. Eager to woo the company, Dongguan officials offered Huawei a prime 1.2-square-kilometer tract of verdant land on the south shore of a lake.

Ren's younger brother, Steven Ren, was put in charge of the construction of these new Dongguan R&D grounds, which they called Ox Horn Campus. They hired Japan's Nikken Sekkei, the world's second-largest architectural firm, which produced a fever dream of a design: Ox Horn would be built to look like twelve miniature European cities, including Paris, Verona, Bruges, and Oxford. They would re-create some of the greatest hits of Western civilization, including Germany's Heidelberg Castle and France's Palace of Versailles. "What is important is not simply to copy certain architectural styles but to make them truly beautiful," Steven Ren wrote of the project.[1]

Huawei would overlook no detail.[2] The architects were proud that none of the roofs of the 108 buildings were identical. Reflecting an eye for historical accuracy, some of the shingles were slate, others terracotta or copper. The pitches of the roofs ranged from twenty to ninety degrees. The buildings were faced in a range of materials, including granite, sandstone, limestone, dolomite, brick, and stucco (for Verona and Grenada). There were, of course, some concessions to modernity, such as treating the porous stones to prevent mildew and algae growth. Facial-recognition gates were installed at the entrances.[3]

Replicating iconic Western buildings was widespread in China at the time, amid a broad fascination with the world among a rising Chinese middle class; Xi's administration would later discourage the practice as suggestive of a lack of cultural confidence.[4] At Huawei, Ren thought the striking structures with historic resonances would inspire his engineers to think globally and aspire to greatness.[5] Huawei hired 150 Russian painters to cover the halls' ceilings and walls with Renaissance-style murals, with the painters joking that even the Kremlin didn't have such beautiful corridors.[6] Someone stocked

A Huawei smartphone ad featuring Hollywood superstar Scarlett Johansson.

the lake by the castle with black swans—a reference to the financial term for worst-case scenarios that are hard to forecast. Ren so frequently warned his staff to look out for black-swan events that, at some point, the bird became Huawei's unofficial mascot.

On a balmy night in southern China in 2016, a singer in a glittering dress crooned in front of a three-piece band. A bartender sliced fresh pineapple for the cocktails. Piles of sashimi gleamed on ice. The room shimmered pink and purple under the spotlights. Then Hollywood superstar Scarlett Johansson walked out onto the stage.[7]

The promotional event for Huawei's new P9 smartphone was billed as a "fan party" for Chinese devotees of Scarlett Johansson. The audience of mostly young Chinese women cheered, waving signs with slogans like I GOT SCARLETT FEVER. It was one among a string of glamorous soirees that Huawei was hosting around the world with the aim of getting consumers to not only recognize the name Huawei but also associate it with sophistication and luxury.

Huawei was pulling out all the stops as it sought to catch up with the world's smartphone kings—Samsung and Apple. To close the gap with Samsung would be a formidable challenge: Samsung was pouring $14 billion a year into advertising, more than Iceland's GDP.[8] With the help of top-tier marketing agencies, Huawei rolled out billboards everywhere from London's Heathrow Airport, to the banks of the Seine River in Paris, to New York's Times Square. Huawei signed on A-listers like Johansson, Gal Gadot, and Henry Cavill to appear in its smartphone commercials. The company also became a sponsor of sports teams, including the Washington Redskins, the Canberra Raiders, and Arsenal Football Club.

This lavish spending would not be a waste. Indeed, it would help Huawei achieve a pretty incredible transformation. A company that hawked telephone switches, undersea cables, and surveillance gear to dictators and strongmen was being reborn in soft focus as a fun and fashionable brand.

In Huawei's early days, Ren had been less than enthused at the idea of hawking handsets—which were called "terminals" in Huawei-speak—as he considered it too far afield from the company's core businesses of switches, routers, and base stations. "Huawei will not make a mobile phone," Ren once insisted indignantly. "Anyone who talks this nonsense is going to get laid off!"[9] Even after Huawei began pursuing smartphones seriously, Ren feared wasting money on marketing and was often harsh on the company's head of consumer products, Richard Yu, or Yu Chengdong. "People always say I criticize Yu Chengdong," Ren remarked to staff. "Actually, my criticism of him is my way of caring for him."[10]

By 2015, it was becoming impossible to dismiss mobile phones. More than half of China's population was online, with most connecting through a smartphone in lieu of a computer.[11] It was increasingly clear to Huawei's executives—and equally clear to tech execs in Silicon Valley—that smartphones should be viewed not so much as tele-

Huawei's consumer products head, Richard Yu.

phones but as the most powerful personal computers in history, and as gold mines in terms of consumer data. William Xu, Huawei's strategic marketing chief, explained the company's expansion into smartphones as following the data "from the ocean to the rivers to the faucets around the world."[12]

Huawei had introduced a smartphone brand called Honor back in 2011, spinning it out in 2013 as a stand-alone brand aimed at the youth market.[13] The inspiration came from the Chinese startup Xiaomi, which had seen overnight success by selling a sleek iPhone-esque smartphone for less than half the price of an Apple device in buzzy "flash sales." Huawei thought it could beat Xiaomi at its own game, staging publicity stunts such as destroying seventeen thousand brand-new phones for allegedly falling a little short of Huawei's stringent quality standards. "We weren't after the sales themselves; we just needed to generate some headlines," Honor CEO Zhao Ming wrote.[14] Xiaomi never had a chance under Huawei's crushing weight. "Huawei is really good at copying," a friend of Xiaomi's founder, Lei Jun, bemoaned.[15] Huawei stampeded past Xiaomi in sales in 2015, the year it launched Honor. Only Samsung and Apple were ahead now.

In 2016, Huawei launched two gem-encrusted watches in partnership with Swarovski. The company hired legendary tenor Andrea Bocelli to sing at a private event and partnered with the National Opera of Paris. When Ren met with Huawei executives in North Africa, he encouraged them to follow the US military's example of buying top-of-the-line stuff. "That includes buying a brand-new car. Don't just go rent used ones," he told them. "Buy a house, then buy the land next to it to build facilities like a basketball court and swimming pool." He green-lit them to splash out on these expenses across Africa.[16]

As Huawei's smartphone business boomed, it began to draw attention to an obscure corner of the company's business empire. Gadget reviewers began noticing, with intrigue, that some of Huawei's phones ran on processors designed by Huawei's in-house HiSilicon label. These chips were surprisingly good for a brand that Huawei did little to promote. The ability of a telecom company to design its own chips reflected an advanced technical level, with few smartphone makers aside from Apple and Samsung able to do so. In 2014, reviewers reported that the HiSilicon processor in Huawei's Honor 6 smartphone was outperforming even the iPhone in certain benchmarks, though it had marked problems in areas like power consumption. "This is a very interesting result," one reviewer remarked.[17]

Ren was wary of HiSilicon getting too much attention. It risked disrupting Huawei's relationships with third-party chip suppliers like Qualcomm; the companies might start to see Huawei as a rival instead of a partner. HiSilicon was also still a major supplier for the surveillance-camera industry, something Huawei didn't tend to talk too much about.[18]

A reporter at China's national broadcaster, CCTV, once told Ren it was a pity that more people didn't know about HiSilicon. "Why does the outside world need to know?" Ren replied. "The outside world doesn't need to know this."[19]

H uawei's AI-focused research center, Noah's Ark Lab, had more than fifty full-time researchers and engineers by 2015,[20] and it was forging research partnerships with top-tier universities around the world. Beijing officials had begun expressing their hopes that China would become a global AI leader in the near future, perhaps as soon as the year 2025. Huawei employees excitedly de-bated the prospects of AI. "No matter how smart machines become, the human mind will evolve more," one commented in a discussion on Huawei's online employee forum. Another countered: "There is no doubt that this level of technology in the wrong hands can cause mass destruction where robots could perhaps malfunction or be cor-rupted."

Since Huawei's earliest days, it had relied heavily on research partnerships with Chinese universities, such as the Huazhong Uni-versity of Science and Technology in Wuhan. Now Huawei was woo-ing universities around the world with research dollars. Few were saying no. Academic researchers generally considered themselves to be engaging in intellectual inquiry for the benefit of the world, with their research findings published for all to read. They didn't see a problem in partnering with a Chinese company on research that would be published publicly in a scientific journal. The researchers at Noah's Ark Lab were working with international universities to study hot emerging topics like natural language processing, which would allow computers to "understand" text or speech in a more hu-manlike way. They were studying techniques such as image quality enhancement, data mining, and action recognition in video clips.

Huawei's long list of research partners was prestigious indeed. It included Oxford and Stanford and UC Berkeley and a host of other universities. The company was working on research projects with the European Commission. It opened a math research center in France, with France's secretary of state for higher education and re-search, Thierry Mandon, showing up for the launch.

Huawei's name was starting to consistently pop up in lists of top lobbying spenders in countries around the world, a sign it had become fluent in the ways of influence buying that its Western rivals had long utilized. In 2014, Huawei was ranked as the number-eight lobbying spender in the EU, with only Microsoft and Germany's Siemens outspending it among tech companies.[21] From 2010 to 2018, Huawei paid for more overseas trips for Australian federal politicians than any other company, according to a tally taken by the Australian Strategic Policy Institute (ASPI).

I n November 2016, Huawei's lead 5G scientist, Wen Tong, and several dozen of his colleagues arrived at the Peppermill in Reno, Nevada.[22] The resort and casino looked like a Roman palace. It boasted indoor and outdoor pools, geothermal-heated spas, and eighty-two thousand square feet of gaming tables and slots. But the Huawei engineers were not there for vacation. The next five days in Reno would determine which nations owned the technology inside the next generation of mobile communications: 5G. Huawei's engineers had toiled for years for this moment, but this was bigger than them. Beijing wanted to reach the front lines of 5G. China had put in more effort than any other nation.[23]

Mobile phones could work globally because companies around the world had agreed to use shared technical standards—first 3G, then 4G, and now 5G. Which companies' patented technologies became part of these standards was a fiercely contentious issue, as it meant that other companies around the world had to pay licensing fees to the standards setters for years to come. The 3rd Generation Partnership Project, or 3GPP, had been set up so that these far-flung companies could hash out the shared standards. The stakeholders who participated ran the gamut, from chipmakers like Qualcomm and Intel, to internet giants like Google and Facebook, to gear makers like Nokia, Ericsson, ZTE, and Huawei.

As one standards representative recalled, 3GPP's meetings were notoriously long and grueling.[24] The group operated by "consensus," which in practice meant that standoffs dragged on for hours until one side or the other broke from sheer exhaustion. "It's hell," said Michael Thelander, a telecom industry consultant who has attended the meetings. "There's no better way to describe it."[25]

Tong had been hired by Huawei out of the ashes of Nortel, where he had been head of the Canadian tech giant's networking technology labs before the company went bankrupt in 2009. He had hundreds of patents to his name. When Tong had joined Huawei, he'd been tasked with the ambitious goal of bringing the company up to the cutting edge of mobile technology by the time 5G was launched, which would be around the year 2020. A decade was a frightfully short amount of time to try to close such a gap. Tong's team got to work.

The advent of 2G had brought text messaging; 3G, mobile photos and video clips; 4G, mobile video. Now mobile engineers expected 5G to bring one-thousand-fold gains in network capacity, making possible data-intensive applications that had previously been the realm of science fiction: self-driving cars, perhaps, or remote surgeries, self-regulating factories, and next-generation surveillance systems.

As the date of the 3GPP summit approached, Tong and his team found themselves on firm footing. Through the help of research partnerships with prestigious institutions across the globe, they had filed for a long list of patents in many areas of 5G technology.

One of the technologies that they were most excited about was something called "polar coding," a new way of cleaning up the noise in data transmissions. As data speeds increased from 4G to 5G, it was crucial to find better ways of reducing the noise. Huawei's advances in polar coding reflected how it was leaning on top academic researchers the world over to help it develop trailblazing technologies. Polar coding had been proposed by a Turkish scientist named Erdal Arıkan in 2008, after he had worked on the problem for decades. The coding scheme laid out in Arıkan's paper was hailed as a theoretical breakthrough in the field. But it required an immense amount of engineering to turn a promising theory into a workable product. "It takes an army of engineers to develop a new technology to the level of maturity required by standardization committees," Arıkan said.

Huawei's engineers knew they were going to come up against opposition at 3GPP. Their polar coding technology was not the only proposal for cleaning up noise. The US chip giant Qualcomm was pushing a rival technology called LDPC. Qualcomm was a formidable foe, owning more key 4G patents than any other company and technologically powering two of every five smartphones in the world. To improve its chances, Huawei had in advance rustled up a coalition of fifty-four companies willing to support polar coding.[26] Virtually all the Chinese companies participating in 3GPP were on board, including Alibaba, Lenovo, and Xiaomi. So were Japan's Toshiba, US chipmaker Broadcom, and Canadian telecom operator Telus. Some of Huawei's rivals were irked. A Samsung representative sniffed that it was "not really fair" that some companies had lined up "a nice combination of supporting companies."[27]

The debate between Huawei and Qualcomm over polar coding versus LDPC took place at an evening session.[28] In anticipation of spectators, 3GPP organizers had moved the meeting into a larger room. Hours passed, with neither side relenting. Both sides had spent significant resources developing their rival technologies, and neither wanted to go home empty-handed. "It was early morning hours," recalled Thelander, who was at the session. "Finally, everybody kind of realized, *You know, look, we gotta get 5G done.*"

The meeting ended in a truce: both Huawei's and Qualcomm's noise-reduction technologies would be adopted for different parts of the 5G standard. From a technological point of view, it was an inelegant and redundant solution. The system would have worked with just one or the other. But telecommunications had never been just a matter of technology. It had always also involved politics.

In the months that followed, there was acknowledgment in the industry that against all odds, Huawei had caught up. For the fifth generation of mobile, Huawei had jumped to number one in standard-essential patents (SEPs), leapfrogging over the likes of Qualcomm and LG. Huawei's long climb had begun in 1987, and now the company had reached the summit.

"There is only one true 5G supplier right now, and that is Huawei," Neil McRae, chief network architect for the UK's BT Group, said at a Huawei-organized conference. "The others need to catch up."[29]

A fter the dust settled, Huawei held a celebration for the key researchers behind its 5G breakthrough, such as its Ottawa-based lead 5G scientist, Tong Wen.[30] Erdal Arıkan, the Turkish inventor of polar coding, also received an invitation. Huawei had not paid him directly for developing a technology that ended up in the company's products, but it had made a donation to his university to support his ongoing research.[31]

A sleek black Mercedes picked him up and drove him down a curving road through Huawei's lush green campus.[32] When the car stopped, two footmen in white suits and gloves opened the door. Guo Ping was standing there, waiting to greet him. A red carpet had been unfurled up the steps into a building that looked like a European-style palace. Two rows of Huawei employees flanked the red carpet, applauding. Inside, the ballroom was adorned with Roman-style pillars and had a pyramidal glass ceiling reminiscent of the Louvre. A row of violinists played classical music. Fresh flowers spilled over the railings. After greeting Arıkan heartily, Ren, Guo, and other Huawei executives sat down in a row of silver-trimmed blue seats. Arıkan was ushered to a golden throne.

As the crowd clapped and cheered, Ren handed Arıkan a golden medal engraved with a victorious goddess. The medal had been crafted by the Monnaie de Paris, the French capital's mint, and it was encrusted with a precious red Baccarat crystal.

Arıkan stepped up to the microphone. "Mr. Ren, you have created the world's largest telecommunications company in the last thirty years. I have spent the last thirty years working at Bilkent University, doing research on a variety of problems that culminated in polar codes. Today, our roads cross on a happy occasion," Arıkan said. "It gives me great pleasure again to acknowledge that without the vision and technical contributions of Huawei directors and engineers, polar codes would not have made it from lab to 5G in less than ten years. And, as engineers, there is no greater reward than seeing our ideas turn into reality. Thank you for making it happen."[33]

Ren looked emotional as he listened to Arıkan through a simultaneous-interpretation headset. He smiled and clapped, blinking his eyes rapidly.

23

The Listening State

THE MODERN SURVEILLANCE
ERA: 2017-2018

B y late 2017, there were growing signs that something was very wrong in China's far-west Xinjiang region.[1] Guards with machine guns manned checkpoints in and out of cities; travelers had to have their faces scanned and walk through full-body scanners. On the streets, pedestrians were stopped by police at random to have their phones checked for illegal political or religious content. Gas stations were barricaded and ringed with razor wire as a precaution against bombings. Officials warned that even modest expressions of Islamic faith, such as growing a beard or wearing a headscarf, would be scrutinized as potential signs of extremism. And a growing number of people—especially members of the Uyghur ethnic minority—were being hauled off without trial to prisonlike sites called "reeducation centers." Estimates of how many people were detained (in either short-term or long-term detention) ranged from the hundreds of thousands to more than a million. Reports of torture, abuse, and deaths trickled out.

Under the banner of counterterrorism, Xinjiang had become the world's most repressive high-tech surveillance state. And Huawei had helped build it. The company's next-generation fast networks, facial-recognition algorithms, and high-definition cameras had all combined to build an invisible net of enormous scale. Huawei was not the only tech company to sell surveillance gear into Xinjiang. But it was certainly among the major suppliers.

In Xinjiang, and across the nation, Huawei was hawking a fulsome portfolio of advanced surveillance technologies, built in cooperation with hundreds of startups and other partner companies. There were smart glasses that police could wear on patrol to scan crowds for faces on a watch list. There were high-definition police body cams that streamed live to a big screen back at the command center.[2] There was a listening device that could monitor and analyze conversations within a ten-meter radius outdoors, day and night.[3] There were biometric scanners that picked up iris patterns in the eyes, which could be used to identify a person, similarly to fingerprints.[4] There was a voiceprint database to match voices on audio recordings against known individuals. These gadgets were often marketed under the brands of Huawei's partner companies, with Huawei satisfied to take a low-key role.

By August 2016, Huawei was named the Xinjiang region's strategic partner for deploying "cloud computing" technologies across the government,[5] a business category that included Huawei's surveillance products. Huawei-based facial-recognition solutions were set up at transportation hubs in Xinjiang's capital, Ürümqi, and along the highways crisscrossing the region. By 2017, Huawei had set up a database for Ürümqi police that the facial-recognition surveillance cameras fed into, which boasted a trove of some fifty million images of faces. A slide deck created by Huawei and one of its partners touted the systems as producing "thousands of accurate alerts to police."[6]

The Xinjiang crackdown—coupled with harsh restrictions against pro-democracy protesters in Hong Kong—would have a significant effect on how the international community viewed China. Since the early 2000s, when China was in the process of joining the WTO, there had been a widespread belief both within and outside the country that the nation's growing economic openness would bring a freer flow of information and a gradual shift toward more democratic governance. Now people had to wonder if they had been wrong.

If Ren Zhengfei had any opinions out of step with the official line on the Xinjiang crackdown, he would have known to keep them to himself. Beijing was warning Chinese nationals of consequences if they were caught "spreading rumors" about the situation in Xinjiang. Years later, pushed by foreign reporters to give his opinion on the Xinjiang repression, Ren largely echoed Beijing's talking points. "Which do you think is better for people—the approach the U.S. has taken toward problems in the Middle East or the approach the Chinese government has taken on the Xinjiang issue?" Ren said to Canada's *The Globe and Mail*. "In the past few years, Xinjiang hasn't seen major social incidents or unrest. Xinjiang is becoming stable."[7] Asked by the UK's Sky News if he agreed with the crackdown, Ren replied, "I am not familiar with government policies in Xinjiang. I only know the overall living standards there are improving. . . . I am not a politician, and I don't study policies."[8]

By the fall of 2017, Huawei's HiSilicon unit had launched its first smartphone chip embedded with AI functions, the Kirin 970, which the company said was capable of recognizing two thousand images per minute.[9] Huawei touted its fledgling AI technologies as helpful to consumers in many ways. These technologies, the company said, had helped China Merchants Bank shorten the time it took to issue a credit card—from fifteen days to five minutes. It was also working with the Chinese startup iFLYTEK on speech-recognition systems, which would be integrated into Huawei smartphones and could help people who spoke different dialects in different parts of China bridge the linguistic gap.

But Huawei was also marketing its AI solutions for advanced internet censorship. In a slide deck, it said its "video fingerprinting" solution could identify similar video clips online, even when someone tried to obscure them by stitching on a different beginning, reversing the images, or overlaying text.[10] Political dissidents were known to use these methods on Chinese social media platforms in an effort to foil censors. Huawei's slide deck said that the company's algorithms were able to do "political detection," which could pick out "sensitive political content and figures" in pictures, text, and video.

What's more, Huawei was pushing AI-equipped surveillance cameras, considering them to be a major market opportunity. In an internal study of 5G use cases, Huawei ranked AI-enabled video surveillance among its top ten AI applications in terms of market potential.[11] In Shenzhen, traffic police began testing out Huawei's AI algorithms on traffic lights at nine intersections; the algorithms adjusted the length of the lights based on real-time traffic flow. Ken Hu, one of Huawei's rotating chairmen, plugged the technology as increasing average vehicle speed by 15 percent. "In the past, drivers looked up at traffic lights to determine whether they should stop or go," he wrote. "Today, traffic lights are looking back at vehicles, counting them up and deciding when to give the green light."

Ren expressed mixed feelings about AI. Speaking to researchers in 2017, he compared AI to nuclear energy, saying it could be used for both good and bad. "I also fear that artificial intelligence will damage human values," he added. "But we cannot stop the progress of human society."[12] After watching a *Star Trek* movie, Ren commented that he found the vision of a spaceship staffed by robots depressing. "I felt really let down when I left the theater," he said. "This movie shows how lonely and horrifying life could be in the AI era. While AI is able to meet some human needs, people will still need a human touch."[13]

Overseas, Huawei's Safe City surveillance solutions were now in use in more than eighty countries, covering some eight hundred million people. As it sought further growth in 2018, the company announced $1.5 billion in financing for African nations to purchase its Safe City solutions. Huawei's technologies were being met with open arms in some countries. After Donald Trump, then president, tweeted that the US had gotten "nothing but lies & deceit" from Pakistan in exchange for billions of dollars in aid, furious Pakistani officials unveiled with fanfare a Safe City project for Punjab Province. At the project's launch, Punjab's chief minister, Shehbaz Sharif, said that Pakistan's answer to the US was that "we do not need your money, loan, or grant. We will eat simple food but will not let our nation be insulted."[14]

But Huawei's growing surveillance footprint was raising alarm in Washington. "This coupling of innovation and authoritarianism is deeply troubling and has spread beyond China itself," Rep. Adam Schiff (D-CA), chairman of the House Permanent Select Committee on Intelligence, said at a hearing. "The export of this technology gives countries the technological tools they need to emulate Beijing's model of social and political control."[15]

Even within China, the growing ubiquity of video surveillance was eliciting some concern. Authorities had discovered with alarm that a number of surveillance cameras in Jiangsu Province had been hacked and were being controlled remotely from overseas. In Shenzhen, officials had Huawei and other local companies publicly pledge that they would not abuse facial recognition and other surveillance technologies.[16]

After returning from the Reno 5G summit, where Huawei had made its breakthrough, Michael Thelander, the telecom industry consultant, got a voicemail from a woman who said she was with the FBI and wanted to talk to him.[17] Thinking it a scam, Thelander didn't reply. Then he got an email from the same FBI agent. She mentioned that she'd dropped by his office, which was also his home. "So I'm getting a visit by the FBI, an email, and a voicemail, all within the period of about two days," he said. Thelander noted that the FBI knew he'd been to the standards meeting and wanted to ask if Huawei's inclusion in 5G raised any espionage concerns. By his own account, he told her that he didn't think it did. A mobile standard was like an open recipe, he said, with everyone knowing the ingredient list. "I said, 'You know, everybody comes together—everybody works together—and there's no secrets being stolen,'" he reported.

The quiet FBI inquiries were an early sign of what was to come. On the campaign trail, Trump had promised to confront China, and now his administration began laying the groundwork for a broad trade war—and, specifically, a war against Huawei. Following the levying of sanctions against ZTE, the Commerce Department had served an administrative subpoena on Huawei, ordering it to turn over all information about its export of US technology to Cuba, Iran, North Korea, Sudan, and Syria. Then, in December 2017, US prosecutors reached out to Huawei's lawyers, telling them that they were going to file criminal charges against Huawei for intellectual-property theft from US companies.

By the start of 2018, US mobile operators were beginning to distance themselves from Huawei's smartphones under pressure from Washington. Some stopped carrying Huawei's handsets—first AT&T, then Verizon.

Then came an explosive report from the French newspaper *Le Monde*. The paper published an exposé revealing that officials at the African Union's headquarters had discovered its servers were mysteriously sending data to China each night between midnight and 2:00 a.m. The futuristic compound, a gift from Beijing, had been constructed by China in Ethiopia's capital, Addis Ababa. "According to several sources within the institution, all sensitive content could have been spied on by China," *Le Monde Afrique* reported. The Australian Strategic Policy Institute (ASPI), a think tank funded by Australia's Department of Defence and the US State Department, published a follow-up piece that expanded on the story: the equipment in question had been supplied by Huawei.

In the media frenzy that followed, Huawei called the allegations of impropriety "completely unsubstantiated" and declared that it had "never" installed a back door in its thirty-year history. "The solutions provided to the AU was controlled, managed, and operated by the organization's IT staff, and Huawei had no access to AU data," Huawei said. The reports of Huawei servers pinging data back to China fell short of a smoking gun, as there was no indication that Huawei was aware of the espionage or participated in it. But to Huawei's critics, the scandal was proof that Huawei gear could contain security risks, whether Huawei's top brass was aware of them or not.

It was amid this string of unfortunate events that Sun Yafang, Huawei's chairwoman for nineteen years, stepped down. Huawei didn't explain the reason. Sun was in her early sixties, which was already past retirement age for many women in China, where the government encouraged early withdrawal from the workforce to make jobs available to younger workers. But perhaps the albatross that was her MSS background had become too much of a liability in light of the growing pressure from Washington.

Sun was going to remain at Huawei, but she would take on a less prominent role. Her successor as chairman was Howard Liang, also known as Liang Hua, a company veteran who had joined in 1995 and worked his way up through positions like president of the supply chain and CFO.

Up through the end, the division of power between Sun and Ren as chairwoman and CEO remained shrouded in mystery to many. "Honestly, I never really understood what the relationship was between them," said one senior industry executive who worked with them both. Another executive at a Huawei vendor remarked: "We were confused as to what her authority was. We had very little direct interaction with her, apart from her being the sign-off person for a bunch of things." After he left the company, William Plummer, a one-time US spokesman for Huawei, said: "To hear it from the Chinese side, she couldn't possibly have any influence [from MSS]. To hear it from the US side, she was groomed and then inserted into this company as the ministry's source. I would imagine there's probably a little truth to all of it."

The Trump administration had begun a diplomatic outreach campaign to try to get other countries to ban Huawei and ZTE from their 5G networks.

Governments around the world were in the middle of testing 5G systems and picking suppliers for their network upgrades, which would freeze them in with those vendors for the next decade or so, until the arrival of 6G. Huawei had a running start, thanks in part to Beijing's early rollout of 5G across China. The company had all but a lock on emerging markets, and it was looking strong in developed markets too: Huawei announced that, in cooperation with local partners, it was moving forward with 5G trials in Germany, France, and Italy. US officials were unsettled. "It looked like Huawei was going to run the tables," recalled Keith Krach, the Trump administration's undersecretary of state for economic growth, energy, and the environment. "Both sides of the aisle were hitting the panic button."

John Bolton, national security adviser to Trump, said that 5G networks were more "flat" than previous generations, which theoretically made it easier for a hacker to burrow from one part of a network into others, elevating the risk of relying on an untrusted supplier. "The threat to 5G was not the physical equipment," he said in an interview. "It was the ability to put programming in that could divert communications and otherwise pick up communications down the line."[18]

Republican lawmakers were ramping up their rhetoric. Speaking on the Senate floor in June 2018, Senator Tom Cotton (R-AR) called for Huawei and ZTE to be blocked from doing business in the US. "These companies have proven themselves to be untrustworthy, and at this point I think the only fitting punishment would be to give them the death penalty—that is, to put them out of business in the United States," he said.[19] Senator Marco Rubio (R-FL) called for the government to "put them out of business by denying them the ability to buy U.S. semiconductors."[20] Eric Xu, Huawei's plainspoken rotating chairman, blasted the lawmakers as "closed-minded and ill-informed" in an interview with the industry publication *Light Reading*. "It seems to me their bodies are in the information age but their minds are still in the agrarian age," Xu said. Huawei later took out ads in *The New York Times* and the *Financial Times* to backpedal Xu's words, supplanting them with more diplomatic ones.

In August 2018, shortly after the trade war officially began, Trump signed into law a defense bill that included a broad ban on US government agencies buying ZTE and Huawei. That month, Australia became the first country in the world to formally ban Huawei and ZTE from its future 5G network. In his memoir, Australian prime minister Malcolm Turnbull recalled wrestling over the issue and talking it over with Trump and US vice president Mike Pence, as well as with Australian intelligence chief Mike Burgess. Turnbull felt that the risk of infrastructure being shut down or infiltrated by a state-sponsored adversary was not one they could ignore.[21]

Ren was adamant that Huawei's work in 5G was not a threat. He said that his company was just trying to contribute apolitically to technological research in a way that could benefit all of humanity. "5G is not an atomic bomb," he insisted.[22]

Z TE's seventy-five-year-old founder and chairman, Hou Weigui, had retired under the cloud of ignominy swept in by US sanctions, though the company said that Hou's retirement was planned and unrelated. In order to get the sanctions lifted, ZTE fired its CEO, pleaded guilty to three felony counts, agreed to pay the US government $1.2 billion in fines, and made other humiliating concessions. And the first time the sanctions were lifted, it turned out to be a false start. In April 2018, the Trump administration again clamped down on ZTE, claiming that the company had not followed through on its agreement to punish employees who violated US sanctions against Iran.

Unexpectedly, ZTE was saved in the end by Trump himself, who did an about-face that people found hard to explain. "President Xi of China, and I, are working together to give massive Chinese phone company, ZTE, a way to get back into business, fast," Trump tweeted in May 2018. "Too many jobs in China lost. Commerce Department has been instructed to get it done!" After extracting an additional monetary penalty of $1.4 billion from ZTE, the administration lifted the sanctions again that July. Some thought Trump had made the concession in hopes of sealing a trade deal with China. "I thought the whole thing was a mistake on his part," Bolton said. "He gave it to Xi Jinping as kind of a gift, which is the way Xi Jinping took it, and I think it sent the wrong signal. You know, if you're going to have a coherent policy, it has to be applied coherently."[23]

There was one part of ZTE's plea deal that would have particularly stung: the company had to assist the US government with any criminal investigations of third parties for three years. ZTE would have to provide the feds with "any document, record, or other materials" for which they asked. For years, ZTE had sought to convince the world that it was not the Chinese government's informant. Now it was compelled to be an informant—but for Washington.

That November, Ren's youngest daughter, Annabel Yao, glided into a Parisian ballroom on the arm of Belgian count Gaspard de Limburg-Stirum. Draped in peach tulle, she was one of only nineteen young women selected to make their debut that year at Le Bal, an exclusive debutante ball, and one of just three who opened the event with a waltz. It was elite company: the other debutantes included Countess Gabrielle de Pourtalès, a descendant of French nobility; Princess Ananya Raje Scindia of the Indian city of Gwalior; True Whitaker, daughter of Oscar-winning actor Forest Whitaker; and Julia McCaw, daughter of AT&T Wireless's founder, Craig McCaw. "I really wanted an opportunity to feel like I've grown up, and to step out into the world," she was quoted as saying in a *Vogue* write-up of the event.[24] She told *Paris Match* that even though she was born into a privileged family, she had worked hard, practicing ballet fifteen hours a week and doing homework until late at night. "My goal is to make the world a better place to live," she said.[25] To mark the occasion, Ren had consented to a rare family photograph with his daughter and her mother, Yao Ling. It was splashed across the press.

At the time of the debutante ball, Annabel Yao was beginning her junior year at Harvard, where she studied computer science. According to the *Paris Match* profile, she had gotten a perfect score on her ACT after attending an international high school in Shanghai. She led an active campus life, serving as finance chair for the Harvard College China Forum and dancing in the student-run Harvard Ballet Company. The piece said that Annabel Yao, discouraged by the grueling training schedules, had once considered giving up ballet, but her father had encouraged her to continue, saying it was not the Ren family way to quit something halfway.

There seemed to be some jealousy between Annabel Yao and Meng Wanzhou—perhaps inevitable for two half sisters whose paths had diverged so thoroughly. Meng had grown up in the early days of material want and patchy education, her wish to study in the US scuttled by her poor command of English. But out of all the children, she had emerged as her father's apprentice at Huawei, and Annabel Yao could never hope to take that place, despite her Harvard degree in computer science. Ren's younger daughter had grown up amid luxury, speaking fluent English effortlessly and moving with ease in international circles. But she wished for more attention from her father. The domestic press didn't help things by constantly comparing the two. "I often wonder, *Why do they speak ill of me?* And why everyone likes my sister but not me," Annabel Yao once told a documentary maker.

In 2018, in a surprise to many, Huawei announced that while Ren was remaining CEO, he was handing over his role as one of the company's four vice-chairs—forty-six-year-old Meng would take on this mantle. People debated if Ren was quietly maneuvering his daughter to succeed him, despite his consistent protests that his children would not be his successors.

Ren would later say that Meng was considering leaving Huawei during this period; perhaps the promotion was a bid to get her to stay. She had occasionally hinted that she wished for more independence. In an essay about the accomplishments of her finance department within Huawei, Meng cited Shu Ting's "To the Oak," a popular contemporary Chinese poem in which Shu writes that she wants to be intertwined with her love yet independent, like a ceiba tree growing alongside an oak. "I am confident that we won't be clinging morning glories hanging on the great oak's branches, nor infatuated birds singing endless praise," Meng wrote. "We are tall and upright ceiba trees in our own right!"[26]

In what might have been her last public appearance in 2018, Meng spoke to university students in her hometown, Chengdu, that autumn. She sounded thoughtful and a bit melancholy. Meng counseled the students that it took ten thousand hours to become great at something, and that a person might have only seventy thousand work hours in their life. "Life is fleeting, and energy is finite," she said. "If we still have dreams, if we still have aspirations, then we have to make choices and focus our limited energy on those choices. The coming days are not endless, and our choices determine our future."[27] Meng didn't know it yet, but a New York court had already issued a sealed warrant for her arrest.

Financial Times editor Lionel Barber recalled Ken Hu, one of Huawei's rotating chairmen, visiting him in London that fall and asking him what he thought about the developments in Washington. Barber told Hu that he wasn't in the business of giving advice but that Huawei certainly had a problem, given the perception of the company as an arm of the Chinese state. Barber said: "You guys are going to get whacked!"[28]

24

Hostage Diplomacy

Meng Wanzhou had not packed light.[1] She'd checked two large suitcases, four cardboard boxes, and a large purple duffel bag for the twelve-day trip.[2] The first stop was Vancouver. She'd be there less than a day before catching an 11:25 p.m. red-eye to Mexico City with her deputy, Ji Hui, Huawei's finance president. From there, she would be continuing on to Costa Rica, Argentina, and France.

She'd kept up her busy travel schedule as 2018 drew to a close. She'd spent much of the year jet-setting across the globe, making stops in Paris, London, Nice, Dublin, Warsaw, Singapore, Vancouver, Tokyo, and Brussels.[3] But as she prepared to squeeze in one more trip, a plan for her detention was being drawn up in Vancouver.

A week before Meng's flight on December 1, 2018, the Vancouver International Airport's police outpost received a phone call from Ottawa asking if it was possible for an arriving passenger to exit the airport without encountering a customs officer. Then, the morning before her departure, the Canadian Justice Department's Vancouver office emailed a unit of the national police service—the Royal Canadian Mounted Police, nicknamed "the Mounties"—that was focused on international organized crime. "Please send an officer this afternoon," the email said. "We expect an urgent request for a provisional arrest from abroad."

Constable Winston Yep had joined the Mounties in 2001, starting out on bicycle patrol.[4] Over the next seventeen years, he slowly climbed the ranks to acting corporal of his unit, which specialized in extradition requests from other countries and cooperation with Interpol. He was already going to the Justice Department that day on other business, so he was selected to handle this mysterious assignment. At the office, Yep was told that Meng was his target. Back on August 22, a New York court had issued a sealed arrest warrant for her. Now US officials were invoking their country's extradition treaty with Canada.

The instructions for Yep were specific. He was to locate her discreetly, confirm her identity, and tell her she was under arrest. After giving her an opportunity to call a lawyer, he needed to make sure she was fingerprinted and booked into jail. The FBI was involved, but it was staying off-site for optics reasons. "FBI will not be present in an effort to avoid the perception of influence," the Canadian Security Intelligence Service wrote in an internal report.[5]

As Yep and his team formulated their plan, one big question was when to arrest her. They could potentially board the plane as soon as it pulled into the gate and haul her off. But they nixed that idea, not wanting to create a scene. Instead, they decided to let border officers stop her. These officers would ask her some questions and check her luggage before Yep stepped in to tell her she was under arrest.

A colleague texted Yep, eagerly observing that they would all earn overtime pay for working on a Saturday: "OT for everyone!"

"Unwanted OT!" Yep typed back. "We didn't want it!"[6]

First thing the next morning, the FBI sent confirmation that Meng had boarded the overnight flight from Hong Kong. She was traveling with a female companion. The FBI sent over a physical description: Meng's hair was slightly longer than shoulder-length, and she was wearing white shoes, dark pants, and a white T-shirt with lettering on the front.[7]

M eng's flight had gone smoothly, pulling into gate 65 of YVR twelve minutes early, at 11:18 a.m. But things went amiss as soon as she stepped into the airport. Two customs officers were at the gate, checking passengers' passports. When they got to her, they asked her for her phones.

When she surrendered her devices, one of the officers slipped them into a shiny silver pouch. They asked her to go with them through customs and immigration, and she ended up at a secondary inspection counter in a deserted corner of the airport. Unbeknownst to Meng, there was a one-way mirror nearby, and Yep was behind it, watching.

The two border agents, Sowmith Katragadda and Scott Kirkland, started questioning her and going through her luggage.[8] They asked if she wanted an interpreter, but she declined. Katragadda, the one who had asked for her phones at the start, was now asking most of the questions while Kirkland scribbled notes in a little notebook.

They searched her purse, which jangled with a key chain of the Eiffel Tower and miniature macarons. They rifled through each suitcase. They pulled out an iPad decorated with a sticker of Winnie-the-Pooh skipping, a MacBook Air embellished with a big sticker of a fairylike woman wearing a flower crown, and a USB stick connected to a pink charm with white flowers. They confiscated all the electronics.

Meng told them that she visited Canada two to three times a year and owned two properties in the country. She also owned three apartments in London, two houses in Hong Kong, and two houses in Shenzhen, she said. She mentioned that she used to have a People's Republic of China passport but relinquished it when she got her Hong Kong passport. The stamps in her passport reflected that she traveled widely, including to the UK, Mexico, Senegal, Germany, Panama, and Brunei.

At some point, Kirkland piped up to ask if Meng was traveling to Argentina for the G20 summit and if she would be meeting with foreign diplomats and telecom representatives there. Meng said that she would not be, and that she was attending strictly internal Huawei meetings. Kirkland scratched this down in his notebook: *4 day Argentina for internal meetings, then on to France.*

Katragadda disappeared for lengths of time, leaving Meng alone with Kirkland. It had now been two hours since she entered the airport, and there was no sign of the interrogation ending. Meng needed to use the washroom, and an officer accompanied her there and back. She was getting more alarmed. She repeatedly asked why she had been selected for secondary inspection. Meng told Kirkland about the time she was questioned by immigration officials at JFK four years ago. They had released her after two hours, she said, allowing her to continue her travels.

Now, Katragadda's supervisor, Sanjit Dhillon, came out and asked her some questions, homing in on finding out if Huawei did business in Iran. "I don't know," Meng replied. Dhillon pushed back, saying that she was the CFO of a multibillion-dollar company and that he didn't believe she wouldn't know such a thing. Meng conceded that Huawei did have an office in Iran.

Then Kirkland asked Meng to provide the PINs for both phones. He wrote them down on a loose sheet of paper.

At 2:11 p.m., nearly three hours after Meng arrived at the airport, Katragadda told her that the customs examination was complete. But she still could not go. The Royal Canadian Mounted Police also wanted to speak with her. Meng agreed, and Yep appeared with a translator.[9] "The reason we're here today is regarding an extradition matter," he said. "We have issued a warrant against Ms. Meng for her arrest and eventually an extradition to the United States." He told her she was accused of fraud.

Meng was confused. "Right, I'm not clear what has happened," she said. "Why would I have an arrest warrant, and I have got involved in fraud?"

"Okay, I don't have the details here. Basically, this charge originated from the United States. They have a fraud charge against you regarding your company, Huawei," Yep said. "This is from the United States, not in Canada." He told her she had a right to counsel.

"Can I tell my family members?"

"You cannot."

"My family members will be worried if they can't find me."

"We will talk about this later."

Meng also asked if she could say a few words to her travel companion before being taken away, and if she could use her iPad in jail. No and no. Just like that, she had been cut off from the outside world.

After she was booked and fingerprinted, Meng was brought to the Alouette Correctional Centre for Women, a low white building hidden behind a thick stand of evergreen trees on the rural outskirts of Vancouver. She would call her time there the worst days of her life.[10]

News of Meng's detention did not reach the wider world until several days later. But at Huawei, Ren Zhengfei and his advisers had to make an immediate decision. Within days, Ren was scheduled to appear in Argentina for business meetings. The plan had been that he would meet Meng there. They debated whether to call off the trip. Meng had sent a note to her father through her husband: "Dad, they are coming after you. Please be careful."[11] Ren decided to go through with the trip, transferring in Dubai and steering clear of stops in Western countries. "It was risky, but if I acted scared, everyone else would too, right? I had to go ahead." Ren's wife was worried. She stayed up late, checking in with him—"Have you crossed out of China yet? Have you boarded the plane?"—and was only able to relax upon his safe return to China.

It would remain a mystery what, exactly, had compelled Ren to keep his travel plans despite such dire extradition risks. China's leader, Xi Jinping, was in Buenos Aires at that moment for G20, along with other Beijing officials. So were other political leaders, including American president Donald Trump and Canadian prime minister Justin Trudeau. It seemed reasonable to think that the urgency of his trip had to do with the high-level officials gathered for G20. But Ren and his team echoed what Meng had told the Canadian border officers: they said the trip was only for internal meetings. Huawei's human-resources chief, Jack Lyu, who had accompanied Ren on the trip, told reporters that Ren did not allow his team to discuss Meng's detention, expecting them to focus on the meeting about the company's transformation of its overseas subsidiary structure. "He thinks this is his personal thing," Lyu said. "He communicated with our lawyer teams in Canada, but all the people should 100 percent engage in the discussion of the transformation project."

News of Meng's detention finally emerged four days later, with the Canadian Justice Department issuing a terse statement. The department said it could not provide more detail, as Meng had sought and been granted a publication ban. China's ambassador to Canada canceled an appearance before Canadian lawmakers that day, though Beijing's response was otherwise cautious. China's Ministry of Foreign Affairs said it had lodged stern requests with Canadian officials, demanding that they clarify the situation and release Meng. As the daughter of Huawei's founder, she was corporate royalty. It was hard to imagine that Beijing would not respond more forcefully. Indeed, the Canadian Security Intelligence Service was warning internally to brace for diplomatic "shock waves." Then, nine days after Meng's arrest, the other shoe dropped.

Chinese authorities detained two Canadian men in China. The first, Michael Kovrig, was a former Canadian diplomat now working for the International Crisis Group. The second, Michael Spavor, led tours to North Korea and had high-level contacts in the country, having facilitated NBA player Dennis Rodman's 2014 meeting with North Korean leader Kim Jong Un. The two men were thrown into detention, kept in cells with the lights on day and night.[12] While Beijing denied that their detainment had anything to do with Meng, it was clear that the two Michaels were Beijing's leverage for negotiating Meng's return.

There would later be varying accounts as to whether or not Trump knew about the plan to detain Meng and who, exactly, made the decision. Trump's national security adviser, John Bolton, said in an interview that it had been the Justice Department's call. "I mean, obviously any issue at the Justice Department is subject to presidential reversal," he stated. "But on something like this, that's really a tactical call on their part." Bolton said that Trump was regularly briefed on the investigation, despite later claiming that he had no advance knowledge of the plan to arrest Meng. "He knew about it. There's no question about that," Bolton maintained. "Whether he remembered or not, it's always an interesting question."

"We had stepped on some big toes," Bolton continued. "You know, he knew everything about this before it happened. But like many examples in Trump's administration, when a decision happened that didn't necessarily go the way he wanted it to—even though he knew about it or had made the decision—he'd find somebody else to try to blame it on."

At the White House Christmas party, Trump seemed conflicted about Meng's detention, describing her as "the Ivanka Trump of China." Asked by Reuters if he would intervene in Meng's case, Trump said he might if it could help him close a trade deal with China. "If I think it's good for what will be certainly the largest trade deal ever made—which is a very important thing—what's good for national security—I would certainly intervene if I thought it was necessary."[13]

O n the continuum of offenses," Meng's attorney was saying, "we're not dealing with military issues, or dual-use goods, or— or murder."[14]

It was several days after Meng's arrest, and she was in court for her bail hearing. Whatever came next, she hoped she could await it in her own home. One of Meng's attorneys, David Martin, was telling the court that she was an upstanding executive who would not risk the embarrassment of attempting to flee.

"Again, I don't trivialize any allegation, but on the continuum of conduct, I'm sure Your Lordship has seen more serious offenses," Martin said.

Meng had written a statement to Justice William Ehrcke. "If this Honourable Court grants me judicial interim release, I will abide by any condition imposed," she wrote. "I will surrender both of my passports. . . . I will scrupulously abide by any curfew. . . . My father founded Huawei and I would never do anything that would cause the company reputational damage."

Meng's bail hearing was the biggest event that the Vancouver courthouse had seen in years. Reporters from around the world poured in, along with protesters. FREE MS. MENG, one protester's sign read. WE LOVE YOU HUAWEI, another said.

Until this moment, Meng had closely guarded her privacy, hardly ever disclosing anything about her personal life. But the stakes were now too high. Her lawyers shared what they hoped was a sympathetic portrait with the court.[15] She was a mother of four, her lawyers said. She had a ten-year-old daughter with her current husband, Liu Xiaozong, and three sons from previous marriages, one of whom was attending school in the United States. She suffered from hypertension and had undergone surgery for thyroid cancer in 2011. She spent two to three weeks each year in Vancouver, where her in-laws summered. She had held permanent residency status in Canada at one point, though she had since relinquished it.

She submitted photos to the court that painted a picture of them as a down-to-earth family. Meng was accustomed to attending work events in designer dresses, but in these snapshots, she hung out with her husband and children, casually dressed in colorful sweatsuits. Here they were sitting in the grass at a park; here, gathered by a piece of driftwood on the beach; here, smiling outside their house on West Twenty-Eighth Avenue, a large, sturdy gray house with a cross-gabled roof and big windows trimmed in black paint.

Several friends submitted character reference letters on her behalf. One was written by Bao Fan, the high-flying Chinese investment banker at China Renaissance who counted many of the nation's buzziest internet companies among his clients. In his letter, he called her "a person of highest professional and moral standards," saying they had worked together. A Vancouver neighbor also penned a letter, sharing that Meng gave the impression of being a "quiet and modest individual" during her brief summer stays there with her family. "I believe that Sabrina would not jeopardize the well-being and future status of her children," the neighbor wrote.

There was some legal uncertainty over whether Meng's husband could guarantee her bail as a noncitizen who was only in Canada on a six-month visitor's visa. Several friends who were permanent Canadian residents stepped in as additional guarantors. One told the court that they had worked with Meng at Huawei in the 1990s and had traveled to Moscow with her in 1997. They had since settled in Vancouver as an insurance agent. "We also understand that should Ms. Meng violate her bail conditions, we might lose one-half million dollars net equity value of our home, which will impact our family's life significantly," they wrote to the court. "We're confident Ms. Meng will not breach any conditions imposed upon her given her character and integrity."

When Justice Ehrcke announced that Meng would be released on bail, she burst into tears. Meng had to wear a GPS tracking anklet at all times, but she would have relative freedom. She could travel around Vancouver between 6:00 a.m. and 11:00 p.m., so long as she was accompanied by security guards.

As Meng walked out into the cold night air in a purple parka, she was swarmed by reporters.

"Ms. Meng! Ms. Meng!"

"Ms. Meng, what's your reaction to being granted bail today?"

Meng tried to avoid eye contact. She looked at her feet, then to the road. There was no car at the curb.

"The vehicle is not in place," someone on her security detail said urgently into their phone. "She's out on the sidewalk. Vehicle's *not* in place."

The press scrum surged forward, cameras flashing. "Back up a bit, please," a security guard said. One of her staffers put his arm around her to try to shield her from view.

"Ms. Meng, what's your reaction to being granted bail today?"

"Ms. Meng, why should people believe you that you won't breach your bail?"

The car finally arrived. Meng scrambled in, out of sight from prying eyes. The big gray house on West Twenty-Eighth Avenue had long been her summer retreat. Now it was her gilded cage. Under the watch of security guards, she walked up the steps.

25

Waterloo

THE TRADE WAR: 2019-2020

I s that everybody?" asked Acting Attorney General Matthew Whitaker, looking to his right and left. Beside him on the stage were a row of officials, including Secretary of Homeland Security Kirstjen Nielsen, Secretary of Commerce Wilbur Ross, and FBI Director Christopher Wray. "Good-looking crew," Whitaker said.[1]

It was hard to think of the last time that so many top officials had shown up just to announce a corporate investigation. None wanted to miss the unsealing of criminal charges against Huawei and its CFO, Meng Wanzhou, at the US Justice Department's headquarters in January 2019. Now Whitaker announced that prosecutors had filed twenty-three charges against "Wah-way"—this pronunciation of Huawei's name, with a silent *h*, had persisted in the West for inscrutable reasons—along with its CFO. Whitaker said that the criminal activity went back at least ten years and extended "all the way to the top."

If Huawei's executives had any lingering hopes that Meng's detention could be smoothed over as a misunderstanding, these were swiftly dashed. Huawei, Meng Wanzhou, and the Huawei shell company Skycom were charged with thirteen counts related to Huawei's business in Iran, including bank fraud and conspiracy to commit wire fraud and money laundering. A second indictment charged Huawei with ten counts tied to theft of trade secrets.

US authorities said they had uncovered a series of shell companies that Huawei was using to obscure its business dealings in Iran. Skycom and Canicula weren't separate companies; they were just Huawei by other names. The prosecutors said a former Skycom employee in Iran had told them that upon showing up for work at Skycom's offices, the employee had discovered that all fellow employees in the building wore Huawei badges and used Huawei email addresses.[2] Two other former Skycom employees had also provided details about the intertwined nature of Huawei and Skycom, including contracting documents that bore Huawei's logo at the top but were signed by an individual on behalf of Skycom. US authorities had also searched the laptop of a Huawei finance manager leaving the United States in 2018, obtaining confidential company spreadsheets that included Skycom and Canicula alongside known Huawei subsidiaries. Prosecutors said this was proof that Skycom and Canicula were viewed internally as part of Huawei, not as third-party companies.[3]

They now revealed just how closely they had been watching Huawei all these years, starting with the FBI's interview of Ren Zhengfei back in 2007 in New York. They accused him of having made false statements all those years ago when he'd said that Huawei complied with US export controls on Iran. They also alleged that Huawei had pinpointed Chinese employees who knew about the company's Iran business and whisked them back to China in an attempt to obstruct the investigation.

The indictment revealed that even as HSBC had been wooing Huawei with more financing, the bank had been cooperating with the US Justice Department, helping it build its case. As it turned out, HSBC was obliged to help the feds, due to an earlier sanctions-violation run-in with the Justice Department in 2012. Under the terms of its deferred prosecution agreement, HSBC had agreed to cooperate with the Justice Department in the future.[4] Now it had handed its books over to the DOJ. According to prosecutors, between 2010 and 2014, Skycom had conducted some $100 million in transactions through HSBC, which ultimately cleared these transactions through the US financial system.

Perhaps most alarming to the Ren family was that prosecutors had zeroed in on Meng. They had gotten their hands on a PowerPoint presentation about Huawei's Iran business that Meng had delivered to HSBC in August 2013. Prosecutors accused Huawei of therein making "numerous misrepresentations" about its Iran unit, Skycom, and its compliance with US laws.

The indictment also revealed that Huawei executives were right in their suspicions that US authorities had copied information off Meng's electronic devices when she was stopped at New York's JFK Airport in 2014. Prosecutors cited a file that had been in the "unallocated space" of one of Meng's devices, which suggested it might have been deleted and recovered. The file read:

SUGGESTED TALKING POINTS

The core of the suggested talking points regarding Iran/Skycom: Huawei's operation in Iran comports with the laws, regulations and sanctions as required by the United Nations, the United States and the European Union. The relationship with Skycom is that of normal business cooperation. Through regulated trade organizations and procedures, Huawei requires that Skycom promises to abide by relevant laws and regulations and export controls. Key information 1: In the past—ceased to hold Skycom shares 1, With regards to cooperation: Skycom was established in 1998 and is one of the agents for Huawei products and services. Skycom is mainly an agent for Huawei.

It seemed clear that prosecutors were trying to build a case that Meng had not only known the details of Huawei's business in Iran but had also actively conspired to mislead others about them.

U p to this point, Ren's public appearances had been so rare that *The Economist* once dubbed him "the Invisible Mr. Ren," describing him as "the most reclusive boss in the technology industry."[5] But the crisis prompted him to do something he'd hardly ever done before: step into the media limelight. A month and a half after his daughter's detention, a seventy-four-year-old Ren walked out to face the international press corps.[6]

He had gone for a dignified but friendly look: a dark-blue sport coat over a light-blue shirt, no tie. Before him were journalists from

The New York Times, The Wall Street Journal, the *Financial Times,* the Associated Press, CNBC, and other major media outlets from around the world. Ren sat down before a microphone, took a breath, and began to tell his life story.

"I joined the military during China's Cultural Revolution," he said. "At that time, there was chaos almost everywhere, including in agriculture and the industry. The country was facing very difficult times."

Asked how he felt about his daughter's detention, Ren said he was declining to comment on the case, as it was best left to the judicial process. But he began reciting a string of thanks. "As Meng Wanzhou's father, I miss her very much. And I'm deeply grateful to the fairness of the Honourable Justice William Ehrcke. I'm also much grateful to prosecutor John Gibb-Carsley and prosecutor Kerry Swift. I also thank the Alouette Correctional Centre for Women for its humane management. Thanks to Meng Wanzhou's cellmates for treating her kindly."

Ren had only praise for Trump, perhaps hoping he was susceptible to flattery. "For President Trump as a person, I still believe he's a great president, in the sense that he was bold to slash taxes," he said. "I think that's conducive to the development of industries in the US."

If Ren had thought he might charm Trump into quickly resolving Meng's case, he would have no such luck. When the soft appeal failed, Huawei began to consider its legal options. In March 2019, Meng's lawyers announced that she was suing the Canadian government, claiming it had been illegal for them to detain, search, and interrogate her without telling her she was under arrest.[7] It wasn't clear if her suit would stand up in court—border agents generally have wide berth to question and search individuals before they enter a country—but it might help public perception of her plight if her lawyers could prove breaches in protocol on the part of the Canadian agents. Soon after, Huawei sued the US government, challenging the constitutionality of the defense bill that Trump had signed into law on August 13, 2018. Section 889 prohibited US government agencies from buying Huawei products. "We are compelled to take this legal action as a proper and last resort," Guo Ping told a packed room of journalists. "We look forward to the court's verdict and trust that it will benefit both Huawei and the American people."

Trump's deputies flooded the zone to declare Huawei a threat. "To say that they don't work with the Chinese government is a false statement," Mike Pompeo said on CNBC's *Squawk Box*. "It is required to by Chinese law."[8] Steve Bannon called Huawei a "dirty bomb inside industrial democracies."[9]

As Huawei's legal team scrambled to build its defense, the fallout began. A number of prominent universities announced they were distancing themselves from the company. First, the University of Oxford said it was suspending all new research grants and donations from Huawei.[10] "This decision will be revisited by the committee in 3–6 months and does not impact existing donations or research projects," the university told its computer science doctoral students in an email. UC Berkeley and Stanford followed suit. "The severity of these accusations raises questions and concerns that only our judicial system can address," a Berkeley administrator wrote to colleagues.[11] These universities had long been under public pressure from politicians on the right to break ties with Huawei. They had resisted, partly because Huawei's donations were welcome funding and partly because they held the loftier belief that science should transcend political squabbles. But the indictments were the last straw.

There was grim news abroad too: a Huawei sales director, Wang Weijing, had just been detained in Poland and charged with espionage. During a trip to Warsaw, US vice president Mike Pence publicly praised Polish president Andrzej Duda for the arrest. The Huawei director was proclaiming his innocence. But reeling from Meng's detention, Huawei decided to cut him loose. A Huawei spokesman told reporters that the company had fired Wang "because the incident in question has brought Huawei into disrepute."[12]

In May 2019, Donald Trump invoked a presidential power generally reserved for wars, terrorist attacks, and pandemics: he declared Huawei a national emergency. "I, Donald J. Trump, President of the United States of America, find that foreign adversaries are increasingly creating and exploiting vulnerabilities in information and communications technology and services," the declaration began.[13] It did not mention Huawei by name, but everyone knew the target. The executive order directed relevant government agencies to take "all appropriate measures" to neutralize Huawei.

The same day, the Commerce Department's Bureau of Industry and Security, which serves as the nation's economic sanctions authority, announced export controls on Huawei.[14] This was the same death blow that ZTE had faced in 2016. Now it was Huawei's turn to confront this existential terror. Like tech companies around the world, Huawei would struggle to make its products without US technology, especially chips and operating systems.

The company relied on Qualcomm and Intel for chips, Google for its Android operating system for smartphones, and Microsoft Windows for laptops. These US companies were reluctant to lose millions of dollars in sales overnight owing to hazy talk of national security. Some executives lobbied the Trump administration behind closed doors, and a few even did so openly. Microsoft's president, Brad Smith, told *Bloomberg Businessweek* that he and his cohorts were pushing US regulators for proof that Huawei was a threat. "Oftentimes, what we get in response is, 'Well, if you knew what we knew, you would agree with us,'" Smith said. "And our answer is, 'Great, show us what you know so we can decide for ourselves. That's the way this country works.'"[15]

Huawei's executives cried foul at this fusillade of attacks. "Politicians in the US are using the strength of an entire nation to come after a private company," Huawei's chief legal officer, Song Liuping, exclaimed to reporters. "They want to put us out of business. This is not normal. Almost never seen in history."[16]

To rally his staff, Ren circulated an old photograph of a World War II–era Soviet bomber jet that was somehow managing to stay aloft despite being riddled with bullets.[17] Ren told them that, like the plane, they would somehow keep flying. Teresa He, the reclusive head of Huawei's chip unit, HiSilicon, also emerged to hearten staff through a rare public letter. If Huawei was really cut off from Qualcomm and Intel, its only hope would be HiSilicon. For years, the unit had worked building "spare tires" for Huawei, He wrote, uncertain if it would ever get to show its full strength, as Huawei prioritized relationships with international vendors. "Now today, it is the decision of history," she wrote. "Overnight, all the spare tires that we built have become the 'main' tires! Our years of blood, sweat, and tears have been cashed in overnight to help the company fulfill its commitment to keep serving customers." Her letter was upbeat, but none of the staff had illusions. The indictment meant that Meng could spend years behind bars. The sanctions meant that Huawei's days might be numbered.

The Commerce Department had given Huawei's US suppliers a grace period of three months to adjust to the sanctions.[18] This was later extended to a year. Huawei seized on this lifeline, rushing to stockpile US chips and other components as it raced to figure out how to survive without US technology. Huawei's US suppliers generally wanted to keep selling to the company. They would be losing big business. Behind closed doors, they lobbied officials in Washington to ease up, warning that sanctions might strengthen China's resolve to develop domestic alternatives to US technology.

Ren told Chinese reporters that Eric Xu, one of the rotating chairs, had phoned him up in the middle of the night to tell him that Huawei's US suppliers were scrambling to fulfill the company's orders. "I was in tears," Ren said. "As a Chinese saying goes, a just cause attracts much support, while an unjust one finds little."[19]

The Trump administration was intensifying its diplomatic campaign to push other governments into excluding Huawei from their upcoming 5G networks.

"Objective number one of the strategic imperative was to take the momentum away from Huawei and replace it with ours," recalled Keith Krach, undersecretary of state for economic growth, energy, and the environment.[20] "You do it by a rolling thunder of announcements, endorsements, wins. I mean, we had a scoreboard."

Krach would develop a sales patter that he would use to try to win over foreign officials. "Even if you're just putting a little bit in your system, you're only as strong as your weakest link," he would say when officials told him they were only using Huawei on the periphery of their networks. Krach would ask them how much cheaper Huawei gear was, then retort, "Well, you're getting ripped off."

"How much is your citizens' personal data worth?" he asked them. "Your companies' proprietary technology and your government's most precious secrets? How much is that worth? Well, that's priceless."

The State Department suffered a setback in April 2019, when the British daily *The Telegraph* reported that Prime Minister Theresa May had given Huawei the green light to build "noncore" parts of the UK's 5G network.[21] The backlash was swift. NSA officials warned that the US would have to reassess its intelligence-sharing relationship with London. An infuriated May launched an internal hunt for the leaker. Within days, she had sacked her defense secretary, Gavin Williamson, telling him in a letter that there was "compelling evidence" pointing to his culpability.[22] It was reflective of just how touchy the Huawei issue had become. The US and UK were close allies, and the company had created a rift between them. Williamson admitted to speaking by phone with Steven Swinford, deputy political editor of *The Telegraph*, on the day the National Security Council had met to discuss the topic, but he swore on his children's lives that he was innocent of leaking.[23]

Pompeo arrived in London soon after to push May on the issue. "Insufficient security will impede the United States' ability to share certain information with trusted networks," Pompeo warned. "This is exactly what China wants. They want to defy Western alliances through bits and bytes, not bullets and bombs."[24]

Trump would later go on *Fox & Friends* to give his own account of the UK push. "With UK, we said, 'We love Scotland Yard very much, but we're not going to do business with you. Because if you use the Huawei system, that means they are spying on you. That would mean they're spying on us.'"[25]

British officials were taken aback by the American saber-rattling. They didn't understand why Huawei was the issue to end all issues, and they didn't understand why the time had to be now to cast them out of the network. With the UK's withdrawal from the European Union imminent, it was a particularly inconvenient time for May's administration to draw swords with China, a major trade partner. They also found the bombast and pushiness of the Trump administration hard to stomach.

"Look, Ambassador," one senior UK security official said, levelly addressing US national security adviser John Bolton during a meeting, "what we can't understand is why, out of all the things—chips, AI, rare earth metals, whatever it is—out of all the things, your administration has decided that a modest amount of base stations on hilltops in England is the epicenter of your new declared tech war with China. Why?"[26]

"You gotta pick something," Bolton replied.

As the year 2019 progressed, Beijing and Washington tallied their wins and losses. Huawei had landed the Philippines, the United Arab Emirates, and Russia among its early 5G customers. Russia's leader, Vladimir Putin, had, in particular, come to Huawei's defense. "There are unceremonious attempts at pushing Huawei away from the global markets," Putin said at a conference in St. Petersburg.[27] The US had won over Australia, New Zealand, and Japan by pledging to shut Huawei out of 5G.

Several key battleground countries remained on the fence. Chief among these was Germany, Europe's largest economy, which was still distrustful of Washington after Edward Snowden revealed that the NSA had tapped German chancellor Angela Merkel's calls for years. Merkel declined to get in line on Huawei. "I tend to trust ourselves to define high security standards, higher than with 4G, 3G, and 2G, but not to shut out vendors from the beginning," Merkel said in a speech, adding that she did not want to isolate the country from entire areas.[28] French president Emmanuel Macron declined to outright exclude Huawei from 5G bidding, though he said he favored European vendors for security reasons. "You would do the same as me," Macron said he told China's leader, Xi Jinping.[29] India's government was allowing Huawei to participate in 5G trials, though it held off on deciding if Huawei could build the actual networks. Canada, which was already up to its eyeballs in political fallout from Meng's detention, was also punting the 5G decision.

For many other countries in the developing world, it didn't matter how persuasively the Trump administration made its pitch. There were hard numbers. They would have to pay significantly more for equipment from other vendors, and they would also incur the wrath of Beijing. "It didn't even make a tiny dent in the emerging markets, or even the middle-income markets that are normally our partners," said Ken Zita, a telecom expert who has, in recent years, helped advise the US government on how to compete against Huawei. "Israel, for example, basically thumbed their nose at Washington. The entire Middle East."[30]

Among those who came to Huawei's defense was Malaysian prime minister Mahathir Mohamad, who declared that Malaysia would use Huawei gear "as much as possible." "Huawei may be powerful in spying or whatever. They can spy as much as they like, because we have no secrets," he said. "America is apparently afraid of the advancement made by Huawei, and they are suspicious that Huawei might be able to, well, spy on them. Maybe that is grounds for condemning. But I think that is not the way to go."[31]

China switched on the world's largest 5G network in November 2019, with most of the West far behind in network construction. There was considerable dismay in the United States. "America is far behind in almost every dimension of 5G," political scientist Graham Allison and former Google CEO Eric Schmidt warned in an op-ed.[32]

Soon after the Trump administration's offensive began in 2019, Huawei purchased a full-page ad in *The Wall Street Journal*. In three lines of large print, it read:

Don't believe everything you hear.
Come and see us.
An open letter to the US media[33]

Beneath this was a signed letter by Catherine Chen, a longtime Huawei executive who was now a senior vice president and head of public and government relations. Chen was willowy, soft-spoken, and a little nervous-looking, but she was one of the most powerful women at Huawei. She had joined the company in 1995, around the

same time as Meng Wanzhou. As head of Huawei's Beijing representative office in the 1990s, she had been the one who smoothed things
over after Ren's gift of cash to a Chinese diplomat had created a ker-
fuffle at the Ministry of Foreign Affairs. Her husband, Cao Yi'an, had
been one of Ren's earliest engineers, back when Huawei was trying
to build its first digital switch. Cao had later left the company and
taken on much of the childcare responsibilities in their family as
Chen continued to climb the corporate ladder. Now, in this open letter published in *The Wall Street Journal*, she wrote that she was seeking greater understanding from the West. "There are only so many
people we can reach out to," she said. "On behalf of Huawei, I would
like to invite members of the US media to visit our campuses and
meet our employees. I hope that you can take what you see and hear
back to your readers, viewers, and listeners, and share this message
with them, to let them know that our doors are always open."

Journalists the world over took her up on the offer: CNN, the *LA
Times*, Sky News, *Handelsblatt, Dagens industri, Kyodo News, Al-
Ahram*. The journalists came in gaggles each week and found a
strange sight. Huawei was a vision of eclectic opulence that would
have put Jay Gatsby himself to shame. At Ox Horn Campus, they
rode the little red train and gawked at the imitations of Heidelberg
Castle and the Palace of Versailles. They saw the black swans gliding
on the lake. There were towering Greek caryatids, the sky-high pillars shaped to look like goddesses. In the conference rooms, the nap-
kins were emblazoned with a cheerful message: "Decent Positive
Enthusiastic."

In the grand European-style hall where Ren generally greeted reporters, there was a painting of the coronation of Napoleon on one
wall and a mural of the 1815 Battle of Waterloo, where Napoleon met

his final defeat. Puzzling at the artwork, a *Der Spiegel* journalist ventured to ask: "Is Huawei a rising or falling empire?"[34] Ren deflected the question lightly, saying that he'd liked the Waterloo mural when he saw it at a Belgium museum, and that the coronation painting had been a gift from a family member of an employee. "Those two paintings don't have anything to do with the situation Huawei faces today," Ren said.

Ren granted each news organization an exclusive interview, an astonishing shift from his previous corporate hermitage. His deputies joked that he was carrying out decades' worth of media engagements in a span of weeks.[35]

It seemed that due to the impossibility of Ren traveling to Canada to testify on his daughter's behalf, his media interviews were a stand-in way for him to serve as a character witness and provide corroborating testimony. Ren praised his daughter as a person with integrity, recounting how she had been careful to repay him the money she borrowed as a college student. "It would be impossible for her to have engaged in any criminal conduct," he said.[36] Ren and his deputies also backed up what Meng had told the border agents—that she was traveling to Argentina purely for internal meetings and not for anything associated with G20. It seemed like an extraordinary timing coincidence, almost defying belief—but that was their story, and they stuck to it.

Ren also used the media interviews to float a modest proposal: that Huawei sell its 5G patents to a Western buyer who could verify and tweak its source code to ensure it was secure, even coming from Huawei.[37]

The company's media blitz coincided with a renewed public controversy over Huawei's obscure ownership structure. In April 2019, a preprint titled "Who Owns Huawei?" had been posted online. Co-written by Christopher Balding of Fulbright University Vietnam and Donald C. Clarke of George Washington University, the paper was stirring up old dust with its striking declaration that Huawei might be "state-controlled and even state-owned," as 98.86 percent of Huawei's shares—all except the 1.14 percent that Ren owned himself—were owned by the company's opaque trade union.[38] "Regardless of who, in a practical sense, owns and controls Huawei, it is clear that the employees do not," the paper concluded. Huawei vociferously disagreed, saying that its employees did indeed own and control the company.

Visiting reporters were now ushered into a gleaming white room with a little sign at the entrance that read ESOP ROOM.[39] ESOP was Huawei shorthand for Employee Stock Ownership Plan. The room had glass-covered display cases that held key Huawei records, like its handwritten corporate registration certificate from 1987 and booklets filled with the names of Huawei's employee shareholders. With only a few moments to peer into the display cases before the tour proceeded, it was hard for visitors to make heads or tails of it.

"It's kind of like Willy Wonka and the Chocolate Factory," one visitor recalled. "You don't really know what you saw. You could see very clean rooms and smiling people."[40]

I f the goal was to charm the press, then Ren seemed to have largely succeeded. "What struck me the most from our roughly one-hour-and-twenty-minute conversation was how candid and frank Ren was," a CNBC reporter remarked.[41] The *New York Times* columnist Thomas Friedman came away from his interview with Ren thinking that Ren's modest proposal was worth consideration if there wasn't proof the company was a threat. "Get to know that name—Huawei," he wrote. "The issues it represents are as important as all the rest of the trade talks combined." Friedman wrote that it was hard to know which side was telling the truth. "If Huawei really is a bad actor, let's get the proof out there and blacklist the hell out of it. If it's not so clear, the Trump team should at least explore Ren's offer to see if there is a pathway for Huawei to assure American intelligence experts and demonstrate good behavior."[42]

In the interviews, Ren continued to praise Trump and his deputies. Asked by a CNN reporter what he would say to Trump, Ren replied, "I would tell him that he is great. No other country in the world can cut taxes in such a short period of time."[43] Speaking with Bloomberg TV, he said, "Even if Huawei collapsed today, we would still be proud. Because it was Trump, not a nobody, that defeated us."[44] Ren called Mike Pence "great" for fighting for his ideals and praised Mike Pompeo as well. "Mike Pompeo is also a great man, with a PhD degree in political science from Harvard University," Ren said to CBS.[45]

Perhaps the one question he got the most was if Huawei helped China's government spy. The journalists asked him that question week after week, sometimes citing China's State Security Law, which says that companies are required to assist in investigations. Each time, Ren denied that Huawei had ever been asked by the Chinese government to aid espionage efforts and said that it would not be willing to do so if asked. "We will certainly say no to any such request," Ren said.[46] He encouraged the reporters to check back in a couple of decades to see if any evidence had come out to the contrary.[47]

Ren was also repeatedly asked about reports that former chair-woman Sun Yafang used to work for China's intelligence agency, the MSS. In 2018, Sun had stepped down as chairwoman but was continuing to play a lower-key role, including serving as Huawei's representative at the Broadband Commission for Sustainable Development, an international organization established by the UN.[48] Ren did not confirm or deny that Sun used to work for the MSS, but he said her background shouldn't disqualify her from working at Huawei. "We cannot say that only people with a spotless record as elementary school students can be employed," he told the BBC. "Our employees come from all different places. We need to assess their behavior, not where they are from."[49]

Ren batted away questions about whether or not he was going to retire. He said that he continued to keep a regular work schedule, having breakfast at 7:30 a.m., then going into the office. "My wife often criticizes me and says that I don't have many friends or hobbies," he told CBS. "I reply that I do have hobbies: reading and writing documents. I especially enjoy working on documents."[50]

26

The Trial

The hills around Vancouver turned flaming red as 2019 waned. Meng Wanzhou was coming up on a year under house arrest. At Huawei, she'd always been in meetings or on the road. Her aides packed her schedule so tightly that she'd sometimes gripe she didn't even have time for a tea break.[1] Now she had nothing but time. She read, painted, looked at the autumn leaves. "If a busy life has eaten away at my time, then hardship has in turn drawn it back out," she wrote.[2] Her husband came for stretches to keep her company, and the children came during breaks from school. Her mother also came to visit. As fall turned to winter, the security guards shoveled the walk. Meng sometimes spoke to her father by phone, though they didn't believe the calls to be private, so they kept the talk at surface level.[3] Her bail terms gave her a long leash, but the leash was still there. When she'd stayed out on her back porch past

11:00 p.m. one night, she and her husband had been obliged to explain to the court that it was a one-off accident.

In China, Meng's detention stirred up patriotic fervor. People put stickers on their cars that read GO HUAWEI, GO CHINA. The Chinese embassy declared it "political persecution."[4] Huawei phones were sold out in shops, as people snatched them up in support. In early 2015, Huawei had unveiled an ad featuring a close-up photograph of a ballet dancer's feet, one in a pointe shoe, the other bare and bruised. Though the ad got mixed reviews from consumers, Huawei executives thought the image conveyed the company's spirit of hard work and perseverance. Now a coffee shop on Huawei's campus began serving drinks in paper cups emblazoned with the infamous bare ballerina foot juxtaposed alongside Meng's foot, her ankle shackled with a monitor. "Meng Wanzhou's foot and the bruised ballerina foot both reflect the hardship of success," read the caption across the cups.

Meng's lawyers felt they had reason for optimism. Wasn't it egregious, after all, that she had been questioned and searched for nearly three hours before being told she was under arrest and had the right to remain silent? The provisional arrest warrant issued by the Canadian court had commanded police to "immediately arrest" her.[5] Was a three-hour delay not a flouting of the court's order? Meng's legal team declared it an illegal search and detention, arguing that since due process was violated, the Vancouver judge was obliged to halt her extradition to the US.

To improve their odds, her defense lawyers were also presenting three other arguments for why the extradition hearings must be halted. First, they said that the Trump administration had corrupted the judicial process by seeking to use Meng as a "bargaining chip" in the trade war. Trump had said himself that he'd consider intervening "if I think

it's good for what will be certainly the largest trade deal ever made."
Second, they said that the Justice Department had misrepresented her
2013 PowerPoint presentation to HSBC, which was focused on Huawei's Iran business, by only citing select parts of it. Third, they argued
that Meng's communication with a British bank about a Chinese company's work in Iran lacked substantial connection to the United States
and should not fall under the jurisdiction of a US court.[6]

Meng only needed to convince the judge that one of these arguments had validity. Some thought her chances were good. In fact,
Canada's ambassador to China, John McCallum, remarked to reporters that Meng might have a strong case against extradition, and that
it would be "great for Canada" if the US dropped the issue.[7] As it
turned out, this was too frank an opinion for a Canadian ambassador
to make aloud. McCallum resigned soon afterward at the request of

*Meng Wanzhou with her husband, Carlos Liu (second right),
outside their house in Vancouver.*

A coffee cup from a Huawei campus café draws a parallel between Meng Wanzhou's wearing of a tracking anklet and the pain that ballerinas suffer to achieve greatness.

Prime Minister Justin Trudeau. Across the border, Huawei's US lawyers were filing a slew of Freedom of Information Act requests with government agencies, seeking to learn what kind of evidence prosecutors might be holding in reserve.

Not everyone saw Meng as a martyr. Some in China quietly said that if she had broken the law, she should face the consequences like anyone else. And scandalous national news had broken that Meng and the two Michaels weren't the only ones who'd been detained in December 2018: so had several former Huawei employees.

One of them, Li Hongyuan, had been jailed for 251 days after Huawei reported him to police for alleged extortion; he was eventually released without charges. Another, Zeng Meng, had been detained while in Thailand on vacation and deported back to Shenzhen, where he was jailed for three months on varying allegations from Huawei before being released. These cases sparked a domestic backlash against the company, with people feeling that it had been exposed as a hypocrite and a bully. Even as it was protesting that its CFO had been unfairly detained, its executives hadn't thought twice about throwing innocent employees behind bars. Too stark was the contrast between Meng's cushy house arrest and the bleak jail conditions that Li and Zeng had endured.

Given the political sensitivities of the issue, it was remarkable that censors allowed the news to be published in China. But Chinese readers would not know that they were getting only half the story. A salient detail the domestic press could not report was that shortly before their detentions, these former Huawei employees had all been in the same online chat group, where they were discussing lodging protests against the company for what they believed was their improper firings. One of them had piped up to say that they had evidence of Huawei's business dealings in Iran and wanted to expose it to the media. Zeng said he believed that their detentions had to do with the WeChat chatter about Iran, because when his colleague's wife hired a lawyer to go see her husband in jail, the police told the lawyer it was a "sensitive case" and wouldn't allow the detainee access to counsel. "This wasn't normal," Zeng said. "I realized this had something to do with my colleague saying in the WeChat group that he was part of the Iran project and was going to report it."[8]

Meanwhile, Canada's Michael Kovrig and Michael Spavor had, by this point, been detained in China for a full year. Kovrig had spent the first five months in Beijing, placed in solitary confinement inside a padded cell, with relentless rounds of interrogation, including questioning about his prior diplomatic work, in apparent violation of the Vienna Convention on Diplomatic Relations. He had then been transferred to a cell with multiple cellmates. In the transfer process, his glasses were confiscated for containing metal, and it was more than a month before he was able to obtain a replacement pair. As for Spavor, he was at a detention center in Dandong, near China's northeast border with North Korea. He shared a cell with up to eighteen other detainees and was only allowed fifteen minutes outside his cell each day.[9] Both men endured sensory manipulation, with the lights in their cells kept on day and night. "They have not had access to a lawyer and have been denied contact with their families and loved ones," Canada's minister of foreign affairs, François-Philippe Champagne, told the public in a statement. "These two Canadians are and will remain our absolute priority."[10]

Meng's extradition hearing began on January 20, 2020, more than a year after her detention in Vancouver. A press gaggle had gathered at daybreak outside her house, and she had given them a polite but distant "Good morning" as she climbed into her black SUV.

When Meng had first begun her house arrest, she'd shied away from the press. On days she had to appear in court, her SUV would whisk her to the courthouse's underground parking garage, and she would try to rush past the TV cameras on her way in, sometimes with her face obscured by a hat. But that day, she walked out of her house with a smile and greeted the press pack. When her SUV arrived at the courthouse, she walked aboveground through the front door. *Wow, where did that one-eighty come from?* thought David Molko, a journalist covering the trial for a Canadian TV station. As Meng strode by, head held high, the reporters saw that there had been a change of strategy. "The Huawei team understood that winning the PR victory among the Canadian public—or at least making that impression—was as important, if not more important, than what was happening inside the courtroom," Molko said.[11]

The first phase of the hearing would be to determine something called "double criminality." This meant that the conduct Meng was accused of had to be illegal in both Canada and the US in order for the extradition to proceed. The double criminality issue helped explain why a case that seemed, at first glance, to be about Iran sanctions was stuck on this question of whether Meng had misled a bank. In 2018, the US had reinstated sanctions on Iran after Trump withdrew from an international nuclear deal in a much-criticized move. Canada had not followed suit. Meng's lawyers now argued that the threshold requirement of double criminality had not been met, as the crux of the US government's case against Huawei had to do with violations of Iran sanctions, which Canada did not enforce. "It's all based on sanctions," defense lawyer Richard Peck said. "Canada is a sovereign nation. We have our own heritage, our own ethos, our own identity, our own standards, our own laws."[12] Prosecutors retorted that the charges against her were for bank fraud, which was clearly illegal in both countries.

Three days into Meng's extradition hearing, a fifty-six-year-old man with a fever and dry cough arrived by ambulance to a Toronto hospital. The man had felt ill since traveling to Wuhan, the Chinese city where many of Huawei's senior executives attended university, and which was about to become known as ground zero of the COVID-19 pandemic. As that first COVID patient was being confirmed in Canada, Wuhan's eleven million residents had just received the shocking news that their city was being locked down. No one was allowed in or out except for emergency vehicles. No one knew what this mysterious disease was or how things would turn out. For its part, Huawei had gotten an urgent phone call. Wuhan was building a massive new field hospital that needed to be completed within two weeks. A team of Huawei engineers was rushed in to set up a 5G connection so that those sealed inside could communicate with the outside. "I won't get infected. I haven't had a girlfriend yet," one young Huawei engineer joked as he prepared to go.[13] Overseas, Huawei adopted its traditional disaster response of throwing itself into relief efforts. It offered up thermal scanners and millions of masks to governments around the world. Officials in Canada and France found themselves pushed to publicly deny that Huawei's mask donations would sway their decisions on 5G suppliers.[14]

In May 2020, as Meng awaited the judge's ruling on the question of double criminality, her team members were upbeat enough that they chartered a plane so she could fly out quickly if there was good news. They also did a group photo shoot on the court steps as a final memento. But the news was disappointing. The judge sided with prosecutors, ruling that since bank fraud was illegal in both Canada and the US, the extradition hearings would continue.[15] Hard on the heels of the ruling, Chinese prosecutors formally charged the two Michaels with espionage—after they had been held for 550 days without charges and without being able to speak to their lawyers. In

China, opaque national security regulations allowed authorities to keep someone detained almost indefinitely before charging them. And once they were charged in a high-profile case like this, the probability that they would be found guilty was close to 100 percent.

Around this time, Meng's younger half sister, Annabel Yao, graduated from Harvard University with a bachelor's degree in computer science.[16] Due to the pandemic, the ceremony was held virtually. "I guess this isn't exactly the senior post that I've rehearsed so many times in my head," she wrote on Instagram, posting an old photo of herself outside Harvard's Widener Library. "Here's to being 'broken up over text' by Harvard after devoting 3.75 years of our souls to this school."[17]

In Vancouver, Meng and her security guards regarded each other with a new distrust, forced to breathe one another's air as they shared car rides and other tight spaces. It did not go unnoticed among her guards that when Meng's husband and their children flew over from Hong Kong for the winter holiday, they did not quarantine separately as they were supposed to. For Christmas, Meng's group booked out a restaurant for a fourteen-person dinner party in disregard of Vancouver's social-distancing rules.[18] Images from Meng's group photo shoot had also leaked, showing Meng and her friends standing in a tight cluster, none of them wearing masks.

Meng's lawyers tried to get her bail terms loosened at one point, arguing that the rotating security detail put her at risk of contracting COVID. Prosecutors pushed back, pointing out that Meng didn't seem overly concerned about COVID, what with her group dinners, shopping sprees to high-end retailers, and hangouts with maskless friends. Some of the details of her lavish lifestyle outraged Canadians, given the plight of the two Michaels. For much of the past year,

Chinese authorities had denied them their monthly consular visits—their only connection to the outside world—citing pandemic-control restrictions. Kovrig had been permitted just two phone calls to family in two years; Spavor, just one.

Meng's request to have her bail conditions loosened was denied.

A year into the sanctions, Huawei was still alive. By some measures, it was even curiously on the ascent. It was still the world's number-one vendor of telecom gear, aided by Beijing's ambitions to construct the world's earliest and largest 5G network. China was already rolling out Huawei and ZTE 5G base stations across the country, even as most nations were still formulating their 5G plans. Huawei had also become the world's number-one smartphone vendor for the first time, in the second quarter of 2020, as rivals like Samsung saw sales plummet during the pandemic. The Trump administration was not pleased. It squeezed harder.

"Any country that uses it, we're not going to do anything in terms of sharing intelligence," Trump said in a rambling appearance on *Fox & Friends*. "Absolutely, Huawei is a disaster. They used to have free rein over our country. They know everything—they knew everything we were doing. Huawei is a way of—is really—I call it 'the Spyway.' What happens is Huawei comes out, and they spy on our country. This is very intricate stuff. You have microchips. You have things that you can't even see. The average person and beyond the average person. The people that do this can't even find it. No, they spy."[19]

In February 2020, the Justice Department filed an expanded indictment against Huawei, accusing the company of lying to banks about not only its business in Iran but also its activities in North Korea. Prosecutors accused Huawei of concealing its North Korea projects, including by instructing a supplier to omit Huawei's logo from shipments to North Korea in 2013, and by referring to the country by the code name "A9."

Weeks later, Trump signed into law a bill earmarking up to $1 billion for small rural US carriers to "rip and replace" Huawei and ZTE gear. As they grasped for more levers to pull, Attorney General William Barr even made the unusual suggestion that the US government should buy a controlling stake in Nokia or Ericsson to counter Huawei, which Vice President Mike Pence and White House economic adviser Larry Kudlow quickly walked back. The US government was "not in the business of buying companies," Kudlow said.

What the US government was in the business of doing was blocking the export of US technology to entities considered a security threat. In May 2020, the Commerce Department tightened the sanctions on Huawei, preventing not only the direct sale of US technology to the company but also the sale of any chips that were made using US technology without a special license. This new rule was wonky, but its implications for Huawei were massive. While Huawei had been designing some of its chips in-house through HiSilicon, it relied on the Taiwan Semiconductor Manufacturing Company, or TSMC, to produce them. When it came to manufacturing advanced chips, TSMC was the very best. One time when Ren met with TSMC's founder, Morris Chang, the two men marveled at how their lives had diverged. Born thirteen years before Ren in mainland China, Chang had also spent his early years in the tumult of war, but had left in 1949 to study at Harvard University. After a flourishing career at Texas Instruments, he'd moved to Taiwan and went on to build the most advanced chip manufacturer in the world. "Why have the two of us walked different paths?" Chang mused.[20] Ren replied that Taiwan was decades ahead of the mainland in opening up to the world, decades ahead in developing technology. TSMC had supplied Huawei for years, but now, under the threat of sanctions, it could not risk losing access to US technology to run its own operations. TSMC shut its doors to Huawei.

Huawei's only hope now was for China's domestic chip foundry, the Semiconductor Manufacturing International Corporation, or SMIC, to learn how to produce advanced chips at lightning speeds. This was a real Hail Mary: SMIC had been endeavoring for two decades to advance its technologies but still lagged several generations behind global leaders in advanced chipmaking.

This second round of US sanctions cut deep. In July 2020, citing the new US sanctions, the UK announced that it was reversing its position on Huawei and would remove all Huawei equipment from the nation's 5G networks by the end of 2027.[21] British officials said that due to the sanctions, Huawei could no longer use trusted international suppliers, increasing the level of its risk. This was a major win for Washington, which for several years had been pushing the UK to quit Huawei. "The British were in an impossible position," said Vince Cable, former UK secretary of state for business, innovation, and skills. "They basically accepted that if the American boycott of sensitive components was operational, the British couldn't act independently. So the government changed its view."[22]

Over the summer, Canada, which had worked with Huawei for 4G, also effectively shut the company out of its 5G networks, with its two major operators, Bell Canada and Telus, opting for Ericsson and Nokia as 5G suppliers. This meant that Washington had succeeded in getting all of the Five Eyes—the intelligence alliance consisting of Australia, Canada, New Zealand, the United Kingdom, and the United States—to ditch Huawei. However, Canada, still suffering from the fallout of Meng's detention and also trying to negotiate the two Michaels' release, did not institute a formal ban.

Much of continental Europe was reluctant to fall in line with a Trump-led Huawei ban. After members of the European Parliament visited Washington in February 2020 to participate in talks on high-tech and security issues, they put this in the summary of their trip: "With today's end-to-end encryption technology, it is possible to run ultra-secure applications on untrusted hardware or potentially inse-cure hardware. The Huawei issue is clearly therefore more political and commercial than technical."[23]

One former senior British security official recalled a heated meet-ing at which a British minister demanded that they work harder with Five Eyes partners to build alternatives to Huawei. "What do you want me to do?" he said he retorted. "Do you want me to phone up Admiral Rogers at the NSA, or General Nakasone at the NSA, and say, 'Do you fancy building a telco to rival Huawei?'"[24]

The Trump administration was now touting a "Clean Network" of global telecom networks that did not use Huawei or ZTE. The term drew swift backlash from some foreign-policy observers, who pointed out its place in the long, racist tradition of suggesting that something foreign is "dirty." "Is it just me or does calling for a 'clean' network and only mentioning removing Chinese tech and companies make China 'dirty' and therefore all racist AF?" asked Simon Shar-wood, Asia-Pacific editor for the British technology publication *The Register*, on Twitter.[25] "The repetition of the word 'clean' . . . Pompeo & his racist dogwhistle at it again," tweeted Juan Ortiz Freuler, an affiliate at Harvard's Berkman Klein Center, a hub for cyberspace research.[26] Susan Ariel Aaronson, an international affairs professor at George Washington University, called the Trump administration's use of the term "racist and paranoid."

Nevertheless, Pompeo announced five "Clean" initiatives to combat Huawei and other Chinese tech companies: Clear Carrier, Clean Store, Clean Apps, Clean Cloud, and Clean Cable. He also encouraged other nations to become "Clean Countries." "We've urged countries to become Clean Countries so that citizens' private information doesn't end up in the hand of the Chinese Communist Party," Pompeo said.[27] The State Department announced in August 2020 that it had built a coalition of thirty "Clean Countries," including the United Kingdom, Canada, Australia, France, Israel, Japan, Sweden, and Vietnam. Some countries were less than thrilled to join the club. In Eswatini, the African country previously called Swaziland, Keith Krach welcomed officials into the Clean Network through a festive ceremony. Weeks later, Eswatini quietly withdrew. An Eswatini official was quoted in Chinese state media as saying that the kingdom believed it should place "equal emphasis on development and security."[28]

Ren Zhengfei's team was putting on a brave face, but Huawei's business was floundering in the face of the Trump administration's multipronged attack. Ren made the bitter decision to cut off some limbs. The first to go was the company's undersea cable joint venture, Huawei Marine Systems Co. The unit had put Huawei in the business of carrying the world's data between continents, in competition with Microsoft, Google, and Facebook. Huawei Marine Systems had laid some thirty-one thousand miles of undersea cable over ninety projects. But with all the geopolitical pressure, it was hard for Huawei Marine Systems to do business. Huawei announced that it was selling its 51 percent stake to a Chinese buyer.

In November 2020, the company revealed that it was also selling off its cherished Honor smartphone line to a consortium. Aggressively priced, sleekly designed, and promoted through viral marketing campaigns to tech-savvy young consumers, Huawei's Honor phones had rocketed the company to number one in smartphone sales globally, dethroning Samsung and Apple. But the US sanctions cut Honor smartphones off from their key components—Qualcomm processors and Google's Android operating system. Ren decided that Honor's hopes for survival depended on it striking out alone. "Become Huawei's strongest global competitor, surpass Huawei, and even shout 'Down with Huawei,'" Ren told the departing team. "Make this a motivational slogan for yourselves."

Behind closed doors, Huawei was racing with SMIC and others to figure out how to make the chips it needed. This was a sensitive project, with national significance, and the company kept a cone of silence around the endeavor in public. Rumors circulated of secret microchip factories. Ren appealed for help from the nation's top scientific minds. "We as a company cannot do two things at once: make products and manufacture chips," he told researchers from China's elite Peking and Tsinghua Universities.[29]

To the outside world, Ren no longer talked too much of defeating rivals or becoming the global leader. He said Huawei's goal was simply to survive.

P rotesters sometimes stood outside Meng's house in Vancouver with a banner calling for the Chinese government to release Uyghur detainees from camps in China's northwestern Xinjiang region.[30] There was growing international horror about the government's Uyghur detention campaign, which reportedly included torture and forced labor. Foreign researchers said the campaign met the United Nations' definition of "crimes against humanity." Some activists and scholars also described it as a "cultural genocide."

There was a vague understanding among China watchers that Huawei might have something to do with the Xinjiang crackdown, though the specifics were largely unknown. Huawei's executives maintained that if the company's products ended up in Xinjiang, it was through third parties, and they didn't know how their customers used them.

From one perspective, Huawei was simply following well-trod footsteps in being purposefully dense about how its technologies were being used. After all, IBM had supplied punch-card computing systems to the Nazis, who used them in their concentration camps during World War II, with IBM executives later protesting that they hadn't known.[31] Cisco had helped China build its Great Firewall, marketing the gear as being able to help Beijing crack down on dissidents.[32] When employees at Nortel's precursor, Bell-Northern Research, were unhappy that the company was hosting the Soviet Union's leader, Leonid Brezhnev, back in the day, the company's president, Don Chisholm, emailed staff to say that anyone who disagreed could take the day off.[33]

In June 2019, Huawei's global cybersecurity officer, John Suffolk, had been hauled before the UK House of Commons' Science and Technology Committee to be grilled on the topic.[34]

"Do you have no concern about being, in a sense, complicit with such outrageous human rights abuses?" asked the committee chair, Norman Lamb, a thin man with a shock of white hair.

"I do not think it is for us to make such judgments," Suffolk replied. "Our judgment is: Is it legal within the countries in which we operate?"

"Should we do business with a company that is complicit in human rights abuses?"

"I think you should do business with all companies that stick to the law."

"There is a lot of law in China, isn't there?" asked Julian Lewis, chair of the Defence Select Committee. "Just like there was a lot of law in Nazi Germany."

"We do not make judgments about whether laws are right or wrong. It is for others to make those judgments."

"Do you have a view as to whether China is a one-party state?"

"China is a one-party state, yes."

"Do you have a view as to whether that Chinese one-party state is repressive of human rights?"

"I don't have a view on that, no."

"You don't have a personal view on that."

"I don't have a personal view on that."

"You are a moral vacuum."

"I don't believe so, no."

I n the latter part of 2020, new details emerged of Huawei's participation in the government's crackdown on Uyghurs. A small Pennsylvania-based research outlet called IPVM published an internal report from Huawei outlining the company's tests of a facial-recognition system.[35]

"Huawei Confidential, No Circulation Without Permission," it said across each page. Dated January 8, 2018, the seven-page PDF was an "interoperability" report outlining the test performance of a facial-recognition tracking system built jointly by Huawei and a partner company, Megvii, one of China's largest facial-recognition providers. It listed dozens of functions they had tested, such as "real-time face capture" and "offline maps." There were two lines that jumped out:

Supports Offline File Uyghur Alarm: Passed
Supports Recognition Based on Age, Sex, Ethnicity and Angle of Facial Images: Passed

The interoperability report showed that Huawei's technology wasn't being used to track Uyghurs by accident. It was by design. Huawei and Megvii engineers had put a "Uyghur alarm" feature into their facial-recognition system to automatically flag faces that appeared to belong to members of the ethnic minority. And they had tested it to make sure it worked.

When news of Huawei's "Uyghur alarm" was published in *The Washington Post* in December 2020, it hit a nerve. Human-rights activists and politicians decried it. The French soccer star Antoine Griezmann announced he was ending his sponsorship deal with Huawei. "Due to strong suspicions that the company Huawei may have contributed to the development of a Uyghur alert through facial recognition software, I'm announcing that I am immediately terminating my partnership with this company," Griezmann said in an Instagram post to his more than thirty million followers. "I take this opportunity to urge Huawei not to merely deny these accusations but to quickly take concrete actions to condemn this mass repression and to use its influence to contribute to the respect of human rights within society."[36]

Huawei tried to downplay the news at first, but with the escalating attention drawn by Griezmann's breaking of ties with the company, Huawei issued a crisis-control statement saying that the language in the interoperability report was "completely unacceptable" and that its technology was not designed to target ethnic groups.[37]

When Tommy Zwicky, vice president of communications at Huawei Denmark, saw the report, he felt distressed.[38] "I had a big hole in my stomach," he said. He had vigorously defended the company when people criticized it in the past, asking where the proof was that Huawei had engaged in the various shadowy misdeeds of which it was accused. But the interoperability report was hard proof that Huawei knew its technology was being used to track an ethnic group, and that executives were okay with it. "This is not something that might have happened," he said. "This happened. Beyond any doubt."

After raising internal protests, he tendered his resignation. He said that Huawei offered him a year's salary in severance if he would leave quietly, but he turned it down. "I couldn't do that," he said. "Then I would still be part of the problem."

I knew it would end up in court," Scott Kirkland said.[39] In the autumn of 2020, Kirkland and the other officers involved in Meng's detention were being hauled onto the witness stand in Vancouver to face questioning from Meng's lawyers about whether they'd followed the law. At issue was her search and interrogation at customs before she was told she was under arrest. On the one hand, border officers had expansive powers to stop and question people entering the country as they saw fit. On the other hand, they should not have been coordinating with police to gather evidence from a suspect before she was informed of her rights.

The officers admitted that such concerns had crossed their minds. Kirkland told the court he'd originally suggested that the police take custody of Meng immediately, out of concern a delay might be seen as a violation of her rights. "Our examination would be argued as a delay in due process," he said. But he had been overridden by colleagues who felt it was both legal and proper for customs to do a thorough exam before handing Meng over to police.

Sowmith Katragadda, the customs officer who had led the questioning of Meng, said he'd also been concerned about the impression of the border agency and police being in cahoots. "I understood this was a serious case. I understood the likelihood of the whole process being reviewed, and I felt we needed to take appropriate measures to ensure the processes were separate and clear," he said.[40]

The border agents denied that police had fed them any of the questions they'd asked Meng. Katragadda said he'd left a couple of times to seek guidance from the customs agency's national security unit, not police, on what to ask Meng. Their supervisor, Sanjit Dhillon, who had come out near the end to ask Meng pointed questions about Iran, also denied that police suggested the interrogatories, claiming he developed them after reading Huawei's Wikipedia page.[41] Katragadda did allow that when he confiscated Meng's phones, he knew that both the police—the Royal Canadian Mounted Police (RCMP)—and the FBI were interested in the devices. "I knew of the RCMP's interest and the FBI's interest," he said.[42]

The border officers had all curiously developed amnesia when it came to some key points, such as who had made the decision for police to delay the arrest, and who had suggested they ask for the passcodes to Meng's phones.[43] The one procedural flaw that Meng's lawyers had managed to pin down was that the sheet of paper with Meng's phone passcodes had ended up in the hands of police. Border officers weren't supposed to just share such information directly with police. Kirkland called it an honest slipup. "It was heart-wrenching to realize I made that mistake," he told the court. It was hard to know what the judge would think. Was the passcode mishap serious enough to throw off the extradition?

Meanwhile, Meng's lawyers were hoping to strike a deal with US prosecutors for her release. In China, Ren had received a visit from the new Canadian ambassador, Dominic Barton, the former managing director of McKinsey & Company. Barton had lived for years in Shanghai while running the consulting firm's Asia practice. Trudeau hoped his extensive China connections could help him break the impasse in negotiating the return of the two Michaels. Indeed, Barton was told that securing their release was one of his top priorities. Though no one liked to publicly admit they were open to a prisoner swap, they all knew that any deal would have to account for both Meng's return to China and the two Michaels' return to Canada.

Once a month, Barton visited the two Michaels at their separate detention centers. This half hour was their only contact with the outside world. Barton spoke to them in a rapid-fire way, trying to cover as much ground as possible.

In March 2021, the two Michaels were tried behind closed doors in separate Chinese courts. Canadian officials said that they were denied access to the courtrooms in violation of diplomatic agreements. There were no immediate verdicts. Nor was there any word about when they would come out. The sword dangled over their necks, and it was clear that their fates were intertwined with Meng's.

In August 2021, Meng's extradition hearings entered the final weeks. Summing up their case, Meng's lead lawyer, Richard Peck, declared that she had been illegally searched and detained at the airport. He said that Trump's willingness to intercede in her case to secure a trade deal was the "very definition of ransom."[44] "When before has a head of state interfered with an extradition?" he asked.[45] Prosecutors asserted that proper procedure had been followed and there was more than enough evidence to warrant her extradition to the US for trial. "No one has received a fairer extradition hearing in this country than Ms. Meng," the Canadian Justice Department's chief counsel, Robert Frater, said.[46]

A week before the end of Meng's extradition hearing, a Chinese court announced that Michael Spavor had been sentenced to eleven years in prison for espionage. There was no word yet on the verdict for Michael Kovrig, though it seemed likely he would face similar punishment: Chinese authorities had tied the two cases together, accusing Spavor of passing sensitive information to Kovrig. And Chinese courts had a near 100 percent conviction rate in prominent political cases.

The week after Spavor's sentencing, Meng's extradition hearings concluded. She had fought extradition tooth and nail for two and a half years. Now there was nothing to do but wait for the judge's decision.

27

A Hero's Welcome

I n the end, the decision did not fall to a judge. US president Joe Biden and Xi had talked by phone in September 2021, and both wished for the prisoners to come home. With a consensus at top levels, Meng Wanzhou's lawyers quickly came to a deferred prosecution agreement with the US Justice Department. She would sign a statement admitting that she had misled HSBC about Huawei's relationship with Skycom, but she would not have to plead guilty. If she abided by the terms of the agreement, the US would drop the charges after a year.

Meng appeared in Vancouver court for the last time on September 24, 2021. Judge Heather Holmes stayed Meng's extradition proceedings, lifted her bail restrictions, and praised her courteousness.

"Thank you, my lady," Meng replied.

China's ambassador to Canada, Cong Peiwu, escorted her onto the flight home. At the same time that Meng left Vancouver, Michael Kovrig and Michael Spavor boarded a plane out of China, accompanied by Canada's ambassador, Dominic Barton.

The usual flight path from Vancouver to Shenzhen would have passed through US airspace over Alaska. The pilot swung wide to avoid it. Watching on flight-tracking websites, thousands followed along as a little plane icon inched across Russia, down through Mongolia, then finally toward the southern coast of China. "The most tracked flight right now is #CA552 (Vancouver–Shenzhen)," a flight-tracking website announced.[1]

Meng gazed out her window at the pitch darkness outside, punctuated by only the flashing navigation lights on the wings. One thought after another rushed through her mind. Nearly three years had passed since she'd last been home. She was forty-nine. As they approached Chinese airspace, Meng felt her vision blur with tears.

She had changed on the plane into a crimson dress, and she emerged on the Shenzhen tarmac to flashing cameras.[2] Two people in hazmat suits, goggles, and latex gloves darted out to present her with red roses. China was still in the depths of the pandemic, with the world's strictest COVID controls. Before she was whisked away for a three-week quarantine, Meng had a brief moment with the cameras. She bowed deeply to a crowd of supporters who stood at a safe distance, wearing masks and waving red flags.

"I've finally returned to the motherland's embrace," Meng said, her voice catching. "It's been full of struggles and difficulties."

Across the nation, she received a hero's welcome. The side of Shenzhen's tallest skyscraper, the Ping An Finance Center, was transformed into a neon billboard that read WELCOME HOME, MENG WANZHOU. Elementary school students were studying the lesson of

Meng Wanzhou's ordeal. Senior officials praised her. Vice Foreign Minister Le Yucheng declared Meng freed not only from the ankle tracker but from "the shackles of hegemony."[3] Now that the operation had succeeded, Chinese officials started to say this too: that President Xi Jinping had personally worked for her release.

Meng's younger half sister, Annabel Yao, posted on her Weibo microblog that she was so excited her hands were shaking. "Thanks to the Party and our great motherland," she wrote. "Sister, you are always my role model, and our whole family's pride."[4]

Although Meng was now safe, US prosecutors were continuing to pursue the cases against Huawei as a company for alleged intellectual-property theft and bank fraud surrounding its business in Iran. Those in Huawei's top leadership used to spend much of their time jet-setting around the world to woo clients, but now they thought twice about leaving Chinese soil. The FBI also fired another warning shot: it filed criminal charges against two Chinese men, calling them intelligence agents posing as magazine employees who had tried to use bribes to obtain nonpublic information about the US government's case against Huawei.

After completing her three-week COVID quarantine, Meng returned to the Huawei office on October 25, Ren Zhengfei's seventy-seventh birthday. She was greeted by a sea of employees who cheered, hugged her, and raised their Huawei smartphones to snap a picture of the thrilling moment.

In March 2022, Meng emerged in her role as CFO to present Huawei's annual results for the first time in four years. "I really feel great

to have this face-to-face communication with you," she told reporters covering the event. "There's no substitute for such interactions."
Meng avoided talking about her detention, but she said that much
had changed while she was gone. "In the few months that I've been
back, I've been trying to catch up. I hope I will catch up."

A few days after the event, Huawei announced that fifty-year-old
Meng Wanzhou was being promoted to one of the company's three rotating chairs, alongside Ken Hu and Eric Xu, with the three taking
turns at six-month stretches to steer the company. To make room for
Meng, Ren's longtime trusted deputy, Guo Ping—who was in his midfif-
ties and not that much older than Meng—had taken a step back to the
supporting role of supervisory board chairman. Ren remained chief
executive. Huawei told the press that the company's succession plan
had not changed and continued to be based on collective leadership.

Ren had repeatedly sworn over the years that Meng would not be
his heir. "Ms. Meng is a manager," he'd said. "My successor will definitely be a fighter." He said his daughter lacked the leadership quality of "pointing the way forward like a beacon." His reassurances
that he would not make succession decisions out of selfish family
considerations had stabilized his executive team, helping him avoid
the sorts of C-suite upheaval that wreaked havoc on many companies. Even so, some of Huawei's staffers always suspected that Ren
had never quite relinquished the idea of a family succession.

Now, after her ordeal in Canada, Meng had finally earned her
place. In the eyes of the Huawei team, she was no longer just the
boss's pampered daughter. She had suffered for the company. She
had put her own neck on the line.

Guo's step back to the supervisory committee marked the end of
an era for Huawei. He had been at the company since 1988, and he'd

been Ren's right-hand man for years. In the 2000s, Guo had been Huawei's point man in its defense against Cisco's lawsuit and in negotiations over possible mergers with Nortel in Canada and Marconi in the UK. Since 2011, he had been one of Huawei's rotating CEOs. At his last appearance at a Huawei annual conference, before the world knew he was stepping down, Guo had looked a little somber and reflective. "Our fight to survive is not over yet," he'd said. Jeffrey Towson, an Asia-based tech consultant, recalled meeting with Guo after he moved to the supervisory committee.[5] "He's working on more, like, institutional memory," he said. "Before, he's hard-charging. Now, he's kind of hanging out in a sweater, you know, having lattes by the lake."

As for Meng, she tried to make up for lost time. China had changed while she was gone. Pop-up COVID test stands now dotted the Shenzhen sidewalks, with residents required to take a test every few days to prevent the spread of the coronavirus. At convenience stores, customers could now pay by scanning their faces. And the rumors about Xi's audacious ambitions turned out to be true: in March 2023, Xi was appointed to an unprecedented third presidential term by a unanimous vote of the rubber-stamp legislature, allowing him time to continue pursuing his dream of transforming China from a developing nation into a world leader.

In April 2023, Meng began her first half-year tenure as rotating CEO of Huawei Technologies.

C anadian prime minister Justin Trudeau was waiting on the tarmac in Calgary when the plane carrying Michael Kovrig and Michael Spavor landed. "These past one-thousand-plus days

Teresa He (left), *head of Huawei's chip division, HiSilicon, and Meng Wanzhou.*

have been terribly arduous for these two men, yet they have shown determination, grace, and resilience at every turn," Trudeau said. "I will be—I always have been—and I always will be moved and impressed by the strength of character these two men possess."[6]

While the two Michaels were detained in China, Canada had put off officially deciding whether to allow Huawei in its 5G network, in a bid to avoid further destabilizing relations. But with the Michaels safely home, Trudeau announced that Canada was officially banning Huawei from its 5G network. "We took the time to carefully analyze the situation, look at all sorts of factors," he said.

After their release, the two Michaels largely kept low public profiles. Michael Kovrig resumed his work with Crisis Group and spent time with his two-year-old daughter, Clara X. Kovrig, whom he was meeting for the first time. His girlfriend, the geopolitical analyst Yanmei Xie, had given birth to Clara in 2019, while he was in detention. Michael Spavor had it tougher—it was hard for him to resume his previous work of organizing business and cultural exchanges in North Korea. His brother, Paul, and close friends organized a fundraiser for him, saying it would help cover his legal costs and living expenses. "This episode could seriously affect his livelihood, possibly result in deportation and loss of possessions," Paul Spavor wrote on the fundraiser's webpage.

In November 2023, astonishing news emerged in Canada's *Globe and Mail*: Michael Spavor was seeking millions of dollars from the Canadian government as compensation for his detention in China. According to the report, he felt that his arrest was due to sensitive information he'd shared with fellow detainee Michael Kovrig, who'd relayed it to Western intelligence agencies without his knowledge. Chinese state media seized on this story to trumpet that China had been right all along—the two Canadians were spies. Kovrig broke his silence to defend himself to Canadian media, saying that China's government was well aware of his work as a diplomat and think-tank analyst, and that he was regularly invited to meet with Chinese officials, analysts, and scholars. "Repeating gaslighting and disinformation about why we were detained only prolongs pain that we're all trying to heal from," Kovrig told the *National Post*.[7]

Within Canada, opinions differed on the lesson of the entire thing, and on whether Ottawa should have helped the US at all when it came to Meng's detention. While the US had a solid case, even Western lawyers agreed it was unusual to make an economic sanctions case personal by detaining a family member of the company's founder. The country certainly hadn't done so in the case of ZTE. "It was definitely a bad move," said Michel Juneau-Katsuya, a former senior Canadian intelligence officer, about Canada's detainment of Meng. "We did the dirty job for the US." Former foreign minister John Manley told Canadian media that officials should have deployed "creative incompetence" to fail to catch Meng.[8] Guy Saint-Jacques, former Canadian ambassador to China, said that in addition to Canada's responsibilities under the bilateral extradition treaty, there was an added factor to contend with: the country was in the middle of trying to renegotiate the North American Free Trade Agreement with Washington. "It would have been difficult to go against the wishes of the US administration, to refuse to extradite Ms. Meng while we were hoping to renegotiate," he said. "That's why we were stuck."

28

Black Swan

As Meng Wanzhou approached the end of her first half-year term at Huawei's helm, the company quietly launched a new smartphone at the end of August 2023. Huawei had skipped the usual fanfare and hadn't even disclosed the Mate 60 Pro's specs. But people were whispering that Huawei had found a way around the US sanctions.[1]

Rarely had so many people bought a brand-new phone just to crack it open and tear it to pieces. Analysts soon confirmed the rumors were right. Huawei had managed to produce a 5G processor through the Chinese foundry SMIC, despite both companies being under US sanctions that were meant to stop them from manufacturing such an advanced chip. No one could say for sure how it had happened. Huawei and SMIC might have achieved the feat by violating sanctions, or they might have managed it by pushing less-advanced tools to the limit. It was like trying to paint a very thin line with the edge of a fat brush: technically possible, but requiring great skill. SMIC and Huawei weren't saying what brushes they were using, or how they'd gotten them.

Many outsiders sought a peek inside Huawei's mysterious chip unit HiSilicon around this time, to no avail. "I was told that any visit to HiSilicon required the approval of Ren Zhengfei himself," said the Washington-based researcher Paul Triolo.[2]

Huawei's new phone created a ruckus in Washington and put the company back in the crosshairs. "The reports about Huawei are incredibly disturbing," Commerce Secretary Gina Raimondo told US lawmakers.[3] She said the Commerce Department needed more resources for sanctions enforcement. Weeks after Huawei's phone launch, the Biden administration tightened its ban on exporting advanced chipmaking tools to China.

If there had been hopes among Huawei's executives that Biden would be softer on China than Trump, they were quickly dispelled. The Biden administration was more careful in its rhetoric to avoid fanning anti-Chinese racism. It didn't use terms like "Clean Network" and "Clean Nations." But in many ways, it was only picking up where the Trump administration had left off and deepening the efforts to contain China. There was no indication that Washington would lift its sanctions against Huawei anytime soon.

The United States was now pushing a new alternative to Huawei. Begun under the Trump administration and taken to the finish line by the Biden administration, Washington now had something called "Open RAN." This was a system of mix-and-match parts for cell towers—sort of like the open Android ecosystem—that could allow upstart US vendors back in the game, even if they could make only one piece of the kit, not the whole set, like Huawei could. Open RAN had plenty of skeptics, with EU officials pointing out that a system with many interconnected vendors was more vulnerable to cybersecurity attacks. But Washington was pushing it full tilt. "This has been a whole-of-government approach," said Alan Davidson, assistant secretary of commerce and an administrator for the National Telecommunications and Information Administration. "We've been working very closely with the State Department, with the White House. . . . We're trying to bring all the tools that we have to bear." In his meetings with world leaders, Biden was personally singing its praises. The US government was subsidizing the technology's rollout around the world, in Indonesia, Nigeria, the Philippines, and even villages of the Amazon rainforest.

Huawei's rise had been a Sputnik moment. It had changed the way that people around the world thought about innovation, trade, and their own pasts and futures. "A country without its own program-controlled switches is like one without an army," Ren Zhengfei had told General Secretary Jiang Zemin back in 1994, as he argued for China's central government to increase investment in telecommunications gear. Similar calls were now being made in nations worldwide. Across the United States, terms like "industrial policy" and "strategic technologies" were suddenly on lots of lips. After decades of believing that the end of history had arrived with free markets and democracy, people came to the realization that history hadn't, in fact, ended. And the future was starting to look like the past.

It wasn't a complete retreat from globalization. That was impossible. But it was an acknowledgment that stock prices and balance

Huawei's largest data center in China, designed to look like a European town and built in the Guizhou hills, began operating in 2021 with one million servers.

sheets could not fully capture the societal value of a nation's technological competency—nor could they fully express the feeling of loss when that was gone.

With Meng's safe return, Ren's string of remarkable press interviews came to an end. The company reverted to its former inscrutable self. For two years, a brief, extraordinary window into the company had been open. Now it had slammed shut again. Ren's younger daughter, Annabel Yao, who had for years chronicled her jet-setting life and ballet dancing on Instagram, abruptly removed all her posts. Ren announced a company-wide policy of writing shorter emails and deleting older records that did not need to be retained. Huawei scrubbed old posts from its website. The company's party secretary, Zhou Daiqi, had retired quietly at some point. It was unclear from the outside who had been named as his successor.[4] In 2024, Huawei opted to skip an annual press conference, a yearslong tradition.

The diplomatic battles continued behind closed doors. In July 2024, Germany's government announced that its major telecom companies would stop using Huawei and ZTE 5G equipment within five years, a big victory for Washington. The West was continuing to grow more inhospitable toward Huawei. Yet—almost incredibly—Huawei was still number one in the world in 5G gear sales. Buoyed by patriotic domestic purchases and continued brisk demand in emerging markets, Huawei was holding its own.

L ong before anyone had heard of Ren Zhengfei or Huawei, Wan Runnan had been China's star entrepreneur in the 1980s, with his company, the Stone Group, touted as "China's IBM." Wan had believed that economic change could lead to political change. He had thrown his support behind the pro-democracy protesters in 1989. As a result, he had to flee to France, with an arrest warrant hanging over his head. He was never able to return home.

Now, decades later and in failing health in Paris, Wan recalled something that had happened one day in the late 1980s, when he was still living in Beijing.[5] Local officials had invited him to dinner. This was unusual. He was usually the one to invite officials to dine, so as to curry favor with the show of hospitality. Over the meal, the officials told Wan that the Ministry of State Security was going to send agents to work undercover at his company in positions dealing with international relations. The officials cast the move to embed these minders as an act of protection for Wan and the company's other executives, a security measure that would keep them from stumbling into unseen risks in their dealings with foreigners. "You have a lot of international business, which raises security issues for you. There are situations that you don't understand," Wan recalled the officials telling him. "They said, 'We are sending some people over. You can just treat them like regular employees.'"

Wan said he knew that around this time, state intelligence also contacted other tech companies in Beijing with the same request. He couldn't say what the situation was for Huawei, which was still a little startup far to the south in Shenzhen, not yet on anyone's radar. But Wan said he didn't believe that Huawei would have been able to escape similar demands. "That is a certainty," he said. "Telecommunications is an industry that has to do with keeping control of a nation's lifeline . . . and actually in any system of communications, there's a back-end platform that could be used for eavesdropping."

It was a rare moment of an executive lifting the cone of silence surrounding the MSS's relationship with China's high-tech industry. It was rare, in fact, in any country. Around the world, such spying operations rank among governments' closest-held secrets. When Edward Snowden had exposed the NSA's operations abroad, he'd ended up in exile in Russia. Wan, too, might have risked arrest had he still been living in China.

Over the years, foreign government officials and journalists had repeatedly asked Huawei's executives if they were willing to stand up against China's government and refuse to help with overseas surveillance. In truth, it was an unanswerable question. Governments around the world, including in both China and the United States, do compel tech companies to assist in investigations, and they also compel them to keep silent about it. Google has notably criticized the frequency of court-issued "gag orders" that prevent it from disclosing government demands for user data.

And while the practices are shrouded in secrecy, there has also been acknowledgment that governments not only hack into networking equipment but also use "direct access" to tap data from telecommunications networks without the network operators knowing the details.

A 2016 report by the UN's special rapporteur on the promotion and protection of the right to freedom of opinion and expression describes such practices this way:

States may also covertly tap into the technical infrastructure belonging to service providers and content platforms in order to intercept a wide variety of information, including communications, user account information, and telephone and Internet records. States reportedly tamper with computer hardware while en route to customers, infiltrate private networks and platforms with malicious software, hack into specific devices, and exploit other digital security loopholes.[6]

When speaking in confidence, industry executives often express a belief that networks are hacked and surveilled to a much greater degree than the general public may suspect. They also acknowledge the difficulty of ascertaining if a back door exists in millions of lines of code. When AT&T conducted a survey of cybersecurity professionals in 2016, 64 percent said they did not expect to be able to have a private conversation on any device.[7]

For Huawei, this means that concerns about its equipment being exploitable by China's intelligence agencies are unlikely to abate—in the same way that China will continue to be wary of Western-made technologies.

"I think there is a genuine fear that there is a back door in Huawei equipment that the Chinese government can access if they want to get whatever information they need. I think that's a genuine fear," said Michael Joseph, founder of the Kenyan mobile operator Safaricom. "You know, well, so what? What are you going to do?" He added: "You also don't know what other governments are up to. And all governments—can you trust any government?—might be listening to your conversations and doing whatever they do."[8]

Little is definitively known by the public about the MSS's overseas wiretapping operations, partly because the MSS does not widely declassify its older records the way that US intelligence agencies do. Nor has there emerged from within the system a massive whistle-blowing effort or a leaker the likes of Edward Snowden. "No defector yet has taken the Mitrokhin path to document past Chinese intelligence operations and the seepage of classified material out of China remains glacial," writes David Ian Chambers, a former British government official who has extensively researched China's intelligence operations.[9]

What's worth pointing out is that the knowledge that such risks exist in telecommunications gear is not new. Policymakers have always known about these risks, and in the heyday years of globalization, they factored them into their considerations.

"I'm quite sure for a long time, the CIA, for example, have been reporting on everything that is done in Malaysia and China," Malaysian prime minister Mahathir Mohamad told reporters when asked about Huawei. "We did not carry out a boycott of America because of that. They have that capacity; now Huawei has got that capacity. Let them do their worst."[10]

What is new is the onset of a fresh cold war between the United

States and China, which has changed calculations. Now the assumption on both sides is that the other nation sees the competition as a zero-sum game and believes that it will not act in good faith, that it will be willing to go to extreme lengths to come out ahead, and that if backed into a corner, it will be willing to entertain pushing the big red button for mutually assured destruction, simply out of spite.

"It depends on what threat you're trying to manage, right?" said Charles Clancy, the former NSA cybersecurity researcher, about why Western governments had until recently largely considered Huawei equipment safe enough to use. "If the threat you're managing does not presume China activating their intelligence law and going much more aggressively against adversaries across the globe, then the threat is manageable. But if you do not have sufficient confidence . . ."[11]

Clancy added that the rip-and-replace program to take out Huawei gear was based on some of these disastrous but unlikely scenarios—the kinds of things that economists call black-swan events.

"We don't know how to quantify that risk," Clancy said. "It really is more of a geopolitical lever that China could pull if they need to or wanted to, perhaps as part of a Taiwan invasion scenario."

This was similar to former Australian prime minister Malcolm Turnbull's stance when banning Huawei from the country's 5G networks: not *innocent until proven guilty*, but *better safe than sorry*. "That didn't mean we thought Huawei was currently being used to interfere with our telecommunication networks," Turnbull wrote in his memoir. "Our approach was a hedge against a future threat: not the identification of a smoking gun but a loaded one."[12]

Black-swan events can come in flocks. One highly unlikely event triggers another thing that no one thought could happen. That Meng Wanzhou would be detained in Vancouver over sanctions violations committed by her company years ago was an extremely unlikely scenario. And yet unlikelier still was that a little switchmaker in Shenzhen could become successful enough for anyone to care at all.

So what happens next? Huawei has survived Washington's offensives, perhaps better than anyone could have expected. It has emerged stronger in some ways, developing its own alternatives to US technologies that it had long relied on. The crisis has revealed Huawei as the apple of Beijing's eye, with officials willing to move mountains to ensure the company escapes death. Huawei looks poised to remain an important actor in world affairs for some time.

But make no mistake: The US government has succeeded in halting Huawei's rise. Huawei is no longer setting new sales records each year but is instead working to regain its 2020 levels. It is no longer expanding farther into the West but is instead defending its turf in emerging markets. The company has lost valuable R&D partnerships with US and European universities, which had helped drive its innovation. Huawei is still on the cutting edge of technology today—a testament to the research work it began many years ago on emerging sectors like artificial intelligence. But with walls up against it in every direction, it remains to be seen if Huawei can maintain its place as an R&D leader in the next generation, and the one after that.

Then there is the matter of Ren himself. Ren has fretted over succession planning for well over two decades, implementing one system after another to try to insulate the company from the missteps of any individual executive, himself included. "If the soul of an enterprise is its entrepreneur, then it's the most miserable, hopeless, and unreliable of enterprises," Ren once told his staff. "If I were a bank, I'd never give him a loan. Why? Who knows, maybe when he gets on a plane tomorrow, he'll fall out of the sky."[13] In recent years, Ren has maintained that he has already passed on much of the power to his colleagues and is no more than a "mascot." But it remains an open question how Huawei will fare without Ren there to inspire staff and remind them of their mission. His successors face a formidable test in carrying on the most successful corporate enterprise that has ever arisen in their nation.

Some years ago, Huawei had tweaked its organizational chart in its annual reports. It had added something at the very top called the "Shareholders' Meeting," which Huawei mysteriously called its "highest authority."[14] The board of directors reported up to the Shareholders' Meeting. So did the CEO. So did everyone else. And it was perhaps more than met the eye, regarding the perennial question of who exactly controlled Huawei.

Huawei's claim that the company is controlled by its more than 150,000 employee shareholders through this "Shareholders' Meeting" is often dismissed out of hand by foreign observers, as it seems patently untrue. After all, the average Huawei engineer or salesperson has no say in the company's grand strategy. But to dismiss the Shareholders' Meeting outright may be hasty. Interestingly, a select few of these shareholders actually do hold real power.

Every five years, a few dozen shareholders are officially anointed as "Representatives," giving them the power to make decisions in the name of all shareholders. These Representatives pass judgment on major company decisions. They also pick Huawei's board of directors, which in turn picks the CEO.

What is curious is who these Representatives are. They are

supposedly elected by an open vote of Huawei's employees, which might lead one to surmise that some random lucky engineers who have rallied votes from their buddies will take turns participating in the company's rule by employees. This is not the case. Since 2014, when Huawei started disclosing the list of shareholder Representatives, this group has remained largely stable, consisting of Huawei's most powerful executives.[15] Indeed, the list of Representatives may even better reflect the power dynamic within the company than lists of the board of directors and the executive management team. People who are known to have influence within the company appear on this list, even when they don't hold other top titles: Ren's brother, Ren Shulu; his son, Ren Ping; and the party secretary, Zhou Daiqi, for instance, have consistently been listed as Representatives. There is also Sun Yafang. After retiring from her role as chairwoman in 2018, she remained at Huawei but did not appear in other senior management positions. But in the 2023 Representatives list, her name continues to come second, just after Ren's and ahead of that belonging to the new, less forceful chairman, Liang Hua.[16] Other respected company elders also appear among the Representatives, including Jiang Xisheng, who negotiated the buyout of the company's original investors.

The Representatives' Commission "decides on, manages, and monitors major company matters," and elects the board of directors and supervisory committee, according to the company's corporate materials. And as it turns out, the Representatives almost invariably elect themselves to directorial and supervisory posts. The directors elect the CEO, always picking Ren, who is also a Representative.

Such a system might sound utterly bewildering to foreigners. But it would ring familiar in China: It is strikingly similar to how the nation operates as a whole. Every five years, the National Congress of the Communist Party of China is held, with some two thousand delegates elected by grassroots vote in party units across the nation.[17] These delegates elect a smaller group of around two hundred officials to the party's Central Committee, which in turn picks twenty-four among them for the Politburo, a subset of seven for the Politburo Standing Committee, and one for general secretary, the party's highest office. Despite this complex system of elections, scholars of China's political systems generally believe that the selection of China's top leaders is predetermined in closed-door meetings among the nation's most powerful officials.

As for Huawei's internal elections, it is unclear why the elected Representatives have remained so consistent. One explanation is that the number of votes an employee gets is weighted to the number of shares held, which would mean that Ren and other senior executives have many more votes than junior staffers. Another explanation is that Ren's team has succeeded in producing steady dividends for Huawei's staff, making many of them wealthy, so workers have little incentive to vote him out. Or, perhaps, in a nation that has elections of a sort but is not a democracy, people have developed the survival skill of making sure votes turn out the way they are supposed to.

This parallel to China's governance system offers a lens through which an answer to the question of who controls Huawei can finally be hazarded. Here is what we know about China's government: the collective governance model obscures who, exactly, is making decisions, and this is by design. Many times, it is the core leader making the decisions, due to his centralized power, but esteemed elders often wield considerable influence in the wings. It can even be possible for them to override the nominal leader on decisions. The party's internal disciplinary mechanism—present for both the government and for Huawei—serves as a powerful stick to keep individual officials in line, as it allows the party to oust those who are ideologically out of step.

Huawei's goal, like the party's, is to ensure its own long-term survival. Achieving this goal requires winning enough buy-in from its workers. But maximizing shareholder value—or individuals' well-being—is not the end in and of itself.

Such a system has strengths and weaknesses. A strength is its ability to accomplish titanic tasks at almost impossible speeds by getting everyone to pull in unison. A weakness is that such a system is often strong but brittle, and its success can come at crushing costs for the individuals involved.

In the 1990s, as they were drafting the Huawei Basic Law, Ren and his deputies asked themselves what sort of company Huawei was.

The answer is now clear: Huawei is a company made in the image of its nation, in all its fearsomeness and flaws, in all its courage and poetry.

ACKNOWLEDGMENTS

I'm immensely grateful to my editors and colleagues at *The Washington Post* for their support of this project and for all that they have taught me. A great big thank-you to Douglas Jehl, Anna Fifield, David Crawshaw, Lily Kuo, and Cameron Barr for their encouragement of my work on this project as I finished my stint in China in 2022, and to Lori Montgomery, Mark Seibel, Alexis Sobel Fitts, Jamie Graff, and Yun-Hee Kim for finding a home for me on *The Washington Post*'s tech policy team in Washington. I have enjoyed working with both teams so much, and my *Post* colleagues have helped shape my understanding of China and the world in so many ways. Thanks especially to Kendra Nichols, Katerina Ang, Christian Shepherd, Lyric Li, Pei-Lin Wu, Alicia Chen, Min Joo Kim, Grace Moon, Emily Rauhala, Ellen Nakashima, Drew Harwell, Cate Cadell, Amanda Coletta, Cat Zakrzewski, and Cristiano Lima-Strong for their insights and camaraderie.

John Pomfret was kind enough to read an early version of my book proposal, and he introduced me to my brilliant agents, Peter and Amy Bernstein, who have guided this idea into concrete reality with expertise and deftness. My editor, Noah Schwartzberg at Portfolio, believed in this story from the start, and I'm very much indebted to him for his thoughtful edits, inspired vision, and staunch support through the many months and vagaries of the project. I'm grateful to Portfolio's leadership, including Adrian Zackheim and Niki Papadopoulos, for their support and guidance. It has been a delight to work with the Portfolio team, and I've appreciated the expertise and attention to detail of Brian Borchard, Nina Brown, Meighan Cavanaugh, Anna Dobbin, Linda Friedner, Jessica Regione, Chris Welch, and Lauren Morgan Whitticom. Brian Lemus designed the beautiful and striking cover. Leila Sandlin has skillfully shepherded the manuscript and kept track of many moving pieces. Ritsuko Okumura has worked tirelessly to bring this book to readers around the world, and Richard Beswick at Abacus has been a champion for it in the UK and Commonwealth markets.

My gratitude goes to Christina Larson, James Palmer, Dan Wang, Matthew Miller, Donald C. Clarke, and Duncan Clark, who read drafts of the manuscript and offered smart critiques that greatly improved it. Sincere appreciation also goes to a person who fell asleep reading the early versions of the 5G passages.

I have had many mentors in the archival research process—new terrain for me as a newspaper reporter. I want to thank Joseph Torigian, Marc Opper, Joshua Seufert, and the experts of the Library of Congress's Asian Reading Room for their generosity in sharing their knowledge of the ins and outs of archives. Without their guidance, the early chapters would have been a shadow of themselves. Daniel

Bailly, Christophe Bélorgeot, and Philippe Robin from the Association des Retraités de Technip (ARTP) provided some fascinating insights on the Liaoyang Petrochemical Fiber Factory, and Zhou Fengsuo, Maya Wang, Christine Choy, and Ben Klein kindly helped me with research leads. With patience and good cheer, Danica Raguz at the Supreme Court of British Columbia assisted me for weeks with my records requests.

I'm deeply grateful to all the telecommunications engineers, executives, government officials, and subject-matter experts who opened up their memories and generously shared their stores of knowledge, insights, and opinions. They include Erdal Arıkan, Christoph Becker, John Bolton, Vince Cable, Duncan Clark, Robert Fox, Gary Garner, George Gilder, Dan Hesse, Dan Hutchison, Michael Joseph, Michel Juneau-Katsuya, Andy Keiser, John Kotter, Michael Kovrig, Keith Krach, Tony Kwong, Richard Kurland, James Lewis, Dongqing Li, Graham Lovelace, Edgar Masri, Simon Murray, Riccardo Nanni, Bill Owens, Jake Parker, Vishu Paul, William Plummer, Chris Powell, Robert Read, Diane Rinaldo, Charles Rollet, Guy Saint-Jacques, Brian Shields, Eric Steinmann, John Strand, Leo Strawczynski, Niels ten Oever, Michael Thelander, Jeffrey Towson, Paul Triolo, John F. Tyson, Wan Runnan, Steve Waterhouse, Eric Zeng, Ken Zita, and Tommy Zwicky. Many others spoke on an anonymous basis. I am especially grateful to the current and former Huawei employees who took the time to share their memories. Any names missing from this list are certainly inadvertent. This project could not have been done without all of you.

David Molko and Amanda Coletta generously shared their notes and insights from the Vancouver trial. Steve Stecklow, Bruce Gilley, and Lionel Barber took the time to share recollections of their encounters with Huawei at key junctures in its history.

My gratitude goes to Mr. Ren Zhengfei and other Huawei executives for answering the questions of my *Wall Street Journal* team in 2019, and for giving us a look inside the grand halls of Huawei. Thanks to Huawei's public relations colleagues—especially Guy Henshilwood, Evita Cao, and Di Fan—for their professionalism in fielding my fact-checking requests over several years. Huawei ultimately decided not to provide comment directly for this project, which I regret but understand, given the uncertainty of the current US-China political environment.

This work owes a major intellectual debt to the Chinese and foreign scholars who have studied Huawei over the years, including Tian Tao, Wu Chunbo, Huang Weiwei, Johann Peter Murmann, Yang Shaolong, Yun Wen, and Donald C. Clarke. Their works are cited in the endnotes, and I encourage anyone with a deeper interest in the company to study their writings. Tian Tao's work on Huawei is, in particular, unparalleled, and it forms a cornerstone for anyone seeking to understand the company.

Mr. Ren has cultivated a unique Renaissance-man strain of corporate culture at Huawei, where employees are encouraged to study history, literature, and philosophy, as well as express their thoughts elegantly on paper. The writings and essays of Huawei's employees have been my constant companion these past few years. I tip my hat to those at Huawei who have put their own thoughts to paper, and to the many people who have done the extensive work of keeping a detailed record of history through Huawei's internal periodicals.

My thanks go out to my former *Wall Street Journal* colleagues, who were my early teachers on Asia's high-tech industry. When I was based in Taipei, Aries Poon and Yun-Hee Kim showed me the ropes, along with my dear colleagues Jenny Hsu, Lorraine Luk, and

Fanny Liu. I'm grateful for all that I learned from the late Carlos Tejada, as well as from Gillian Wong, Josh Chin, Sofia McFarland, John Corrigan, Charles Hutzler, Jeremy Page, Yoko Kubota, Alyssa Abkowitz, Chao Deng, Kersten Zhang, Yang Jie, and many others.

Further gratitude goes to Jake Adelstein, Chun Han Wong, Josh Chin, Liza Lin, Ted Anthony, James Zimmerman, Bethany Allen, Shibani Mahtani, and Steven Lee Myers for kindly sharing their insights on the brass tacks of a book project. And I thank Chiara Capitanio, Jasmine Tillu, Ryan Morgan, Brian Jackson, Vincent Lee, Yuan Li, Jen Kwon, and Yuan Ren for friendship, commiseration, hot pots, and intellectual exchange.

I have had wonderful teachers over the years. The late Jeffrey Nardone was my first journalism teacher, who taught me and my fellow students to be curious about the world, to aspire for change for the better, and to hold an irreverence for authority figures of all stripes. Joe Grimm, Jim Wilhelm, M. L. Elrick, and Jim Schaefer gave me my first glimpse into serious investigative reporting at the *Detroit Free Press*. Lynda Kraxberger, Amy Simons, Jim MacMillan, Karen Mitchell, and other professors at the Missouri School of Journalism taught me to see the stories in the world around me, and to be scrupulous in note-taking and fact-checking. David Mandy and Jeffrey Milyo at the MU Department of Economics taught me how to start looking at how the world works through the flow of goods and currency. I've been exploring it with wonder ever since.

My deepest thanks go to my parents for the opportunities they gave me, and to my brother, Dan, for cheering me on. They are an inspiration.

Last and most, thank you to my beloved husband, Michael, for his love and support throughout this project and in our lives together.

He has been a champion of this book from the start, an insightful critic of the early drafts, an unstoppable fount of puns, and a thoughtful interlocutor on issues of history and international affairs. His insights have made this book smarter and better in many ways. He and our sweet cats have rallied me when I felt uncertain, lifted me up when I was down, and pulled me across the finish line.

HUAWEI'S CORPORATE
STRUCTURE

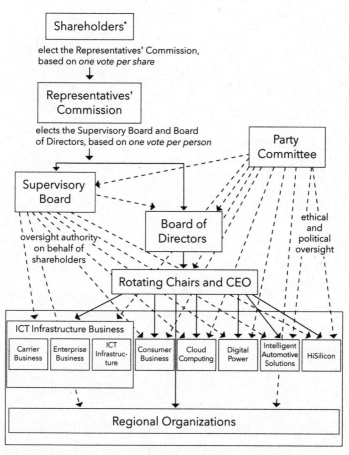

Shareholders*

elect the Representatives' Commission,
based on *one vote per share*

Representatives'
Commission

elects the Supervisory Board and Board
of Directors, based on *one vote per person*

Party
Committee

Supervisory
Board

Board of
Directors

oversight authority
on behalf of
shareholders

ethical
and
political
oversight

Rotating Chairs and CEO

ICT Infrastructure Business

Carrier
Business

Enterprise
Business

ICT
Infrastruc-
ture

Consumer
Business

Cloud
Computing

Digital
Power

Intelligent
Automotive
Solutions

HiSilicon

Regional Organizations

*Huawei's shareholders consist of Ren Zhengfei (0.73%) and Huawei's union
(99.27%), with the union representing 151,796 current and former engineers.

TIMELINE OF EVENTS

July 7, 1937:   The Marco Polo Bridge incident, a clash between Japanese and Chinese troops near Beijing, marks the start of World War II in the Pacific theater.

1937:   Ren Moxun arrives in Rongxian, Guangxi Province, and opens the July Seventh Bookstore.

1939:   Nationalists shut down the July Seventh Bookstore.

October 25, 1944:   Ren Zhengfei is born.

September 2, 1945:   Japan surrenders; World War II ends.

1946:   The Chinese Civil War resumes.

October 1, 1949:   Mao Zedong proclaims the establishment of the People's Republic of China.

1950:	Ren Moxun arrives in the Guizhou town of Zhenning with an assignment to set up a middle school for children of the Bouyei ethnic minority.
October 1957:	The Soviet Union launches Sputnik 1, the world's first artificial satellite, into orbit.
1958:	The Ren family moves to Duyun in Guizhou Province, where Ren Moxun becomes dean of Duyun Minority Teachers' College and joins the Communist Party.
1958:	Mao Zedong begins the Great Leap Forward campaign.
1959–1961:	The Great Chinese Famine takes hold.
1963:	Ren Zhengfei is accepted into the Chongqing Institute of Architecture and Engineering.
May 1966:	The decade-long Cultural Revolution begins. Ren Moxun and Meng Dongbo are put into labor camps during this period.
1968:	Ren Zhengfei graduates from the Chongqing Institute of Architecture and Engineering and afterward goes to work at Base 011.
February 13, 1972:	Meng Wanzhou is born.
1974:	Ren Zhengfei trains at the Xi'an Instruments Factory. He is later dispatched to Liaoyang with the PLA Engineering Corps to build a nylon and polyester factory.
September 9, 1976:	Mao Zedong dies, ending the Cultural Revolution.

Around 1977:   Meng Wanzhou goes to live with her paternal grandparents in Guizhou.

1978:   At the nation's first National Science Conference, attended by Ren Zhengfei, China's new leader, Deng Xiaoping, declares the return of science following the Cultural Revolution. Ren joins the Chinese Communist Party. With the construction of the Liaoyang Petrochemical Fiber Factory largely complete, Ren's troop moves south to Jinan, where Ren becomes deputy director of a research institute.

1979:   Ren Zhengfei publishes *A Floating-Ball Precision Pressure Generator—Air Pressure Balance*, a book about his invention. Ren Moxun becomes principal of Duyun No. 1 Middle School. Meng Dongbo travels to Europe.

May 1980:   The Shenzhen Special Economic Zone is established.

January 8, 1982:   The US Justice Department orders the breakup of AT&T, which at the time was the world's leader in telecommunications research.

September 1982:   Ren Zhengfei attends the Twelfth National Congress of the Chinese Communist Party. Deng Xiaoping announces the disbandment of the PLA Engineering Corps.

1982–1984:   Ren Zhengfei and Meng Jun move to Shenzhen (date uncertain), and Ren begins work at South Sea Oil.

1984:   Ren Moxun retires from the middle school and

devotes his time to compiling a history of the local schools.

February 1987: Shenzhen allows individuals to set up minjian private tech companies.

September 15, 1987: Huawei Technologies Co. is founded.

Spring 1988: Ren Zhengfei travels to the Huazhong Institute of Technology in Wuhan to try to recruit researchers to build a switch.

Autumn 1988: Guo Ping, a Huazhong Institute graduate student, arrives at Huawei for an internship.

1990: Huawei holds a shareholder meeting at which there is a severe dispute between Ren Zhengfei and his five original investors.

1990: Meng Wanzhou graduates from high school and enrolls at Shenzhen University as an accounting major.

1990: Ken Hu joins Huawei.

1991: Military engineer Wu Jiangxing develops the "04 switch," China's first homegrown advanced digital switch.

1991: Huawei sets up its chip design center, which is later renamed HiSilicon.

1991–1992: Huawei registers as a jitisuoyouzhi, or collectively owned company (exact date unclear).

1992: Steven Ren joins Huawei.

1993:   Li Yinan and Eric Xu join Huawei.

1993:   Huawei begins developing the C&C08, its first advanced digital switch.

March 4, 1993:   Huawei establishes its first US subsidiary, Ran Boss Technologies, in Santa Clara, California, to work on R&D.

April 1993:   Huawei launches Mobeco, a domestic joint venture with provincial telecommunication bureaus, promising them high annual investment returns.

1994:   Sun Yafang is promoted to vice-chairwoman at Huawei.

May 1994:   A first test unit for Huawei's C&C08 digital switch is set up in Yiwu, Zhejiang.

June 1994:   Ren Zhengfei meets the nation's leader, Jiang Zemin, in Shenzhen and makes his now-famous statement that "a country without its own program-controlled switches is like one without an army."

November 1994:   China Merchants Bank announces a new financial product called "domestic buyer's credit"; Huawei is the first company in the nation able to offer it to customers.

January 1, 1995:   The World Trade Organization is established; due to US obstruction, China is not a founding member.

April 3, 1995:   The Ministry of Posts and Telecommunications approves Huawei's C&C08 switch for mass production.

June 1995: Ren Moxun passes away.

September 1995: Huawei opens its Hong Kong branch.

1996: Huawei is one of eight companies selected by Beijing for a $1 billion national semiconductor development program.

January 28, 1996: Huawei's sales team holds a "mass resignation ceremony" led by Sun Yafang.

March 1996: Huawei sets up its internal Communist Party branch.

April 1996: China and Russia announce a strategic partnership, and Ren Zhengfei travels to Moscow to open Huawei's office in the country.

June 1996: Huawei seals a deal to sell C&C08 switches to Hutchison Telecom, breaking into the Hong Kong market.

November 1996: While visiting Huawei, Vice-Premier Wu Bangguo suggests that the company try to re-create its success in landline telephone switches with mobile telephony.

1997: Huawei says it changed its legal structure to a limited liability company this year. Huawei also begins negotiating the buyout of its five original investors, a process that takes several years; it cracks into the Beijing market with its first sales of C&C08 switches to the city; and it begins deployment of its first videoconferencing and video-surveillance system, ViewPoint.

February 20, 1997: Deng Xiaoping passes away.

April 1997: Huawei's first international joint venture, Beto-Huawei, is set up in the Russian city of Ufa.

July 1, 1997: The Hong Kong handover ends 156 years of British colonial rule.

September 1997: As a workaround to China's Company Law, which restricts the number of shareholders in a limited liability company to fifty, the Shenzhen government suggests that local companies adopt an employee ownership model in which employee shares are held by a "union" that counts as a single shareholder. Around this time, Huawei adopts the suggested structure.

December 1997: Ren Zhengfei visits IBM and decides to hire the company to consult Huawei on how to grow its international business.

1998: Huawei institutes a new policy that requires executives to complete an overseas posting in order to be eligible for promotion.

January 1998: Ren Zhengfei's daughter Annabel Yao is born.

March 1998: Huawei adopts its "Huawei Basic Law" after two years of drafting.

August 1998: IBM consultants begin to arrive at Huawei,

where they will remain in residence for a
decade.

1999: Sun Yafang becomes Huawei's chairwoman.

September 1999: Sun Yafang attends Harvard Business School's
Advanced Management Program for mid-career
executives.

1999–2000: Anonymous letters accuse Huawei of illegal
business practices, prompting the National Audit
Office to audit Huawei's books.

March 2000: The dot-com bubble bursts.

August 2000: Huawei opens offices in Mexico and Sweden.

November 2000: *Forbes* puts Ren Zhengfei at number three on its
list of China's fifty richest entrepreneurs.

January 2001: Huawei sets up a subsidiary in Plano, Texas,
called Futurewei Technologies, aimed at selling
into the US market.

January 2001: Ren Zhengfei accompanies Vice President Hu
Jintao on a state visit to Iran.

February 16, 2001: The Pentagon orders an air strike on a fiber-optic
cable network that Huawei is constructing in Iraq,
with Huawei accused of violating UN sanctions by
working on the project.

February 25, 2001: Following the death of his mother the previous
month, Ren Zhengfei publishes an essay titled
"My Father and Mother," recounting his family
history.

September 2001: Huawei is criticized in the foreign media for allegedly building a phone system for the Taliban in Afghanistan.

October 2001: Huawei sells Avansys Power—the unit previously named Mobeco that aided its early domestic expansion by bringing municipal telecom bureaus on board as investors—to Emerson Electric in the United States for $750 million.

December 2001: China is accepted into the World Trade Organization.

February 2003: Cisco sues Huawei, alleging intellectual-property violations.

March 2003: The United States invades Iraq.

July 2003: With sanctions lifted after the deposing of Saddam Hussein, Iraq issues its first mobile network licenses to three companies, including Asiacell, which Huawei had wooed. Huawei is contracted to supply Asiacell's network.

2004: Huawei's chip design center is formalized as a subsidiary called HiSilicon.

July 2004: Cisco drops its lawsuit against Huawei.

December 2004: Huawei launches a network for its first US customer, the small cellular operator ClearTalk, operating in Southern California and Arizona.

2005: The China Development Bank allocates $10 billion

in financing for overseas customers to purchase Huawei products.

April 2005: Huawei lands its first major contract in the West when the UK operator BT picks the company as a supplier for its major network upgrade from dial-up internet to broadband.

2006: Huawei's chip unit, HiSilicon, launches its first surveillance-camera chip.

January 2006: North Korea's leader, Kim Jong Il, visits Huawei.

April 2006: A twenty-five-year-old Huawei engineer named Hu Xinyu dies from a brain infection after weeks of overtime work, sparking public backlash against Huawei's work culture.

November 2006: Huawei strikes a deal to sell its stake in H3C, its joint venture with 3Com, back to the US company. Huawei agrees not to compete directly with 3Com's enterprise networking business for eighteen months.

2007: Huawei begins selling "managed services," whereby it helps run customers' networks for a fee.

May 2007: Huawei enters the submarine cable market with the launch of Huawei Submarine Networks, a joint venture with the UK's Global Marine Systems.

July 2007: The FBI interviews Ren Zhengfei at a hotel in New York.

September 2007: News breaks that Huawei was planning to buy a stake in 3Com as part of Bain Capital's takeover of the networking company, sparking controversy in Washington and a review of the deal by CFIUS.

Autumn 2007: Huawei engineers begin working to set up cell service on Mount Everest ahead of the Olympics.

December 2007: Through *Management Optimization*, an in-house newspaper, Huawei announces to staff that the company's Communist Party committee will now have veto power over executive appointments.

2008: Huawei is number one worldwide in patent application filings, the first time a Chinese company has held the title.

2008: Huawei names a new party secretary, Zhou Daiqi, after Madam Chen Zhufang retires.

2008: Meng Wanzhou registers as a director of Skycom.

January 2008: China's Labor Contract Law goes into effect, providing employment protections for employees who have worked at the same company for more than a decade. Just before the deadline, sixty-five hundred Huawei employees resign and rejoin the company, wiping out their seniority.

February 2008: Huawei gives up plans to buy a stake in 3Com after CFIUS indicates it will block the deal.

May 8, 2008: The Olympic torch ascends Mount Everest, with Huawei helping to broadcast the images to the world.

2009: After extensive delays, China finally rolls out 3G mobile networks, allowing smartphones to fully function in the nation.

2009: Huawei starts selling its Safe City surveillance systems internationally.

2010: Meng Wanzhou becomes Huawei's CFO.

August 2010: Republican lawmakers write to the Obama administration, urging it to block Huawei's bid to supply Sprint's network.

November 2010: Sprint rejects Huawei's bid to supply its 4G network.

November 2010: The Huawei Cyber Security Evaluation Centre (HCSEC), where Huawei will allow the UK government to examine its equipment for cybersecurity vulnerabilities, opens in the United Kingdom.

February 2011: Ken Hu, Huawei's deputy chairman, pens an open letter inviting the US government to investigate the company so that it can clear its name by proving it is "a normal commercial institution and nothing more."

December 2011: Huawei announces a shift to a rotating CEO system, with Guo Ping, Ken Hu, and Eric Xu taking turns at the helm of the company for six-month stints.

March 2012: Australia bans Huawei from bidding for its next-generation broadband network.

September 2012: The House Permanent Select Committee on Intelligence (HPSCI) holds a hearing on Huawei and ZTE.

October 2012: The HPSCI issues its report on Huawei and ZTE, recommending that US companies stop buying from the two.

2013: Huawei carves out Honor as a stand-alone smartphone brand aimed at the youth market.

January 2013: In Beijing, Meng Wanzhou holds her first press conference as Huawei's CFO, promising that the company will be more transparent.

January 2013: Reuters reports that Meng Wanzhou was a Skycom board member.

August 22, 2013: Meng Wanzhou meets with HSBC executives and presents a slide deck about Huawei's Iran business.

March 2014: *The New York Times* and *Der Spiegel* report that, based on documents leaked by Edward Snowden, the NSA has been infiltrating Huawei for years through a program called "Shotgiant."

April 2014: A bomb attack at a train station in Ürümqi triggers the start of a counterterrorism crackdown in Xinjiang.

June 2014: Meng Wanzhou is detained for secondary questioning at New York's JFK Airport, and her electronics are copied by US authorities.

2015: Huawei surpasses Xiaomi in smartphone sales, with only Apple and Samsung ahead of it.

October 2015: Xi Jinping visits Huawei's offices in the UK.

2016: In Dongguan, Huawei begins constructing its Ox Horn Campus, which will have twelve "towns" designed after European cities and regions.

March 2016: The US Commerce Department sanctions ZTE.

November 2016: Huawei gets its polar coding technology included in the 5G standard.

2017: China announces its goal to become a world AI power by 2030.

January 2018: AT&T and Verizon stop carrying Huawei smartphones.

January 2018: French newspaper *Le Monde* reports that the servers at the African Union's headquarters were sending data to China each night.

March 2018: After serving as Huawei's chairwoman for nineteen years, Sun Yafang steps down and is replaced by Liang Hua.

July 2018: The Australian Strategic Policy Institute reports that the servers at the African Union's headquarters were produced by Huawei.

August 2018: President Trump signs into law a defense bill that bans US government agencies from buying Huawei and ZTE equipment.

August 2018: Australia becomes the first country in the world to formally ban Huawei and ZTE from its future 5G network.

November 2018: Annabel Yao appears as a debutante at Le Bal in Paris.

December 1, 2018: Meng Wanzhou is detained at the Vancouver International Airport.

December 10, 2018: The Canadians Michael Kovrig and Michael Spavor are detained in China.

December 11, 2018: Meng Wanzhou is released on bail.

January 16, 2019: Ren Zhengfei holds his first press conference with international media.

January 28, 2019: US prosecutors announce criminal charges against Huawei and Meng Wanzhou.

May 2019: President Trump declares a national emergency in telecommunications, ordering federal agencies to take "all appropriate measures." The Commerce Department's Bureau of Industry and Security announces sanctions on Huawei.

June 2019: Huawei decides to sell its undersea cable subsidiary, Huawei Marine Systems, to a Chinese buyer.

January 20, 2020: Meng Wanzhou's extradition hearing begins in Vancouver.

Second quarter 2020: For the first time, Huawei becomes the world's number-one smartphone vendor in sales.

May 2020:	The Commerce Department tightens sanctions on Huawei.
July 2020:	The UK announces a reversal of its position on Huawei and says that it will remove all Huawei equipment from the nation's 5G networks by the end of 2027.
November 16, 2020:	Huawei announces that it will sell its Honor phone brand.
March 22, 2021:	Michael Kovrig and Michael Spavor are tried behind closed doors.
September 24, 2021:	Huawei's CFO, Meng Wanzhou, enters into a plea agreement with the US Justice Department and is allowed to return to China. On the same day, Beijing allows Michael Kovrig and Michael Spavor to return to Canada.
March 2022:	Meng Wanzhou is promoted, joining Ken Hu and Eric Xu as one of Huawei's three rotating chairs. Guo Ping becomes chairman of the supervisory board.
April 2023:	Meng Wanzhou begins her first half-year tenure as a rotating CEO at Huawei.
September 2023:	Huawei launches the Mate 60 Pro smartphone, which runs on a 5G chip made domestically despite US sanctions.

ADDITIONAL READING

For readers interested in a deeper understanding of these topics, I would like to highlight the following works for further reading. This list is far from comprehensive. The below are books unless otherwise noted.

Other Works on Huawei in English

The Huawei Way, by Tian Tao with Wu Chunbo, is an early work that explains Huawei's philosophy and corporate culture to a global audience and, in many ways, remains the standard-bearer for books written with direct input from senior Huawei executives.

The Management Transformation of Huawei, by Xiaobo Wu, Johann Peter Murmann, Can Huang, and Bin Guo, is an excellent detailed resource on the obscurities of Huawei's management structure, and its appendix includes a full translation of the Huawei Basic Law.

The Huawei Stories series (*Pioneers, Explorers, Visionaries, Adventurers,* and *Spirit*), edited by Tian Tao and Yin Zhifeng, is a selection of essays by Huawei employees, many originally published in *Huawei People*, that offer first-person accounts of key moments in the company's history.

Huidu: Inside Huawei, by William B. Plummer, the company's former US spokesman, is a colorful memoir that sheds light on the company's response to the House investigation and other crises in the US.

Huawei Inside Out, by Joseph Smith, presents an interesting view on Huawei from the perspective of one of the early IBM consultants who helped the company internationalize.

Those interested in exploring varying viewpoints on Huawei's ownership should start with Christopher Balding and Donald C. Clarke's paper on Huawei's corporate structure, "Who Owns Huawei?" (http://dx.doi.org/10.2139/ssrn.3372669), and the detailed rejoinder paper from Chinese professor Wang Jun, as translated by Zichen Wang (https://www.pekingnology.com/p/who-really-owns-huawei-a-response).

Other Works on Huawei in Chinese

The two volumes of *Huawei Interviews* [华为访谈录], by Tian Tao, reflect many years of study and research, and they are unparalleled in their insight into the early days of Huawei's history and the experiences of key members of Ren's executive team.

Former Huawei executive Li Yuzhuo's memoir, *Straight Down the Path: My Business Ideals* [一路直行：我的企业理想], is a frank and colorful account of life at Huawei and other Chinese high-tech firms, featuring anecdotes about Li's humorous run-ins with Ren Zhengfei and other industry titans, as well as an explanation of how Huawei's early domestic joint ventures helped its sales expansion.

Huawei's World [华为的世界], by Wu Jianguo and Ji Yongqing, is a vivid narrative of Huawei's early rise based partly on the personal experiences of Wu, who served as a deputy to chief engineer Zheng Baoyong at Huawei.

Liu Ping's [刘平] memoir, *Bygone Times at Huawei* [华为往事], and Cao Yi'an's [曹贻安] *Miscellaneous Notes on Striving at Huawei* [在华为打拼杂记], which both appear to be published only online, provide insights into the personalities and work culture at Huawei. Penned by former Huawei executives, they are well worth reading in their entirety for those interested in the company.

Zhang Lihua's [张利华] *Huawei R&D* [华为研发] provides a detailed account of Huawei's early switches and other products and how they were developed.

Other Works on the Telecommunications Industry

The essay "Who Lost Lucent? The Decline of America's Telecom Equipment Industry," by Robert D. Atkinson, is a good place to start for those looking to understand the other half of the story: the long decline of the United States as the unquestioned leader of the industry. See https://americanaffairsjournal.org/2020/08/who-lost-lucent-the-decline-of-americas-telecom-equipment-industry.

The Deal of the Century: The Breakup of AT&T, by Steve Coll, explains the origins of the US Justice Department's 1982 order for the dismantling of AT&T's telephone monopoly, which in retrospect was the beginning of the end of US reign over the global telecom sector.

Adventures in Innovation: Inside the Rise and Fall of Nortel, by John Tyson, explores the journey of one of Huawei's most storied Western rivals and the factors that led to its bankruptcy.

Wireless Wars: China's Dangerous Domination of 5G and How We're

Fighting Back, by Jonathan Pelson, provides a colorful account of the recent history of the global telecom sector from the perspective of a former executive at US giant Lucent.

3Com, by Jeff Chase with Jon Zilber, includes an insightful chronicle of 3Com's joint venture with Huawei, which helped Huawei defend itself against the Cisco lawsuit, and also details Huawei's ill-fated attempt to purchase a stake in 3Com as part of Bain's attempted takeover.

Standing Up to China: How a Whistleblower Risked Everything for His Country, by Ashley Yablon, ZTE's former general counsel in the United States, offers a vivid account of the author's decision to become a whistleblower to the FBI over the company's sanctions violations. The book also includes passages about Yablon's prior work at Huawei.

Other Works on State Surveillance and Technological Espionage

Permanent Record, by Edward Snowden, explains Snowden's studies of China's surveillance capabilities while he was at the NSA and how they led him to investigate what powers the US government had in this regard.

The Secret Sentry: The Untold History of the National Security Agency, by Matthew M. Aid, is a deeply researched history of the NSA based largely on US government records released through Freedom of Information Act requests. It includes an account of the 2001 US bombing of Huawei's fiber-optic network in Iraq.

No Place to Hide: Edward Snowden, the NSA, and the U.S. Surveillance State, by Glenn Greenwald, reports explosive details about how the NSA implanted back-door surveillance tools in Cisco routers being sent to overseas customers. Greenwald's reportage is based on classified records leaked by Edward Snowden.

Surveillance State: Inside China's Quest to Launch a New Era of Social

Control, by Josh Chin and Liza Lin, is a deep dive into contemporary China's high-tech surveillance apparatus, with a detailed account of the crackdown in the Xinjiang region and a chapter about Huawei's assistance with state surveillance in Uganda.

The Sentinel State: Surveillance and the Survival of Dictatorship in China, by Minxin Pei, provides historical perspective on China's intelligence-gathering operations and an explanation of how the country has evolved into its current high-tech state.

Chinese Spies: From Chairman Mao to Xi Jinping, by Roger Faligot, is a deeply researched account of China's intelligence activities at home and abroad. It is written by a French investigative journalist who has been chipping away at the subject for decades.

The Secret History of the Five Eyes: The Untold Story of the International Spy Network, by Richard Kerbaj, devotes a chapter to the closed-door negotiations between the Trump administration and the United Kingdom over Huawei.

Other Works on China's High-Tech Industry

The Shenzhen Experiment: The Story of China's Instant City, by Juan Du, is a vivid and richly researched account of the rise of the Shenzhen Special Economic Zone.

China's Telecommunications Revolution, by Eric Harwit, chronicles the construction of China's phone and internet networks from 1949 to the modern era.

Alibaba: The House that Jack Ma Built, by Duncan Clark, is a fascinating window into the Chinese internet giant, told by a real expert on China's tech industry.

Other Works on US-China Relations

The Beautiful Country and the Middle Kingdom: America and China, 1776 to the Present, by John Pomfret, is a nuanced and epic account of how US-China relations have evolved over centuries.

Superpower Showdown: How the Battle Between Trump and Xi Threatens a New Cold War, by Bob Davis and Lingling Wei, provides a fly-on-the-wall account of the trade war negotiations between Washington and Beijing, as well as broader context on the history of the US-China relationship.

China-US 2039: The Endgame?, by Bill Owens, is a thought-provoking reflection on the risks of a US-China war and how to mitigate them. It is written by the former vice-chairman of the Joint Chiefs who represented Huawei in its 2010 bid for a Sprint contract.

Governmental Reports

The House Permanent Select Committee on Intelligence's 2012 report on Huawei and ZTE remains one of the most detailed and frequently cited public US government reports on the companies. The report can be found at https://intelligence.house.gov/sites/intelligence.house.gov/files/docu ments/huawei-zte%20investigative%20report%20(final).pdf.

The Huawei Cyber Security Evaluation Centre Oversight Board's annual reports for the UK's national security adviser make for interesting reading, laying out security issues found in tested Huawei equipment each year. The reports can be found at https://www.gov.uk/search/all?keywords=huawei+ cyber+security+evaluation+centre+oversight+board+annual+reports&or der=relevance.

PHOTO CREDITS

Page xxx, bottom: Photo by the author.

Page xxxi, top: Photo by the author.

Page xxxi, middle: Photo by Heinz Ruckemann / UPI via Alamy.

Page xxxi, bottom: Photo by Jin Liwang / Imago via Alamy.

Page 11: Photo from the 1959 booklet 重庆建筑工程学院, an internally published overview of the Chongqing Institute of Architecture and Engineering.

Page 23: Photo from the *Sichuan Daily*.

Page 33: Photo by the author.

Page 49: Photo courtesy of Wan Runnan.

Page 128: Photo by David de la Paz / Xinhua News Agency via Imago / Alamy.

Page 163: Photo by Joerg Boethling / Alamy.

Page 218: Photo by J. Scott Applewhite / Associated Press.

Page 261: Photo by ImagineChina Limited / Alamy.

Page 263: Photo by Marcel Thomas / ZUMA Press, Inc. / Alamy.

Page 317: Photo by Darryl Dyck / The Canadian Press via Associated Press.

Page 318: Photo by the author.

Page 342: Photo by STR/AFP via Getty Images.

Page 348: Photo by Tao Liang / Imago via Alamy.

INDEX

Swarovski, 264
Sweden, 138, 158, 328, 374
Swift, Kerry, 301
Switzerland, 31
Symantec, 211–12
Syria, 278

Taiwan, 24, 95, 190, 191, 353
Taiwan Semiconductor Manufacturing
 Company (TSMC), 325–26
Taiwan Strait Crisis of 1995–1996, 105–6
Taliban, 145–46, 165, 375
Target, 253
TASS Russian News Agency, 106
Taylorism, 119
Technip and Speichim, 25–27
technology transfer, 60, 69, 169–70
Telefónica, 160, 243
telegraphs, 58–59
telephones, 59–60. *See also* smartphones
 wiretapping, 76, 154–55, 240–41, 352
telephone switches, 42–48, 53–54, 56,
  59–64, 67–71, 74, 80–81, 92–93, 98
  04 switch, 60–61, 63, 80, 81, 139, 370
  BH-01, 43–44, 47, 128
  BH-03, 47–48
  C&C08, 63–64, 65, 68–69, 75, 81, 93,
   107, 371
  SP30, 81
Telus, 269, 326–27
Teng Hongfei, 252
"terminals," 262–63
Texas Instruments, 325–26
Thailand, 158, 319
Thatcher, Margaret, 96
Thelander, Michael, 268, 270, 277–78
3rd Generation Partnership Project
 (3GPP), 267–70
"Thirteen Rooms of the Ren Family,"
  13–14
Thomas, Alan, 234–35
Thompson, Terry, 241–42
Thought Guards, 21, 22–23
3Com Corporation, 152–53, 170–72, 227,
 376, 377
Tiananmen Square protests, 49, 50, 51, 57,
  66, 70, 75–76, 89, 90, 91, 105, 115
Tianjin, 81
Tian Qingjun, 252
Tian Tao, 45, 47, 48, 123, 136

Tibet, 7, 190–91
Time (magazine), 159
Timperlake, Edward, 195
Toshiba, 269
trade war. *See* US-China trade war
traffic surveillance, 275–76
Triolo, Paul, 346
Troop 00229, 35–36
Trudeau, Justin, 291, 318, 335, 341–42
Trump, Donald
 Meng's case, 291, 292–93, 301, 316–17,
  321, 336
 Pakistan and, 276
 trade war and bans, 278, 280–83, 297–
  98, 301–10, 313, 316–17, 321, 324–25,
  327–29, 336, 346–47, 380, 381
Trump, Ivanka, 293
Tsinghua University, 11, 254, 329
tuberculosis, 28
Tunisia, 208
Turkey, 205, 206–7, 240
Turnbull, Malcolm, 281, 353
Twitter, 203, 212, 255, 327

UK (United Kingdom)
 handover of Hong Kong, 91–92,
  95–98, 373
 Huawei and, 159–60, 198–202, 224–25,
  306–7, 327, 328, 376, 378, 382
 HSBC and Iran, 233–35, 299,
  317, 379
 Meng's visit, 31–32
 Official Secrets Act, 200
 Vodafone and, 240
 Xi Jinping visit, 249–50, 380
Ukraina Hotel, 107
Ukraine, 106, 112
United Arab Emirates (UAE), 154, 166,
 168, 206, 208, 219, 307
United Nations (UN), 24, 104, 129, 351
 Iraq sanctions, 141–42, 147–48, 164
 Oil-for-Food Programme, 104
 Security Council, 144–45
United Wireless, 219
University of California, Berkeley, 266,
 302–3
University of Electronic Science and
 Technology, 130
University of Manchester, 250
University of Oxford, 266, 302